MW01027299

ON SHEDDING
AN OBSOLETE PAST

Bidding Farewell to the American Century

Also in the Dispatch Books Series

ON SHEDDING
AN OBSOLETE PAST

Bidding Farewell to the American Century

ANDREW BACEVICH

A TomDispatch Book

Haymarket Books
Chicago, Illinois

© 2022 Andrew Bacevich

Published in 2022 in cooperation with TomDispatch.com by
Haymarket Books
P.O. Box 180165
Chicago, IL 60618
773-583-7884
www.haymarketbooks.org
info@haymarketbooks.org

ISBN: 978-1-64259-834-6

Distributed to the trade in the US through Consortium Book Sales and
Distribution (www.cbsd.com) and internationally through Ingram Publisher Services International (www.ingramcontent.com).

This book was published with the generous support of Lannan Foundation and Wallace Action Fund.

Special discounts are available for bulk purchases by organizations and
institutions. Please call 773-583-7884 or email info@haymarketbooks.org
for more information.

Cover design by Steve Leard. Cover photograph of US Air Force load-
ing Afghan evacuees onto an aircraft in August 2021 © Senior Airman
Taylor Crul/US Air Force via AP.

Printed in Canada by union labor.

Library of Congress Cataloging-in-Publication data is available.

10   9   8   7   6   5   4   3   2   1

To Lawrence Kaplan

Contents

II The Blob Goes Haywire

III On and On They Go

Introduction

This book collects essays written for *TomDispatch* during the interval between the presidential election campaign of 2016 and the first year of the Biden administration in 2021. More than a few observers have referred to this brief period as the Age of Trump, implicitly assigning to Donald Trump's single term as US president significance comparable to the reign of Caesar Augustus or Charlemagne. While flattery of this sort likely finds favor with Trump himself, such a comparison is beyond wrong. It's blasphemous, on a par with equating a circus act to the religious rituals of Good Friday or Yom Kippur.

The pieces included in this book make the case that there was no Age of Trump, any more than there was an Age of George W. Bush or an Age of Barack Obama, or for that matter an Age of Harry Truman or Dwight D. Eisenhower. To indulge in the conceit of the American commander in chief presiding over any such eponymous age is to undervalue or ignore factors that play a far more important role in shaping reality. Whatever the presumption of gullible or lazy American media commentators, US presidents do not direct history; they merely respond to its imperatives, with varied degrees of acumen or success.

That said, any figure in any era who achieves even transitory prominence, whether political, military, intellectual, corporate, or cultural, testifies to the prevailing zeitgeist. If President Trump stands apart from other recent US presidents, it is because he so exquisitely embodied even while exacerbating the contradictions defining the United States as it lurched drunkenly into the third millennium.

In a memorable poem written at the outset of the Second World War, W. H. Auden branded the 1930s as a "low dishonest decade." A comparable judgment could well apply to the period that began with the collapse of the Soviet Union in 1991 and culminated with Trump's elevation to the White House twenty-five years later. Yet "low" and "dishonest" fall short in capturing the fall from grace that Americans experienced during this quarter-century. Commencing in a torrent of self-congratulations, the period ended in a welter of consternation, confusion, and recrimination.

Rather than merely low, this post–Cold War period was all but devoid of redeeming value. Rather than simply dishonest, it was febrile and deluded. Rarely in world history has an ostensibly great nation—in this case, a self-anointed "sole superpower"—so quickly and definitively flung away an advantageous position.

At the beginning of this period, ostensibly sane and serious Americans took it as given that the United States—deemed a colossus of incomparable stature—had ascended to a position empowering it to determine history's future course. According to those in the know, it had become the "indispensable nation."

By the time Trump took possession of the Oval Office in 2017, however, the indispensable nation's propensity for shooting itself in the foot had long since become apparent. By the time President Trump boarded Marine One four years later for one final flight from the White House lawn, events had definitively exposed expectations of the United States exercising political, ideological, economic, or military preeminence as positively daft. In this context, the coronavirus pandemic that in 2020 took the lives of hundreds of thousands of Americans while the sitting president dithered serves as the ultimate expression of the folie de grandeur that comprised the era's abiding theme.

Some might object that describing this period as devoid of redeeming value goes too far. After all, even while subjected to repeated deployments to distant combat zones, US troops have displayed exemplary perseverance. As COVID-19 wreaked havoc, medical professionals and first responders stayed at their posts and performed heroically. Meanwhile, on behalf of justice, equality, and fairness, various progressives organized, marched, protested, and occupied. Yet neither the bravery displayed by the troops, nor the tenacity of the anti-COVID warriors, nor the passion of left-wing reformers yielded anything remotely like a moral consensus around which all Americans could rally.

Just the opposite was true. Battered by multiple, mutually reinforcing sources of stress, mostly rooted in doubts about the long-term viability of the (real or imagined) American Dream, the nation watched as its last vestiges of unity trickled away.

Beginning on a note of exalted expectations, the post–Cold War period culminated with the nation disintegrating into warring factions, a reality vividly displayed in the assault on the Capitol resulting from the contested presidential election of 2020. Although Trump cynically attempted to exploit those divisions to his own benefit, he did not create them. Now that Trump is gone, those divisions remain as entrenched as ever. So too does the work of deciphering their origins and assessing their implications. In that regard, we have a long way to go.

"We are two countries." *Atlantic* magazine staff writer George Packer penned those words on election night 2020. In the circles where big name journalists travel, such a verdict passes for cutting-edge analysis. Two countries: one bigoted and ignorant, the other tolerant and enlightened; one passionately pro-Trump, the other virtuously opposed to all that Trumpism signified; one inhabited by deplorables, the other by my kind of people. Four years of relentlessly obsessing about Donald Trump culminated in this sort of judgment—which is too convenient by half.

Trump did not divide America. Events over which Trump exercised minimal influence shattered whatever precarious unity the nation had cobbled together during World War II and managed to sustain during the subsequent Cold War.

Today we are not two countries. We are several, perhaps many— and we don't get along.

There will be no restoration of unity until Americans first negotiate a ceasefire. By inviting readers to frame the recent past as something other than an Age of Trump, this book represents a tentative and preliminary effort at addressing that requirement.

Taken together, the essays that follow seek to occupy a place between "Breaking News!" ephemera and the perspective of future generations who will view the past with the benefit of far greater knowledge and detachment. In that sense, *On Shedding an Obsolete Past* constitutes a foray into contemporary history.

The task of the contemporary historian is to see beyond the klieg lights of the moment—TV reporters breathlessly relaying the latest half-truth from on high—and to make a start at unearthing the context in which the present is unfolding. Contemporary history necessarily has a limited shelf life. It is a start point rather than a destination. For all that, it performs an essential function.

Given my own scholarly training and professional background, I tend to view the past through a lens that emphasizes events in the realm of war and statecraft. As a result, the essays in this collection pay particular attention to the consequences stemming from the militarization of US policy. Dating from the end of the Cold War and reaching its zenith in the years following 9/11, the militarization of basic US policy played a key role in facilitating Donald Trump's preposterous rise to national political prominence and in exacerbating the divisions that afflict us.

As president, Trump inherited this militarized approach to policy, professed to despise it, and promised to end it. Needless to say, he failed, much as he failed in almost every other domestic or foreign policy initiative he undertook, apart from those benefiting pals and fellow plutocrats. Yet as these essays attempt to show, his failure is itself instructive. The inability of the so-called "most powerful man in the world" to end the endless wars that he denounced hints at deeper explanations for the nation's penchant for ill-conceived military misadventures.

Understanding the predicament in which the United States finds itself at present requires fundamentally recasting our understanding of America's past. My hope is that the essays included here will provide a useful first step toward doing just that.

Walpole, Massachusetts
January 2022

I
TWISTING THE PAST

1
Angst in the Church
of America the Redeemer

David Brooks on Making America Great Again

February 23, 2017

part from being a police officer, firefighter, or soldier engaged in one of this nation's endless wars, writing a column for a major American newspaper has got to be one of the toughest and most unforgiving jobs there is. The pay may be decent (at least if your gig is with one of the major papers in New York or Washington), but the pressures to perform on cue are undoubtedly relentless.

Anyone who has ever tried cramming a coherent and ostensibly insightful argument into a mere 750 words knows what I'm talking about. Writing op-eds does not perhaps qualify as high art. Yet, like tying flies or knitting sweaters, it requires no small amount of skill. Performing the trick week in and week out without too obviously recycling the same ideas over and over again—or at least while disguising repetitions and concealing inconsistencies—requires notable gifts.

David Brooks of the *New York Times* is a gifted columnist. Among contemporary journalists, he is our Walter Lippmann, the closest thing we have to an establishment-approved public intellectual. As was the case with Lippmann, Brooks works hard to suppress the temptation to rant. He shuns raw partisanship. In his frequent radio and television appearances, he speaks in measured tones. Dry humor and ironic references abound. And like Lippmann, when circumstances change, he makes at least a show of adjusting his views accordingly.

For all that, Brooks remains an ideologue. In his columns, and even more so in his weekly appearances on NPR and PBS, he plays the role of the thoughtful, non-screaming conservative, his very presence affirming the ideological balance that, until November 8, 2016, was a prized hallmark of "respectable" journalism. Just as that balance always involved considerable posturing, so, too, with the ostensible conservatism of David Brooks: it's an act.

Praying at the Altar of American Greatness

In terms of confessional fealty, his true allegiance is not to conservatism as such, but to the Church of America the Redeemer. This is a virtual congregation, albeit one possessing many of the attributes of a more traditional religion. The Church has its own Holy Scripture, authenticated on July 4, 1776, at a gathering of fifty-six prophets. And it has its own saints, prominent among them the Good Thomas Jefferson, chief author of the sacred text (not the Bad Thomas Jefferson who owned and impregnated enslaved people); Abraham Lincoln, who freed said enslaved people and thereby suffered martyrdom (on Good Friday no less); and, of course, the duly canonized figures most credited with saving the world itself from evil: Winston Churchill and Franklin Roosevelt, their status akin to that of saints Peter and Paul in Christianity. The Church of America the Redeemer even has its own Jerusalem, located on the banks of the Potomac, and its own hierarchy, its members situated nearby in high temples of varying architectural distinction.

This ecumenical enterprise does not prize theological rigor. When it comes to shalts and shalt nots, it tends to be flexible, if not altogether squishy. It demands of the faithful just one thing: a fervent belief in America's mission to remake the world in its own image. Although in times of crisis Brooks has occasionally gone a bit wobbly, he remains at heart a true believer.

In a March 1997 piece for the *Weekly Standard,* his then-employer, he summarized his credo. Entitled "A Return to National Greatness," the essay opened with a glowing tribute to the Library of Congress and, in particular, to the building completed precisely a century earlier to house its many books and artifacts. According to Brooks, the structure itself embodied the aspirations defining America's enduring purpose. He called particular attention to the dome above the main reading room decorated with a dozen "monumental figures" representing the advance of civilization and culminating in a figure representing America itself. Contemplating the imagery, Brooks rhapsodized:

> The theory of history depicted in this mural gave America impressive historical roots, a spiritual connection to the centuries. And it assigned a specific historic role to America as the latest successor to Jerusalem, Athens, and Rome. In the procession of civilization, certain nations rise up to make extraordinary contributions . . . At the dawn of the 20th century, America was to take its turn at global supremacy. It was America's task to take the grandeur of past civilizations, modernize it, and democratize it. This common destiny would unify diverse Americans and give them a great national purpose.

Twenty years later, in a column with an identical title, but this time appearing in the pages of his present employer, the *New York Times*, Brooks revisited this theme. Again, he began with a paean to the Library of Congress and its spectacular dome with its series of "monumental figures" that placed America "at the vanguard of the great human march of progress." For Brooks, those twelve allegorical figures convey a profound truth: "America is the grateful inheritor of other people's gifts. It has a spiritual connection to all people in all places, but also an exceptional role. America culminates history. It advances a way of life and a democratic model that will provide people everywhere with dignity. The things Americans do are not for themselves only, but for all mankind."

In 1997, in the midst of the Clinton presidency, Brooks had written that "America's mission was to advance civilization itself." In 2017, as Trump gained entry into the Oval Office, he embellished and expanded that mission, describing a nation "assigned by providence to spread democracy and prosperity; to welcome the stranger; to be brother and sister to the whole human race."

Back in 1997, "a moment of world supremacy unlike any other," Brooks had worried that his countrymen might not seize the opportunity that was presenting itself. On the cusp of the twenty-first century, he worried that Americans had "discarded their pursuit of national greatness in just about every particular." The times called for a leader like Theodore Roosevelt, who wielded that classic "big stick" and undertook monster projects like the Panama Canal. Yet Americans were stuck instead with Bill Clinton, a small-bore triangulator. "We no longer look at history as a succession of golden ages," Brooks lamented. "And, save in the speeches of politicians who usually have no clue what they are talking about," America was no longer fulfilling its "special role as the vanguard of civilization."

By early 2017, with Trump in the White House and Steve Bannon whispering in his ear, matters had become worse still. Americans had seemingly abandoned their calling outright. "The Trump and Bannon Anschluss has exposed the hollowness of our patriotism," wrote Brooks, inserting the now-obligatory reference to Nazi Germany. The November 2016 presidential election had "exposed how attenuated our vision of national greatness has become and how easy it was for Trump and Bannon to replace a youthful vision of American greatness with a reactionary, alien one." That vision now threatens to leave America as "just another nation, hunkered down in a fearful world."

What exactly happened between 1997 and 2017, you might ask? What occurred during that "moment of world supremacy" to reduce the United States from a nation summoned to redeem humankind to one hunkered down in fear?

Trust Brooks to have at hand a brow-furrowing explanation. The fault, he explains, lies with an "educational system that doesn't teach civilizational history or real American history but instead a shapeless multiculturalism," as well as with "an intellectual culture that can't imagine providence." Brooks blames "people on the left who are uncomfortable with patriotism and people on the right who are uncomfortable with the federal government that is necessary to lead our project."

An America that no longer believes in itself—that's the problem. In effect, Brooks revises Norma Desmond's famous complaint about the movies, now repurposed to diagnose an ailing nation: it's the politics that got small.

Nowhere does he consider the possibility that his formula for "national greatness" just might be so much hooey. Between 1997 and 2017, after all, egged on by people like David Brooks, Americans took a stab at "greatness," with the execrable Donald Trump now numbering among the eventual results.

Invading Greatness

Say what you will about the shortcomings of the American educational system and the country's intellectual culture, they had far less to do with creating Trump than did popular revulsion prompted by specific policies that Brooks, among others, enthusiastically promoted. Not that he is inclined to tally up the consequences. Only as a sort of postscript to his litany of contemporary American ailments does he refer even in passing to what he calls the "humiliations of Iraq."

A great phrase, that. Yet much like, say, the "tragedy of Vietnam" or the "crisis of Watergate," it conceals more than it reveals. Here, in short, is a succinct historical reference that cries out for further explanation. It bursts at the seams with implications demanding to be unpacked, weighed, and scrutinized. Brooks shrugs off Iraq as a minor embarrassment, the equivalent of having shown up at a dinner party wearing the wrong clothes.

Under the circumstances, it's easy to forget that, back in 2003, he and other members of the Church of America the Redeemer devoutly supported the invasion of Iraq. They welcomed war. They urged it. They did so not because Saddam Hussein was uniquely evil—although he was evil enough—but because they saw in such a war the means for the United States to accomplish its salvific mission. Toppling Saddam and transforming Iraq would provide the mechanism for affirming and renewing America's "national greatness."

Anyone daring to disagree with that proposition they denounced as craven or cowardly. Writing at the time, Brooks disparaged those opposing the war as mere "marchers." They were effete, pretentious, ineffective, and absurd. "These people are always in the streets with their banners and puppets. They march against the IMF and World Bank one day, and against whatever war happens to be going on the next. . . They just march against."

Perhaps space constraints did not permit Brooks in his recent column to spell out the "humiliations" that resulted and that even today continue to accumulate. Here in any event is a brief inventory of what that euphemism conceals: thousands of Americans needlessly killed; tens of thousands grievously wounded in body or spirit; trillions of dollars wasted; millions of Iraqis dead injured, or displaced; this nation's moral standing compromised by its resort to torture, kidnapping, assassination, and other perversions; a region thrown into chaos and threatened by radical terrorist entities like the Islamic State that US military actions helped foster. And now, if only as an oblique second-order bonus, we have Donald Trump's elevation to the presidency to boot.

In refusing to reckon with the results of the war he once so ardently endorsed, Brooks is hardly alone. Members of the Church of America the Redeemer, Democrats and Republicans alike, are demonstrably incapable of rendering an honest accounting of what their missionary efforts have yielded.

Brooks belongs, or once did, to the Church's neoconservative branch. But liberals such as Bill Clinton, along with his secretary of state Madeleine Albright, were congregants in good standing, as were Barack Obama and his secretary of state Hillary Clinton. So, too, are putative conservatives like Senators John McCain, Ted Cruz, and Marco Rubio, all of them subscribing to the belief in the singularity and indispensability of the United States as the chief engine of history, now and forever.

Back in April 2003, confident that the fall of Baghdad had ended the Iraq War, Brooks predicted that "no day will come when the enemies of this endeavor turn around and say, 'We were wrong. Bush was right.'" Rather than admitting error, he continued, the war's opponents "will just extend their forebodings into a more distant future."

Yet it is the war's proponents who, in the intervening years, have choked on admitting that they were wrong. Or when making such an admission, as did both John Kerry and Hillary Clinton while running for president, they write it off as an aberration, a momentary lapse in judgment of no particular significance, like having guessed wrong on a TV quiz show.

Rather than requiring acts of contrition, the Church of America the Redeemer has long promulgated a doctrine of self-forgiveness, freely available to all adherents all the time. "You think our country's so innocent?" the nation's forty-fifth president recently barked at a TV host who had the temerity to ask how he could have kind words for the likes of Russian president Vladimir Putin. Observers professed shock that a sitting president would openly question American innocence.

In fact, Trump's response and the kerfuffle that ensued both missed the point. No serious person believes that the United States is "innocent." Worshippers in the Church of America the Redeemer do firmly believe, however, that America's transgressions, unlike those of other countries, don't count against it. Once committed, such sins are simply to be set aside and then expunged, a process that allows American politicians and pundits to condemn a "killer" like Putin with a perfectly clear conscience while demanding that Trump do the same.

What the Russian president has done in Crimea, Ukraine, and Syria qualifies as criminal. What American presidents have done in Iraq, Afghanistan, and Libya qualifies as incidental and, above all, beside the point.

Rather than confronting the havoc and bloodshed to which the United States has contributed, those who worship in the Church of America the Redeemer keep their eyes fixed on the far horizon and the work still to be done in aligning the world with American expectations. At least they would, were it not for the arrival at center stage of a manifestly false prophet who, in promising to "make America great again," inverts all that "national greatness" is meant to signify.

For Brooks and his fellow believers, the call to "greatness" emanates from faraway precincts—in the Middle East, East Asia, and Eastern Europe. For Trump, the key to "greatness" lies in keeping faraway places and the people who live there as far away as possible. Brooks et al. see a world that needs saving and believe that it's America's calling to do just that. In Trump's view, saving others is not a peculiarly American responsibility. Events beyond our borders matter only to the extent that they affect America's well-being. Trump worships in the Church of America First, or at least pretends to do so in order to impress his followers.

That Trump inhabits a universe of his own devising, constructed of carefully arranged alt-facts, is no doubt the case. Yet, in truth, much the same can be said of Brooks and others sharing his view of a country providentially charged to serve as the "successor to Jerusalem, Athens, and Rome." In fact, this conception of America's purpose expresses not the intent of providence, which is inherently ambiguous, but their own arrogance and conceit. Out of that conceit comes much mischief. And in the wake of mischief come charlatans like Trump.

2

The Age of Great Expectations and the Great Void

History after "the End of History"

January 8, 2017

The fall of the Berlin Wall in October 1989 abruptly ended one historical era and inaugurated another. So, too, did the outcome of the 2016 US presidential election. What are we to make of the interval between those two watershed moments? Answering that question is essential to understanding how Donald Trump became president and where his ascendency leaves us.

Hardly had this period commenced before observers fell into the habit of referring to it as the "post–Cold War" era. Now that it's over, a more descriptive name might be in order. My suggestion: America's Age of Great Expectations.

Forgive and Forget

The end of the Cold War caught the United States completely by surprise. During the 1980s, even with Mikhail Gorbachev running the Kremlin, few in Washington questioned the prevailing conviction that the Soviet-American rivalry was and would remain a defining feature of international politics more or less in perpetuity. Indeed, endorsing such an assumption was among the prerequisites for gaining entrée to official circles. Virtually no one in the American establishment gave serious thought to the here-today, gone-tomorrow possibility that the Soviet threat, the Soviet empire, and the Soviet Union itself might someday vanish. Washington had plans aplenty for what to do should a Third World War erupt, but none for what to do if the prospect of such a climactic conflict simply disappeared.

Still, without missing a beat, when the Berlin Wall fell and two years later the Soviet Union imploded, leading members of that establishment wasted no time in explaining the implications of developments they had totally failed to anticipate. With something close to unanimity, politicians and policy-oriented intellectuals interpreted the unification of Berlin and the ensuing collapse of communism as an all-American victory of cosmic proportions. "We" had won; "they" had lost—with that outcome vindicating everything the United States represented as the archetype of freedom.

From within the confines of that establishment, one rising young intellectual audaciously suggested that the "end of history" itself might be at hand, with the "sole superpower" left standing now perfectly positioned to determine the future of all humankind. In Washington, various powers that be considered this hypothesis and concluded that it sounded just about right. The future took on the appearance of a blank slate upon which Destiny itself was inviting Americans to inscribe their intentions.

American elites might, of course, have assigned a far different, less celebratory meaning to the passing of the Cold War. They might have seen the outcome as a moment that called for regret, repentance, and making amends.

After all, the competition between the United States and the Soviet Union, or more broadly between what was then called the Free World and the Communist bloc, had yielded a host of baleful effects. An arms race between two superpowers had created monstrous nuclear arsenals and, on multiple occasions, brought the planet precariously close to Armageddon. Two singularly inglorious wars had claimed the lives of many tens of thousands of American soldiers and literally millions of Asians. One, on the Korean peninsula, had ended in an unsatisfactory draw; the other, in Southeast Asia, in catastrophic defeat. Proxy fights in Asia, Africa, Latin America, and the Middle East killed so many more and laid waste to whole countries. Cold War obsessions led Washington to overthrow democratic governments, connive in assassination, make common cause with corrupt dictators, and turn a blind eye to genocidal violence. On the home front, hysteria compromised civil liberties and fostered a sprawling, intrusive, and unaccountable national security apparatus. Meanwhile, the military-industrial complex and its beneficiaries conspired to spend vast sums on weapons purchases that somehow never seemed adequate to the putative dangers at hand.

Rather than reflecting on such somber and sordid matters, however, the American political establishment together with ambitious members of the country's intelligentsia found it so much more expedient simply to move on. As they saw it, the annus mirabilis of 1989 wiped away the sins of former years. Eager to make a fresh start, Washington granted itself a plenary indulgence. After all, why contemplate past unpleasantness when a future so stunningly rich in promise now beckoned?

Three Big Ideas and a Dubious Corollary

Soon enough, that promise found concrete expression. In remarkably short order, three themes emerged to define the new American age. Informing each of them was a sense of exuberant anticipation toward an era of almost unimaginable expectations. The twentieth century was ending on a high note. For the planet as a whole but especially for the United States, great things lay ahead.

Focused on the world economy, the first of those themes emphasized the transformative potential of turbocharged globalization led by US-based financial institutions and transnational corporations. An "open world" would facilitate the movement of goods, capital, ideas, and people and thereby create wealth on an unprecedented scale. In the process, the rules governing American-style corporate capitalism would come to prevail everywhere on the planet. Everyone would benefit, but especially Americans who would continue to enjoy more than their fair share of material abundance.

Focused on statecraft, the second theme spelled out the implications of an international order dominated as never before—not even in the heydays of the Roman and British Empires—by a single nation. With the passing of the Cold War, the United States now stood apart as both supreme power and irreplaceable global leader, its status guaranteed by its unstoppable military might.

In the editorial offices of the *Wall Street Journal*, the *Washington Post*, the *New Republic*, and the *Weekly Standard*, such "truths" achieved a self-evident status. Although more muted in their public pronouncements than Washington's reigning pundits, officials enjoying access to the Oval Office, the State Department's seventh floor, and the E-ring of the Pentagon generally agreed. The assertive exercise of (benign!) global hegemony seemingly held the key to ensuring that Americans would enjoy safety and security, both at home and abroad, now and in perpetuity.

The third theme was all about rethinking the concept of personal freedom as commonly understood and pursued by most Americans. During the protracted emergency of the Cold War, reaching an accommodation between freedom and the putative imperatives of national security had not come easily. Cold War–style patriotism seemingly prioritized the interests of the state at the expense of the individual. Yet even as thrillingly expressed by John F. Kennedy—"Ask not what your country can do for you, ask what you can do for your country"—this was never an easy sell, especially if it meant wading through rice paddies and getting shot at.

Once the Cold War ended, however, the tension between individual freedom and national security momentarily dissipated. Reigning conceptions of what freedom could or should entail underwent a radical transformation. Emphasizing the removal of restraints and inhibitions, the shift made itself felt everywhere, from patterns of consumption and modes of cultural expression to sexuality and the definition of the family. Norms that had prevailed for decades if not generations—marriage as a union between a man and a woman, gender identity as fixed at birth—became passé. The concept of a transcendent common good—which during the Cold War had taken a backseat to national security—now took a backseat to maximizing individual choice and autonomy.

Finally, as a complement to these themes, in the realm of governance, the end of the Cold War cemented the status of the president as quasi-deity. In the Age of Great Expectations, the myth of the president as a deliverer from (or, in the eyes of critics, the ultimate perpetrator of) evil flourished. In the solar system of American politics, the man in the White House increasingly became the sun around which everything seemed to orbit. By comparison, nothing else mattered much.

From one administration to the next, of course, presidential efforts to deliver Americans to the Promised Land regularly came up short. Even so, the political establishment and the establishment media collaborated in sustaining the pretense that out of the next endlessly hyped "race for the White House," another Roosevelt or Kennedy or Reagan would magically emerge to save the nation. From one election cycle to the next, these campaigns became longer and more expensive, drearier and yet ever more circus-like. No matter. During the Age of Great Expectations, the reflexive tendency to see the president as the ultimate guarantor of American abundance, security, and freedom remained sacrosanct.

Blindsided

Meanwhile, between promise and reality, a yawning gap began to appear. During the concluding decade of the twentieth century and the first decade-and-a-half of the twenty-first, Americans endured a seemingly endless series of crises. Individually, none of these merit comparison with, say, the Civil War or World War II. Yet never in US history has a sequence of events occurring in such close proximity subjected American institutions and the American people to greater stress.

During the decade between 1998 and 2008, they came on with startling regularity: one president impeached and his successor chosen by the direct intervention of the Supreme Court; a massive terrorist attack on American soil that killed thousands, traumatized the nation, and left senior officials bereft of their senses; a mindless, needless, and unsuccessful war of choice launched on the basis of false claims and outright lies; a natural disaster (exacerbated by engineering folly) that all but destroyed a major American city, after which government agencies mounted a belated and half-hearted response; and finally, the worst economic downturn since the Great Depression, bringing ruin to millions of families.

For the sake of completeness, we should append to this roster of seismic occurrences one additional event: Barack Obama's election as the nation's first Black president. He arrived at the zenith of American political life as a seemingly messianic figure called upon not only to undo the damage wrought by his predecessor, George W. Bush, but somehow to absolve the nation of its original sins of slavery and racism.

Yet during the Obama presidency, race relations, in fact, deteriorated. Whether prompted by cynical political calculations or a crass desire to boost ratings, race baiters came out of the woodwork—one of them, of course, infamously birthered in Trump Tower in mid-Manhattan—and poured their poisons into the body politic. Even so, as the end of Obama's term approached, the cult of the presidency itself remained remarkably intact.

Individually, the impact of these various crises ranged from disconcerting to debilitating to horrifying. Yet to treat them separately is to overlook their collective implications, which the election of Donald Trump only now enables us to appreciate. It was not one president's dalliance with an intern *or* "hanging chads" *or* 9/11 *or* "Mission Accomplished" *or* the inundation of the Lower Ninth Ward *or* the collapse of Lehman Brothers *or* the absurd birther movement that undermined the Age of Great Expectations. It was the way all these events together exposed those expectations as radically suspect.

In effect, the various crises that punctuated the post–Cold War era called into question key themes to which a fevered American triumphalism had given rise. Globalization, militarized hegemony, and a more expansive definition of freedom, guided by enlightened presidents in tune with the times, *should* have provided Americans with all the blessings that were rightly theirs as a consequence of having prevailed in the Cold War. Instead, between 1989 and 2016, things kept happening

that weren't supposed to happen. A future marketed as all but foreordained proved elusive, if not illusory. As actually experienced, the Age
of Great Expectations became an Age of Unwelcome Surprises.

A Candidate for Decline

True, globalization created wealth on a vast scale, just not for ordinary
Americans. The already well-to-do did splendidly, in some cases unbe-
lievably so. But middle-class incomes stagnated and good jobs became
increasingly hard to find or keep. By the election of 2016, the United
States looked increasingly like a society divided between haves and
have-nots, the affluent and the left-behind, the 1 percent and everyone
else. Prospective voters were noticing.

Meanwhile, policies inspired by Washington's soaring hegemonic
ambitions produced remarkably few happy outcomes. With US forces
continuously engaged in combat operations, peace all but vanished as a
policy objective (or even a word in Washington's political lexicon). The
acknowledged standing of the country's military as the world's best-
trained, best-equipped, and best-led force coexisted uneasily with the
fact that it proved unable to win.

Instead, the national security establishment became conditioned to
the idea of permanent war, high-ranking officials taking it for granted
that ordinary citizens would simply accommodate themselves to this
new reality. Yet it soon became apparent that, instead of giving ordinary Americans a sense of security, this new paradigm induced an
acute sense of vulnerability, which left many susceptible to demagogic
fearmongering.

As for the revised definition of freedom, with autonomy emerging
as the national summum bonum, it left some satisfied but others adrift.
During the Age of Great Expectations, distinctions between citizen and
consumer blurred. Shopping became tantamount to a civic obligation,
essential to keeping the economy afloat. Yet if all the hoopla surrounding
Black Friday and Cyber Monday represented a celebration of American
freedom, its satisfactions were transitory at best, rarely extending beyond
the due date printed on a credit card statement. Meanwhile, as digital

connections displaced personal ones, relationships, like jobs, became more contingent and temporary. Loneliness emerged as an abiding affliction. Meanwhile, for all the talk of empowering the marginalized—people of color, women, LGBTQ+ people—elites reaped the lion's share of the benefits while ordinary people were left to make do. The atmosphere was rife with hypocrisy and even a whiff of nihilism.

To these various contradictions, the establishment itself remained stubbornly oblivious, with the 2016 presidential candidacy of Hillary Clinton offering a case in point. As her long record in public life made abundantly clear, Clinton embodied the establishment in the Age of Great Expectations. She believed in globalization, in the indispensability of American leadership backed by military power, and in the post–Cold War cultural project. And she certainly believed in the presidency as the mechanism to translate aspirations into outcomes.

Such commonplace convictions of the era, along with her vanguard role in pressing for the empowerment of women, imparted to her run an air of inevitability. That she deserved to win appeared self-evident. It was, after all, her turn. Largely overlooked were signs that the abiding themes of the Age of Great Expectations no longer commanded automatic allegiance.

Gasping for Air

Senator Bernie Sanders offered one of those signs. That a past-his-prime, self-professed socialist from Vermont with a negligible record of legislative achievement and tenuous links to the Democratic Party might mount a serious challenge to Clinton seemed, on the face of it, absurd. Yet by zeroing in on unfairness and inequality as inevitable by-products of globalization, Sanders struck a chord.

Knocked briefly off balance, Clinton responded by modifying certain of her longstanding positions. By backing away from free trade, the ne plus ultra of globalization, she managed, though not without difficulty, to defeat the Sanders insurgency. Even so, he, in effect, served as the canary in the establishment coal mine, signaling that the Age of Great Expectations might be running out of oxygen.

A parallel and far stranger insurgency was simultaneously wreaking havoc in the Republican Party. That a narcissistic political neophyte stood the slightest chance of capturing the GOP seemed even more improbable than Sanders taking a nomination that appeared Clinton's by right.

Coarse, vulgar, unprincipled, uninformed, erratic, and with little regard for truth, Trump was *sui generis* among presidential candidates. Yet he possessed a singular gift: a knack for riling up those who nurse gripes and are keen to pin the blame on someone or something. In post–Cold War America, among the millions that Hillary Clinton was famously dismissing as "deplorables," gripes had been ripening like cheese in a hothouse.

Through whatever combination of intuition and malice aforethought, Trump demonstrated a genius for motivating those deplorables. He pushed their buttons. They responded by turning out in droves to attend his rallies. There they listened to a message that they found compelling.

In Trump's pledge to "make America great again" his followers heard a promise to restore everything they believed had been taken from them in the Age of Great Expectations. Globalization was neither beneficial nor inevitable, the candidate insisted, and he vowed, once elected, to curb its effects along with the excesses of corporate capitalism, thereby bringing back millions of lost jobs from overseas. He would, he swore, fund a massive infrastructure program, cut taxes, keep a lid on the national debt, and generally champion the cause of working stiffs. The many complications and contradictions inherent in these various prescriptions would, he assured his fans, give way to his business savvy.

In considering America's role in the post–Cold War world, Trump exhibited a similar impatience with the status quo. Rather than allowing armed conflicts to drag on forever, he promised to win them (putting to work his mastery of military affairs) or, if not, to quit and get out, pausing just long enough to claim as a sort of consolation prize whatever spoils might be lying loose on the battlefield. At the very least, he would prevent so-called allies from treating the United States like some patsy.

Henceforth, nations benefiting from American protection were going to foot their share of the bill. What all of this added up to may not have been clear, but it did suggest a sharp departure from the usual post-1989 formula for exercising global leadership.

No less important than Trump's semi-coherent critique of globalization and American globalism, however, was his success in channeling the discontent of all those who nursed an inchoate sense that post–Cold War freedoms might be working for some, but not for them.

Not that Trump had anything to say about whether freedom confers obligations, or whether conspicuous consumption might not actually hold the key to human happiness, or any of the various controversies related to gender, sexuality, and family. He was indifferent to all such matters. He was, however, distinctly able to offer his followers a grimly persuasive explanation for how America had gone off course and how the blessings of liberties to which they were entitled had been stolen. He did that by fingering as scapegoats Muslims, Mexicans, and others "not like me."

Trump's political strategy as president would overturn the conventions that had governed right thinking since the end of the Cold War. To the amazement of an establishment grown smug and lazy, his approach worked. Even while disregarding all received wisdom when it came to organizing and conducting a presidential campaign in the Age of Great Expectations, Trump won. He did so by enchanting the disenchanted, all those who had lost faith in the promises that had sprung from the bosom of the elites that the end of the Cold War had taken by surprise.

Adrift Without a Compass

Within hours of Trump's election, among progressives, expressing fear and trepidation at the prospect of what he might actually do upon assuming office became de rigueur. Yet those who had actually voted for Trump were also left wondering what to expect. Both camps assign him the status of a transformative historical figure. However, premonitions of incipient fascism and hopes that he will engineer a new American

Golden Age are likely to prove similarly misplaced. To focus on the man himself rather than on the circumstances that produced him is to miss the significance of what occurred.

Note, for example, that his mandate is almost entirely negative. It centers on rejection: of globalization, of counterproductive military meddling, and of the post–Cold War cultural project. Yet neither Trump nor any of his surrogates has offered a coherent alternative to the triad of themes providing the through line for the last quarter-century of American history. Apart from a lingering conviction that forceful—in The Donald's case, blustering—presidential leadership can somehow turn things around, "Trumpism" is a dog's breakfast.

In all likelihood, his presidency will prove less transformative than transitional. As a result, concerns about what he may do, however worrisome, matter less than the larger question of where we go from here. The principles that enjoyed favor following the Cold War have been found wanting. What should replace them?

Efforts to identify those principles should begin with an honest accounting of the age we are now leaving behind, the history that happened after "the end of history." That accounting should, in turn, allow room for regret, repentance, and making amends —the very critical appraisal that ought to have occurred at the end of the Cold War but was preempted when American elites succumbed to their bout of victory disease.

Don't expect Trump to undertake any such appraisal. Nor will the establishment that candidate Trump so roundly denounced, but which President-elect Trump, at least in his senior national security appointments, now shows signs of accommodating. Those expecting Trump's election to inject courage into members of the political class or imagination into inside-the-Beltway "thought leaders" are in for a disappointment. So the principles we need—an approach to political economy providing sustainable and equitable prosperity; a foreign policy that discards militarism in favor of prudence and pragmatism; and an enriched, inclusive concept of freedom—will have to come from somewhere else.

"Where there is no vision," the Book of Proverbs tells us, "the people perish." In the present day, there is no vision to which Americans collectively adhere. For proof, we need look no further than the election of Trump.

The Age of Great Expectations has ended, leaving behind an ominous void. Yet Trump's own inability to explain what should fill that great void provides neither excuse for inaction nor cause for despair. Instead, Trump himself makes manifest the need to reflect on the nation's recent past and to think deeply about its future.

A decade before the Cold War ended, writing in *democracy*, a short-lived journal devoted to "political renewal and radical change," the historian and social critic Christopher Lasch sketched out a set of principles that might lead us out of our current crisis. Lasch called for a politics based on "the nurture of the soil against the exploitation of resources, the family against the factory, the romantic vision of the individual against the technological vision, [and] localism over democratic centralism." Nearly a half-century later, as a place to begin, his prescription remains apt.

3
Kissing the Specious Present Goodbye

Did History Begin Anew Last November 8?

June 22, 2017

Forgive me for complaining, but recent decades have not been easy ones for my peeps. I am from birth a member of the WHAM tribe, that once proud, but now embattled conglomeration of white, heterosexual American males. We have long been—there's no denying it—a privileged group. When the blessings of American freedom get parceled out, WHAMs are accustomed to standing at the head of the line. Those not enjoying the trifecta of being white, heterosexual, and male get what's left.

Fair? No, but from time immemorial those have been the rules. Anyway, no real American would carp. After all, the whole idea of America derives from the conviction that some people (us) deserve more than others (all those who are not us). It's God's will—so at least the great majority of Americans have believed since the Pilgrims set up shop just about four hundred years ago.

Lately, however, the rules have been changing in ways that many WHAMs find disconcerting. True, some of my brethren—let's call them one percenters—have adapted to those changes and continue to do very well indeed. Wherever corporate CEOs, hedge fund managers, investment bankers, tech gurus, university presidents, publishers, politicians, and generals congregate to pat each other on the back, you can count on WHAMs—reciting bromides about the importance of diversity!—being amply represented.

Yet beneath this upper crust, a different picture emerges. Further down the socioeconomic ladder, being a WHAM carries with it disadvantages. The good, steady jobs once implicitly reserved for us—lunch pail stuff, yes, but enough to keep food in the family larder—are increasingly hard to come by. As those jobs have disappeared, so too have the ancillary benefits they conferred, self-respect not least among them. Especially galling to some WHAMs is being exiled to the back of the cultural bus. When it comes to art, music, literature, and fashion, the doings of Blacks, Latinx people, Asian people, LGBTQ+ folks, and women generate buzz. By comparison, white heterosexual males seem bland, uncool, and passé, or worst of all simply boring.

The Mandate of Heaven, which members of my tribe once took as theirs by right, has been cruelly withdrawn. History itself has betrayed us.

All of which is nonsense, of course, except perhaps as a reason to reflect on whether history can help explain why, today, WHAMs have worked themselves into such a funk in Donald Trump's America. Can history provide answers? Or has history itself become part of the problem?

Paging Professor Becker

"For all practical purposes history is, for us and for the time being, what we know it to be." So remarked Carl Becker in 1931 at the annual meeting of the American Historical Association. Professor Becker, a towering figure among historians of his day, was president of the AHA that year. His message to his colleagues amounted to a warning of sorts: Don't think you're so smart. The study of the past may reveal truths, he allowed, but those truths are contingent, incomplete, and valid only "for the time being."

Put another way, historical perspectives conceived in what Becker termed "the specious present" have a sell-by date. Beyond their time, they become stale and outmoded, and so should be revised or discarded. This process of rejecting truths previously treated as authoritative is inexorable and essential. Yet it also tends to be fiercely contentious. The present may be specious, but it confers real privileges, which a particular reading of the past can sustain or undermine. Becker believed it inevitable that "our now valid versions" of history "will in due course be relegated to the category of discarded myths." It was no less inevitable that beneficiaries of the prevailing version of truth should fight to preserve it.

Who exercises the authority to relegate? Who gets to decide when a historical truth no longer qualifies as true? Here, Becker insisted that "Mr. Everyman" plays a crucial role. For Becker, Mr. Everyman was Joe Doakes, John Q. Public, or the man on the street. He was "every normal person," a phrase broad enough to include all manner of people. Yet nothing in Becker's presentation suggested that he had the slightest interest in race, sexual orientation, or gender. His Mr. Everyman belonged to the tribe of WHAM.

In order to "live in a world of semblance more spacious and satisfying than is to be found within the narrow confines of the fleeting present moment," Becker emphasized, Mr. Everyman needs a past larger than his own individual past. An awareness of things said and done long ago provides him with an "artificial extension of memory" and a direction.

Memories, whether directly or vicariously acquired, are "necessary to orient us in our little world of endeavor." Yet the specious present that we inhabit is inherently unstable and constantly in flux, which means that history itself must be pliable. Crafting history necessarily becomes an exercise in "imaginative creation" in which all participate. However unconsciously, Everyman adapts the past to serve his most pressing needs, thereby functioning as "his own historian."

Yet he does so in collaboration with others. Since time immemorial, according to Becker, purveyors of the past—the "ancient and honorable company of wise men of the tribe, of bards and story-tellers and minstrels, of soothsayers and priests, to whom in successive ages has been entrusted the keeping of the useful myths"—have enabled him to "hold in memory . . . those things only which can be related with some reasonable degree of relevance" to his own experience and aspirations. In Becker's lifetime it had become incumbent upon members of the professoriate, successors to the bards and minstrels of yesteryear, "to enlarge and enrich the specious present common to us all to the end that 'society' (the tribe, the nation, or all mankind) may judge of what it is doing in the light of what it has done and what it hopes to do."

Yet Becker took pains to emphasize that professional historians disdained Mr. Everyman at their peril:

> Berate him as we will for not reading our books, Mr. Everyman is stronger than we are, and sooner or later we must adapt our knowledge to his necessities. Otherwise he will leave us to our own devices . . . . The history that does work in the world, the history that influences the course of history, is living history . . . . It is for this reason that the history of history is a record of the "new history" that in every age rises to confound and supplant the old.

Becker stressed that the process of formulating new history to supplant the old is organic rather than contrived; it comes from the bottom up, not the top down. "We, historians by profession, share in this necessary effort," he concluded. "But we do not impose our version of the human story on Mr. Everyman; in the end it is rather Mr. Everyman who imposes his version on us."

Donald Trump as Everyman's Champion?

Becker offered his reflections on "Everyman His Own Historian," the title of his AHA presentation, in the midst of the Great Depression. Perhaps because that economic crisis found so many Americans burdened with deprivation and uncertainty, he implicitly attributed to his everyman a unitary perspective, as if shared distress imbued members of the public with a common outlook. That was not, in fact, the case in 1931 and is, if anything, even less so in our own day.

Still, Becker's construct retains considerable utility. Today finds more than a few white heterosexual American males, our own equivalent of Mr. Everyman, in a state of high dudgeon. From their perspective, the specious present has not panned out as it was supposed to. As a consequence, they are pissed. In November 2016, to make clear just how pissed they were, they elected Trump as president of the United States.

This was, to put it mildly, not supposed to happen. For months prior to the election, the custodians of the past in its "now valid version" had judged the prospect all but inconceivable. Yet WHAMs (with shocking support from other tribes) intervened to decide otherwise. Rarely has a single event so thoroughly confounded history's self-assigned proctors. One can imagine the shade of Professor Becker whispering, "I warned you, didn't I?"

Those deeply invested in drawing a straight line from the specious present into the indefinite future blame Trump himself for having knocked history off its prescribed course. Remove Trump from the scene, they appear to believe, and all will once again be well. The urgent imperative of doing just that—immediately, now, no later than this afternoon—has produced what *New York Times* columnist Charles Blow aptly calls a "throbbing anxiety" among those who (like Blow himself) find "the relentless onslaught of awfulness erupting from this White House" intolerable. They will not rest until Trump is gone.

This idée fixe, reinforced on a daily basis by ever more preposterous presidential antics, finds the nation trapped in a sort of bizarre do-loop. The media's obsession with Trump reinforces his obsession with the media and between them they simply crowd out all possibility of thoughtful reflection. Their fetish is his and his theirs. The result is a cycle of mutual contempt that only deepens the longer it persists.

Both sides agree on one point only, which is that history began anew November 8, 2016, when (take your pick) America either took leave of its senses or chose greatness. How the United States got to November 8 qualifies, at best, as an afterthought or curiosity. It's almost as if the years and decades that had preceded Trump's election had all disappeared into some vast sinkhole.

Where, then, are we to turn for counsel? For my money, Charles Blow is no more reliable as a guide to the past or the future than is Donald Trump himself. Much the same could be said of most other newspaper columnists, talking heads, and online commentators (contributors to *Tom-Dispatch* notably excepted, of course). As for politicians of either party, they have as a class long since forfeited any right to expect a respectful hearing.

God knows Americans today do not lack for information or opinion. On screens, over the airways, and in print, the voices competing for our attention create a relentless cacophony. Yet the correlation between insight and noise is discouragingly low.

What would Carl Becker make of our predicament? He would, I think, see it as an opportunity to "enlarge and enrich the specious present" by recasting and reinvigorating history. Yet doing so, he would insist, requires taking seriously the complaints that led our latter-day everyman to throw himself into the arms of Donald Trump in the first place. Doing *that* implies a willingness to engage with ordinary Americans on a respectful basis.

Unlike President Trump, I do not pretend to speak for Everyman or for his female counterpart. Yet my sense is that many Americans have an inkling that history of late has played them for suckers. This is notably true with respect to the post–Cold War era, in which the glories of openness, diversity, and neoliberal economics, of advanced technology and unparalleled US military power, all promised in combination to produce something like a new utopia in which Americans would indisputably enjoy a privileged status globally.

In almost every respect, those expectations remain painfully unfulfilled. The history that "served for the time being" and was endlessly reiterated during the presidencies of Bush 41, Clinton, Bush 43, and Obama no longer serves. It has yielded a mess of pottage: grotesque inequality, worrisome insecurity, moral confusion, an epidemic of self-destructive behavior, endless wars, and basic institutions that work poorly if at all. Nor is it just WHAMs who have suffered the consequences. The history with which Americans are familiar cannot explain this outcome.

Alas, little reason exists to expect Becker's successors in the guild of professional historians to join with ordinary Americans in formulating an explanation. Few academic historians today see Everyman as a worthy interlocutor. Rather than berating him for not reading their books, they ignore him. Their preference is to address one another.

By and large, he returns the favor, endorsing the self-marginalization of the contemporary historical profession. Contrast the influence wielded by prominent historians in Becker's day—during the first third of the twentieth century, they included, along with Becker, such formidables as Henry Adams, Charles and Mary Beard, Alfred Thayer Mahan, and Frederick Jackson Turner—with the role played by historians today. The issue here is not erudition, which today's scholars possess in abundance, but impact. On that score, the disparity between then and now is immense.

In effect, professional historians have ceded the field to a new group of bards and minstrels. So the bestselling "historian" in the United States today is Bill O'Reilly, whose books routinely sell more than a million copies each. Were Trump given to reading books, he would likely find O'Reilly's both accessible and agreeable. But O'Reilly is in the entertainment business. He has neither any interest nor the genuine ability to create what Becker called "history that does work in the world."

Still, history itself works in mysterious ways known only to God or to Providence. Only after the fact do its purposes become evident. It may yet surprise us.

Owing his election in large part to my fellow WHAMs, Trump is now expected to repay that support by putting things right. Yet as events make it apparent that Trump is no more able to run a government than O'Reilly is able to write history, they may well decide that he is not their friend after all. With that, their patience is likely to run short. It is hardly implausible that Trump's assigned role in history will be once and for all to ring down the curtain on our specious present, demonstrating definitively just how bankrupt all the triumphalist hokum of the past quarter-century—the history that served "for the time being"—has become.

When that happens, when promises of American greatness restored prove empty, there will be hell to pay. Joe Doakes, John Q. Public, and the man on the street will be even more pissed. Should that moment arrive, historians would do well to listen seriously to what Everyman has to say.

4
On Seeing America's Wars Whole

Six Questions for A. G. Sulzberger

March 20, 2018

Dear Mr. Sulzberger:

Congratulations on assuming the reins of this nation's—and arguably, the world's—most influential publication. It's the family business, of course, so your appointment to succeed your father doesn't exactly qualify as a surprise. Even so, the responsibility for guiding the fortunes of a great institution must weigh heavily on you, especially when the media landscape is changing so rapidly and radically.

Undoubtedly, you're already getting plenty of advice on how to run the paper, probably more than you want or need. Still, with your indulgence, I'd like to offer an outsider's perspective on "the news that's fit to print." The famous motto of the *Times* insists that the paper is committed to publishing "all" such news—an admirable aspiration even if an impossibility. In practice, what readers like me get on a daily basis is "all the news that *Times* editors deem worthy of print."

Of course, within that somewhat more restrictive universe of news, not all stories are equal. Some appear on the front page above the fold. Others are consigned to page A17 on Saturday morning.

And some topics receive more attention than others. In recent years, comprehensive coverage of issues touching on diversity, sexual preference, and the status of women has become a *Times* hallmark. When it comes to Donald Trump, "comprehensive" can't do justice to the attention he receives. At the *Times* (and more than a few other media outlets), he has induced a form of mania, with his daily effusion of taunts, insults, preposterous assertions, bogus claims, and decisions made, then immediately renounced, all reported in masochistic detail. Throw in salacious revelations from Trump's colorful past and leaks from the ongoing Mueller investigation of his campaign and our forty-fifth president has become for the *Times* something akin to a Great White Whale, albeit with a comb-over and a preference for baggy suits.

In the meantime, other issues of equal or even greater importance—I would put climate change in this category—receive no more than sporadic or irregular coverage. And, of course, some topics simply don't make the cut at all, like just about anything short of a school shooting that happens in that vast expanse west of the Hudson that Saul Steinberg years ago so memorably depicted for the *New Yorker*.

The point of this admittedly unsolicited memo is not to urge the *Times* to open a bureau in Terre Haute or in the rapidly melting Arctic. Nor am I implying that the paper should tone down its efforts to dismantle the heteronormative order, empower women, and promote equality for transgender persons. Yet I do want to suggest that obsessing about this administration's stupefying tomfoolery finds the *Times* overlooking one particular issue that predates and transcends the Trump Moment. That issue is the normalization of armed conflict, with your writers, editors, and editorial board having tacitly accepted that, for the United States, war has become a permanent condition.

Let me stipulate that the *Times* does devote an impressive number of column-inches to the myriad US military activities around the planet. Stories about deployments, firefights, air strikes, sieges, and casualties abound. Readers can count on the *Times* to convey the latest White House or Pentagon pronouncements about the briefly visible light at the end of some very long tunnel. And features describing the plight of veterans back from the war zone also appear with appropriate and commendable frequency.

So anyone reading the *Times* for a week or a month will have absorbed the essential facts of the case, including the following:

- Over six thousand days after it began, America's war in Afghanistan continues, with *Times* correspondents providing regular and regularly repetitive updates.

- In the seven-year-long civil war that has engulfed Syria, the ever-shifting cast of belligerents now includes at least two thousand (some sources say four thousand) US special operators, the rationale for their presence changing from week to week, even as plans to keep US troops in Syria indefinitely take shape.

- In Iraq, now liberated from ISIS, itself a byproduct of US invasion and occupation, US troops are now poised to remain in place, more or less as they did in West Germany in 1945 and in South Korea after 1953.

- On the Arabian Peninsula, US forces have partnered with Saudi Crown Prince Mohammad bin Salman Al Saud in brutalizing Yemen, thereby creating a vast humanitarian disaster despite the absence of discernible US interests at stake.

- In the military equivalent of whacking self-sown weeds, American drones routinely attack Libyan militant groups that owe their existence to the chaos created in 2011 when the United States impulsively participated in the overthrow of Muammar Gaddafi.

- More than a quarter-century after American troops entered Somalia to feed the starving, the US military mission there continues, presently in the form of recurring air strikes.

- Elsewhere in Africa, the latest theater to offer opportunities for road-testing the most recent counterterrorism techniques, the US military footprint is rapidly expanding, all but devoid of congressional (or possibly any other kind of) oversight.

- From the Levant to South Asia, a flood of American-manufactured weaponry continues to flow unabated, to the delight of the military-industrial complex, but with little evidence that the arms we sell or give away are contributing to regional peace and stability.

- Amid this endless spiral of undeclared American wars and conflicts, Congress stands by passively, only rousing itself as needed to appropriate money that ensures the unimpeded continuation of all of the above.

- Meanwhile, President Trump, though assessing all of this military hyperactivity as misbegotten—"Seven trillion dollars. What a mistake."—is effectively perpetuating and even ramping up the policies pioneered by his predecessors.

This conglomeration of circumstances, I submit, invites attention to several first-order questions to which the *Times* appears stubbornly oblivious. These questions are by no means original with me. Indeed, Mr. Sulzberger (may I call you A. G.?), if you've kept up with *Tom-Dispatch*—if you haven't, you really should—you will already have encountered several of them. Yet in the higher reaches of mainstream journalism they remain sadly neglected, with disastrous practical and moral implications.

The key point is that when it comes to recent American wars, the *Times* offers coverage without perspective. "All the news" is shallow and redundant. Lots of dots, few connections.

To put it another way, what's missing is any sort of Big Picture. The *Times* would never depict Russian military actions in Crimea, eastern Ukraine, and Syria, along with its cyber-provocations, as somehow unrelated to one another. Yet it devotes remarkably little energy to identifying any links between what US forces today are doing in Niger and what they are doing in Afghanistan; between US drone attacks that target this group of "terrorists" and those that target some other group; or, more fundamentally, between what we thought we were doing as far back as the 1980s when Washington supported Saddam Hussein and what we imagine we're doing today in the various Muslim-majority nations in which the US military is present, whether welcome or not.

Crudely put, the central question that goes not only unanswered but unasked is: What the hell is going on? Allow me to deconstruct that in ways that might resonate with *Times* correspondents:

What exactly should we call the enterprise in which US forces have been engaged all these years? The term that George W. Bush introduced back in 2001, "Global War on Terrorism," fell out of favor long ago. Nothing has appeared to replace it. A project that today finds US forces mired in open-ended hostilities across a broad expanse of Muslim-majority nations does, I suggest, deserve a name, even if the commander in chief consigns most of those countries to "shithole" status. A while back, I proposed "War for the Greater Middle East," but that didn't catch on. Surely, the president or perhaps one of his many generals could come up with something better, some phrase that conveys a sense of purpose, scope, stakes, or location. The paper of record should insist that whatever it is the troops out there may be doing, their exertions ought to have a descriptive name.

What is our overall objective in waging that no-name war? After 9/11, George W. Bush vowed at various times to eliminate terrorism, liberate the oppressed, spread freedom and democracy, advance the cause of women's rights across the Islamic world, and even end evil itself. Today, such aims seem like so many fantasies. So what is it we're trying to accomplish? What will we settle for? Without a readily identifiable objective, how will anyone know when to raise that "Mission Accomplished" banner (again) and let the troops come home?

By extension, what exactly is the strategy for bringing our no-name war to a successful conclusion? A strategy is a kind of roadmap aimed at identifying resources, defining enemies (as well as friends), and describing a sequence of steps that will lead to some approximation of victory. It should offer a vision that gets us from where we are to where we want to be. Yet when it comes to waging its no-name war, Washington today has no strategy worthy of the name. This fact should outrage the American people and embarrass the national security establishment. It should also attract the curiosity of the *New York Times*.

Roughly speaking, in what year, decade, or century might this war end? Even if only approximately, it would help to know—and the American people deserve to know—when the front page of the *Times* might possibly carry a headline reading "Peace Secured" or "Hostilities Ended" or even merely "It's Over." On the other hand, if it's unrealistic to expect the ever-morphing, ever-spreading no-name war to end at all, then shouldn't someone say so, allowing citizens to chew on the implications of that prospect? Who better to reveal this secret hidden in plain sight than the newspaper over which you preside?

What can we expect the no-name war to cost? Although the president's estimate of $7 trillion may be a trifle premature, it's not wrong. It may even end up being on the low side. What that money might otherwise have paid for—including infrastructure, education, scientific and medical research, and possibly making amends for all the havoc wreaked by our ill-considered military endeavors—certainly merits detailed discussion. Imagine a running tally of sunk and projected cumulative costs featured on the front page of the *Times* every morning. Just two numbers: the first, a tabulation of what the Pentagon has already spent pursuant to all US military interventions, large and small, since 9/11; the second, a projection of what the final bill might look like decades from now when the last of this generation's war vets passes on.

Finally, what are the implications of saddling future generations with this financial burden? With the sole exception of the very brief Gulf War of 1990–1991, the no-name war is the only substantial armed conflict in American history where the generation in whose name it was waged resolutely refused to pay for it—indeed, happily accepted tax cuts when increases were very much in order. With astonishingly few exceptions, politicians endorsed this arrangement. One might think that enterprising reporters would want to investigate the various factors that foster such irresponsibility.

So that's my take. I'm sure, A. G., that journalists in your employ could sharpen my questions and devise more of their own. But here's a small proposition: just for a single day, confine Donald Trump to page A17 and give our no-name war the attention that the *Times* normally reserves for the president it loathes.

I'm not a newspaperman, but I'm reminded of that wonderful 1940 Hitchcock movie *Foreign Correspondent*. I expect you've seen it. Europe is stumbling toward war, and Mr. Powers, head honcho at the fictitious *New York Globe*, is tired of getting the same old same old from the people he has on the scene. "I don't want any more economists, sages, or oracles bombinating over our cables," he rages. "I want a reporter. Somebody who doesn't know the difference between an ism and a kangaroo."

His rant requires deciphering. What Powers wants is someone with the combination of guts and naiveté to pose questions that more seasoned journalists trapped in a defective narrative of their own creation simply overlook.

So he pulls the decidedly unseasoned and spectacularly uninformed John Jones off the police beat, renames him Huntley Haverstock, sets him up with an expense account, and sends him off to take a fresh look at what gives in Europe. Haverstock proceeds to unearth the big truths to which his more sophisticated colleagues have become blind. Almost singlehandedly, he alerts the American people to the dangers just ahead—and he also gets the girl. Terrific movie (even if, given Hitchcock's well-documented mistreatment of women, it may be politically incorrect to say so).

Anyway, A. G., we need you to do something approximating what Mr. Powers did, but in real life. Good luck. I'm in your corner.

5
Infinite War

The Gravy Train Rolls On

June 7, 2018

"The United States of Amnesia." That's what Gore Vidal once called us. We remember what we find it convenient to remember and forget everything else. That forgetfulness especially applies to the history of others. How could *their* past, way back when, have any meaning for *us* today? Well, it just might. Take the European conflagration of 1914–1918, for example.

You may not have noticed. There's no reason why you should have, fixated as we all are on the daily torrent of presidential tweets and the flood of mindless rejoinders they elicit. But let me note for the record that the centenary of the conflict once known as The Great War is well underway and before the present year ends will have concluded.

Indeed, a hundred years ago this month, the 1918 German spring offensive—code-named Operation Michael—was sputtering to an unsuccessful conclusion. A last desperate German gamble, aimed at shattering Allied defenses and gaining a decisive victory, had fallen short. In early August of that year, with large numbers of our own doughboys now on the front lines, a massive Allied counteroffensive was to commence, continuing until the eleventh hour of the eleventh day of the eleventh month, when an armistice finally took effect and the guns fell silent.

In the years that followed, Americans demoted The Great War. It became World War I, vaguely related to but overshadowed by the debacle next in line, known as World War II. Today, the average citizen knows little about that earlier conflict other than that it preceded and somehow paved the way for an even more brutal bloodletting. Also, on both occasions, the bad guys spoke German.

So, among Americans, the war of 1914–1918 became a neglected stepsister of sorts, perhaps in part because the United States only got around to suiting up for that conflict about halfway through the fourth quarter. With the war of 1939–1945 having been sacralized as the moment when the Greatest Generation saved humankind, the war-formerly-known-as-The-Great-War collects dust in the bottom drawer of American collective consciousness.

From time to time, some politician or newspaper columnist will resurrect the file labeled "August 1914," the grim opening weeks of that war, and sound off about the dangers of sleepwalking into a devastating conflict that nobody wants or understands. Indeed, with Washington today having become a carnival of buncombe so sublimely preposterous that even that great journalistic iconoclast H. L. Mencken might have been struck dumb, ours is perhaps an apt moment for just such a reminder.

Yet a different aspect of World War I may possess even greater relevance to the American present. I'm thinking of its duration. The longer it lasted, the less sense it made. But on it went, impervious to human control like the sequence of Biblical plagues that God had inflicted on the ancient Egyptians.

So the relevant question for our present American moment is this: once it becomes apparent that a war is a mistake, why would those in power insist on its perpetuation, regardless of costs and consequences? In short, when getting *in* turns out to have been a bad idea, why is getting *out* so difficult, even (or especially) for powerful nations that presumably should be capable of exercising choice on such matters? Or more bluntly, how did the people in charge during The Great War get away with inflicting such extraordinary damage on the nations and peoples for which they were responsible?

For those countries that endured World War I from start to finish—especially Great Britain, France, and Germany—specific circumstances provided their leaders with an excuse for suppressing second thoughts about the cataclysm they had touched off. Among them were:

- mostly compliant civilian populations deeply loyal to some version of King and Country, further kept in line by unremitting propaganda that minimized dissent;
- draconian discipline—deserters and malingerers faced firing squads—that maintained order in the ranks (most of the time) despite the unprecedented scope of the slaughter; and
- the comprehensive industrialization of war, which ensured a seemingly endless supply of the weaponry, munitions, and other equipment necessary for outfitting mass conscript armies and replenishing losses as they occurred.

Economists would no doubt add sunk costs to the mix. With so much treasure already squandered and so many lives already lost, the urge to press on a bit longer in hopes of salvaging at least some meager benefit in return for what (and who) had been done in was difficult to resist.

Even so, none of these, nor any combination of them, can adequately explain why, in the midst of an unspeakable orgy of self-destruction, with staggering losses and nations in ruin, not one monarch or president or premier had the wit or gumption to declare: Enough! Stop this madness!

Instead, the politicians sat on their hands while actual authority devolved onto the likes of British field marshal Sir Douglas Haig, French marshals Ferdinand Foch and Philippe Pétain, and German commanders Paul von Hindenburg and Erich Ludendorff. In other words, to solve a conundrum they themselves had created, the politicians of the warring states all deferred to their warrior chieftains. For their part, the opposing warriors jointly subscribed to a perverted inversion of strategy best summarized by Ludendorff as "punch a hole [in the front] and let the rest follow." And so the conflict dragged on and on.

The Forfeiture of Policy

Put simply, in Europe, a hundred years ago, war had become politically purposeless. Yet the leaders of the world's principal powers—including, by 1917, US president Woodrow Wilson—could conceive of no alternative but to try harder, even as the seat of Western civilization became a charnel house.

Only one leader bucked the trend: Vladimir Lenin. In March 1918, soon after seizing power in Russia, Lenin took that country out of the war. In doing so, he reasserted the primacy of politics and restored the possibility of strategy. Lenin had his priorities straight. Nothing in his estimation took precedence over ensuring the survival of the Bolshevik Revolution. Liquidating the war against Germany therefore became an imperative.

Allow me to suggest that the United States should consider taking a page out of Lenin's playbook. Granted, prior to the collapse of the Soviet Union in 1991, such a suggestion might have smacked of treason. Today, however, in the midst of our never-ending efforts to expunge terrorism, we might look to Lenin for guidance on how to get our priorities straight.

As was the case with Great Britain, France, and Germany a century ago, the United States now finds itself mired in a senseless war. Back then, political leaders in London, Paris, and Berlin had abrogated control of basic policy to warrior chieftains. Today, ostensibly responsible political leaders in Washington have done likewise. Some of those latter-day American warrior chieftains who gather in the White House or testify on Capitol Hill may wear suits rather than uniforms, but all remain enamored with the twenty-first-century equivalent of Ludendorff's notorious dictum.

Of course, our post-9/11 military enterprise—the undertaking once known as the Global War on Terrorism—differs from The Great War in myriad ways. The ongoing hostilities in which US forces are involved in various parts of the Islamic world do not qualify, even metaphorically, as "great." Nor will there be anything great about an armed conflict with Iran, should members of the current administration get their apparent wish to provoke one.

Today, Washington need not even bother to propagandize the public into supporting its war. By and large, members of the public are indifferent to its very existence. And given our reliance on a professional military, shooting citizen-soldiers who want to opt out of the fight—once the fate of deserters—is no longer required.

There are also obvious differences in scale, particularly when it comes to the total number of casualties involved. Cumulative deaths from the various US interventions, large and small, undertaken since 9/11 number in the hundreds of thousands. The precise tally of those lost during the European debacle of 1914–1918 will never be known, but the total probably surpassed thirteen million.

Even so, similarities between The Great War as it unspooled and our own not-in-the-least-great war(s) deserve consideration. Today, as then, strategy—that is, the principled use of power to achieve the larger interests of the state—has ceased to exist. Indeed, war has become an excuse for ignoring the absence of strategy.

For years now, US military officers and at least some national security aficionados have referred to ongoing military hostilities as "the Long War." To describe our conglomeration of spreading conflicts as "long" obviates any need to suggest when or under what circumstances (if any) they might actually end. It's like the meteorologist forecasting a "long winter" or the betrothed telling their beloved that theirs will be a "long engagement." The implicit vagueness is not especially encouraging.

Some high-ranking officers of late have offered a more forthright explanation of what "long" may really mean. In the *Washington Post*, the journalist Greg Jaffe recently reported that "winning for much of the U.S. military's top brass has come to be synonymous with staying put." Winning, according to Air Force General Mike Holmes, is simply "not losing. It's staying in the game."

Not so long ago, America's armed forces adhered to a concept called *victory*, which implied conclusive, expeditious, and economical mission accomplished. No more. Victory, it turns out, is too tough to achieve, too restrictive, or, in the words of Army Lieutenant General Michael Lundy, "too absolute." The United States military now grades itself instead on a curve. As Lundy puts it, "winning is more of a continuum," an approach that allows you to claim mission accomplishment without, you know, actually accomplishing anything.

It's like soccer for six-year-olds. Everyone tries hard so everyone gets a trophy. Regardless of outcomes, no one goes home feeling bad.

In the US military's case, every general gets a medal (or, more likely, a chest full of them).

"These days," in the Pentagon, Jaffe writes, "senior officers talk about 'infinite war.'"

I would like to believe that Jaffe is pulling our leg. But given that he's a conscientious reporter with excellent sources, I fear he knows what he's talking about. If he's right, as far as the top brass are concerned, the Long War has now officially gone beyond long. It has been deemed endless and is accepted as such by those who preside over its conduct.

Strategic Abomination

In truth, infinite war is a strategic abomination, an admission of professional military bankruptcy. *Erster Generalquartiermeister* Ludendorff might have endorsed the term, but Ludendorff was a military fanatic.

Check that. Infinite war is a strategic abomination except in the eyes of arms merchants, so-called defense contractors, and the "emergency men" devoted to climbing the greasy pole of what we choose to call the national security establishment. In other words, candor obliges us to acknowledge that, in some quarters, infinite war is a pure positive, carrying with it a promise of yet more profits, promotions, and opportunities to come. War keeps the gravy train rolling. And, of course, that's part of the problem.

Who should we hold accountable for this abomination? Not the generals, in my view. If they come across as a dutiful yet unimaginative lot, remember that a lifetime of military service rarely nurtures imagination or creativity. And let us at least credit our generals with this: in their efforts to liberate or democratize or pacify or dominate the Greater Middle East they have tried every military tactic and technique imaginable. Short of nuclear annihilation, they've played just about every card in the Pentagon's deck—without coming up with a winning hand. So they come and go at regular intervals, each new commander promising success and departing after a couple years to make way for someone else to give it a try.

It tells us something about our prevailing standards of generalship that, by resurrecting an old idea—counterinsurgency—and applying it with temporary success to one particular theater of war, General David Petraeus acquired a reputation as a military genius. If Petraeus is a military genius, so, too, was General George McClellan. After he won the Battle of Rich Mountain in 1861, newspapers dubbed McClellan "the Napoleon of the Present War." But the action at Rich Mountain decided nothing and McClellan didn't win the Civil War any more than Petraeus won the Iraq War.

No, it's not the generals who have let us down, but the politicians to whom they supposedly report and from whom they nominally take their orders. Of course, under the heading of politician, we quickly come to our current commander in chief. Yet it would be manifestly unfair to blame President Trump for the mess he inherited, even if he is presently engaged in making matters worse.

The failure is a collective one, to which several presidents and both political parties have contributed over the years. Although the carnage may not be as horrific today as it was on the European battlefields on the Western and Eastern Fronts, members of our political class are failing us as strikingly and repeatedly as the political leaders of Great Britain, France, and Germany failed their peoples back then. They have abdicated responsibility for policy to our own homegrown equivalents of Haig, Foch, Pétain, Hindenburg, and Ludendorff. Their failure is unforgivable.

Congressional midterm elections are just months away and another presidential election already looms. Who will be the political leader with the courage and presence of mind to declare, Enough! Stop this madness! Man or woman, straight or queer, Black, brown, or white, that person will deserve the nation's gratitude and the support of the electorate.

Until that occurs, however, the American penchant for war will stretch on toward infinity. No doubt Saudi and Israeli leaders will cheer, Europeans who remember their Great War will scratch their heads in wonder, and the Chinese will laugh themselves silly. Meanwhile, issues of genuinely strategic importance—climate change offers one obvious example—will continue to be treated like an afterthought. As for the gravy train, it will roll on.

6

The "Forever Wars" Enshrined

Visiting mar-SAYLZ

May 23, 2019

arlier this month, I spent a day visiting Marseilles to videotape a documentary about recent American military history, specifically the ongoing wars that most of us prefer not to think about.

Lest there be any confusion, let me be more specific. I am not referring to Marseilles (mar-SAY), France, that nation's largest port and second largest city with a population approaching 900,000. No, my destination was Marseilles (mar-SAYLZ), Illinois, a small prairie town with a population hovering around five thousand.

Our own lesser Marseilles nestles alongside the Illinois River, more or less equidistant between Chicago and Peoria, smack dab in the middle of flyover country. I have some personal familiarity with this part of America. More than half a century ago, the school I attended in nearby Peru used to play the Panthers of Marseilles High. Unfortunately, their school closed three decades ago.

Back then, the town had achieved minor distinction for manufacturing corrugated boxes for Nabisco. But that factory was shuttered in 2002 and only the abandoned building remains, its eight-story hulk still looming above Main Street.

Today, downtown Marseilles, running a few short blocks toward the river, consists of tired-looking commercial structures dating from early in the previous century. Many of the storefronts are empty. By all appearances, the rest may suffer a similar fate in the not-too-distant future. Although the US economy has bounced back from the Great Recession, recovery bypassed Marseilles. Here, the good times ended long ago and never came back. The feel of the place is weary and forlorn. Hedge fund managers keen to turn a quick profit should look elsewhere.

Perhaps not too surprisingly, this is Trump country. Marseilles is located in LaSalle County, which in 2016 voted for Donald Trump over Hillary Clinton by a hefty 14 percent margin. It's easy to imagine residents of Marseilles, which is more than 96 percent white, taking umbrage at Clinton's disparaging reference to The Donald's supporters as so many "deplorables." They had reason to do so.

A Midwestern Memorial to America's Wars in the Greater Middle East

Today, Marseilles retains one modest claim to fame. It's the site of the Middle East Conflicts Wall Memorial, dedicated in June 2004 and situated on an open plot of ground between the river and the old Nabisco plant. The memorial, created and supported by a conglomeration of civic-minded Illinois bikers, many of them Vietnam veterans, is the only one in the nation that commemorates those who have died during the course of the various campaigns, skirmishes, protracted wars, and nasty mishaps that have involved US forces in various quarters of the Greater Middle East over the past several decades.

Think about it: any American wanting to pay personal tribute to those who fought and died for our country in World War II or Korea or Vietnam knows where to go—to the Mall in Washington, DC, that long stretch of lawn and reflecting pools connecting the Washington Monument and the Lincoln Memorial. Any American wanting to honor the sacrifice of those who fought and died in a series of more recent conflicts that have lasted longer than World War II, Korea, and Vietnam combined must travel to a place where the nearest public transportation is a Greyhound bus station down the road in Ottawa and the top restaurant is Bobaluk's Beef and Pizza. Nowhere else in this vast nation of ours has anyone invested the money and the effort to remember more than a generation's worth of less-than-triumphant American war making. Marseilles has a lock on the franchise.

Critics might quibble with the aesthetics of the memorial, dismissing it as an unpretentious knockoff of the far more famous Vietnam Wall. Yet if the design doesn't qualify as cutting edge, it is palpably honest and heartfelt. It consists chiefly of a series of polished granite panels listing the names of those killed during the various phases of this country's "forever wars" going all the way back to the sailors gunned down in the June 1967 Israeli attack on the USS *Liberty*.

Those panels now contain more than eight thousand names. Each June, in conjunction with the annual Illinois Motorcycle Freedom Run, which ends at the memorial, more are added. Along with flags and plaques, there is also text affirming that all those commemorated there are heroes who died for freedom and will never be forgotten.

On that point, allow me to register my own quibble. Although my son's name is halfway down near the left margin of Panel 5B, I find myself uneasy with any reference to American soldiers having died for freedom in the Greater Middle East. Our pronounced penchant for using that term in connection with virtually any American military action strikes me as a dodge. It serves as an excuse for not thinking too deeply about the commitments, policies, and decisions that led to all those names being etched in stone, with more to come next month and probably for many years thereafter.

In Ernest Hemingway's famed novel about World War I, *A Farewell to Arms*, his protagonist is "embarrassed by the words sacred, glorious, and sacrifice and the expression in vain." I feel something similar when it comes to the use of *freedom* in this context. Well, not embarrassed exactly, but deeply uncomfortable. Freedom, used in this fashion, conceals truth behind a veil of patriotic sentiment.

Those whose names are engraved on the wall in Marseilles died in service to their country. Of that there is no doubt. Whether they died to advance the cause of freedom or even the wellbeing of the United States is another matter entirely. Terms that might more accurately convey why these wars began and why they have persisted for so long include oil, dominion, hubris, a continuing and stubborn refusal among policymakers to own up to their own stupendous folly, and the collective negligence of citizens who have become oblivious to where American troops happen to be fighting at any given moment and why. Some might add to the above list an inability to distinguish between our own interests and those of putative allies like Saudi Arabia and Israel.

Candidates at the Wall

During the several hours I spent there, virtually no one else visited the Middle East Conflicts Wall Memorial. A single elderly couple stopped by briefly and that was that. If this was understandable, it was also telling. After all, Marseilles, Illinois, is an out-of-the-way, isolated little burg. Touristy it's not. There's no buzz and no vibe and it's a long way from the places that set the tone in present-day America. To compare Marseilles with New York, Washington, Hollywood, Las Vegas, or Silicon Valley is like comparing a Dollar General with Saks Fifth Avenue. Marseilles has the former. The closest Saks outlet is about a two-hour drive to Chicago's Loop.

On the other hand, when you think about it, Marseilles is exactly the right place to situate the nation's only existing memorial to its Middle Eastern wars. Where better, after all, to commemorate conflicts that Americans would like to ignore or forget than in a hollowing-out Midwestern town they never knew existed in the first place?

So, with the campaign for the 2020 presidential election now heating up, allow me to offer a modest proposal of my own—one that might, briefly at least, make Marseilles a destination of sorts.

Just as there are all-but-mandatory venues in Iowa and New Hampshire where candidates are expected to appear, why not make Marseilles, Illinois, one as well? Let all of the candidates competing to oust Donald Trump from the White House (their ranks now approaching two dozen) schedule at least one campaign stop at the Middle East Conflicts Wall, press entourage suitably in tow.

Let them take a page from presidents John F. Kennedy and Ronald Reagan at the Berlin Wall and use the site as a backdrop to reflect on the historical significance of this particular place. They should explain in concrete terms what the conflicts memorialized there signify: describe their relationship to the post–Cold War narrative of America as the planet's "indispensable nation" or "sole superpower"; assess the disastrous costs and consequences of those never-ending wars; fix accountability; lay out to the American people how to avoid repeating the mistakes made by previous administrations, including the present one that seems to be itching for yet another conflict in the Middle East; and help us understand how, under the guise of promoting liberty and democracy, Washington has sown chaos through much of the region.

And, just to make it interesting, bonus points for anyone who can get through their remarks without referring to "freedom" or "supreme sacrifice," citing the Gospel of John, chapter 15, verse 13 ("Greater love hath no man than this . . ."), or offering some fatuous reference to GIs as agents of the Lord called upon to smite evildoers. On the other hand, apt comparisons to Vietnam are not just permitted but encouraged.

I'm betting that the good bikers of Illinois who long ago served in Vietnam will happily provide a mic and a podium. If they won't, I will.

1
The Art of Shaping Memory

Knowing Whom to Remember and How to Forget

June 20, 2019

How best to describe the recently completed allied commemoration of the seventy-fifth anniversary of the D-Day invasion of France? Two words come immediately to mind: heartfelt and poignant.

The aged D-Day veterans gathering for what was probably the last time richly deserved every bit of praise bestowed on them. Yet one particular refrain that has become commonplace in this age of Donald Trump was absent from the proceedings. I'm referring to "fake news." In a curious collaboration, Trump and the media, their normal relationship one of mutual loathing, combined forces to falsify the history of World War II. Allow me to explain.

In a stirring presentation, Trump—amazingly—rose to the occasion and captured the spirit of the moment, one of gratitude, respect, even awe. Ever so briefly, the president sounded presidential. In place of his usual taunts and insults, he managed a fair imitation of Ronald Reagan's legendary "boys of Pointe du Hoc" speech of 1984. "We are gathered here on freedom's altar," Trump began—not exactly his standard introductory gambit.

Then, in a rare display of generosity toward people who were neither Republicans nor members of his immediate family, Trump acknowledged the contributions of those who had fought alongside the GIs at Normandy, singling out Brits, Canadians, Poles, Norwegians,

Australians, and members of the French resistance for favorable mention. He related moving stories of great heroism and paid tribute to the dwindling number of D-Day veterans present.

And as previous presidents had done on similar occasions marking D-Day anniversaries, he placed the events of that day in a reassuringly familiar historical context. "The blood that they spilled, the tears that they shed, the lives that they gave, the sacrifice that they made, did not just win a battle. It did not just win a war. Those who fought here won a future for our nation. They won the survival of our civilization. And they showed us the way to love, cherish, and defend our way of life for many centuries to come," Trump said.

Nor was that all. "Today, as we stand together upon this sacred Earth," Trump concluded, "We pledge that our nations will forever be strong and united. We will forever be together. Our people will forever be bold. Our hearts will forever be loyal. And our children, and their children, will forever and always be free."

Strong and united, together, bold, loyal, and free . . . forever.

It was, in its way, an astonishing performance, all the more so because it was entirely out of character. It was as if Secretary of State Mike Pompeo had published a book of sonnets or National Security Advisor John Bolton had performed a serviceable rendition of *"Nessun dorma"* on the steps of the Lincoln Memorial—wonderful in its way, but given the source startling as well.

Selective Remembering and Convenient Forgetting

If the purpose of Trump's speech was to make his listeners feel good, he delivered. Yet in doing so, he also relieved them of any responsibility for thinking too deeply about the event being commemorated.

Now, let me just say that I hold no brief for Joseph Stalin or the Soviet Union, or Marxism-Leninism. Yet you don't need to be an apologist for communism to acknowledge that the Normandy invasion would never have succeeded had it not been for the efforts of Marshal Stalin's Red Army. For three full years before the first wave of GIs splashed ashore at Omaha Beach, Russian troops had been waging a titanic struggle along a vast front in their own devastated land against the cream of the German military machine.

One data point alone summarizes the critical nature of the Soviet contribution. In May 1944, there were some 160 German divisions tied up on the Eastern Front. That represented more than two-thirds of the armed might of the Third Reich, 160 combat divisions that were therefore unavailable for commitment against the Anglo-American forces desperately trying to establish a foothold in Normandy.

As has been the custom for quite some time now the German chancellor, representing the defeated enemy, attended the D-Day anniversary festivities as an honored guest. Angela Merkel's inclusion testifies to an admirable capacity to forgive without forgetting.

Russian President Vladimir Putin did not, however, make the guest list. In liberal circles, Putin has, of course, made himself persona non grata. Yet excluding him obviated any need for Trump and other dignitaries in attendance to acknowledge, even indirectly, the Soviet role in winning World War II. Although the Red Army was never known for finesse or artfulness, it did kill an estimated four million of Merkel's countrymen, who were thereby not on hand to have a go at killing Trump's countrymen.

If war is ultimately about mayhem and murder, then the Soviet Union did more than any other belligerent to bring about the final victory against Nazi Germany. Without for a second slighting the courage and contributions of our Canadian, Polish, Norwegian, and Australian comrades—bless them all—it was the Red Army that kept General Dwight Eisenhower's expeditionary command from being pushed back into the Channel. In other words, thank God for the godless communists.

So, however heartfelt and poignant, the seventy-fifth anniversary of the D-Day landings was an exercise in selective remembering and convenient forgetting. It was, in other words, propaganda or, in contemporary parlance, fake news. The deception—for that's what it was—did not escape the notice of Russian commentators. Yet members of the American media, otherwise ever alert to Trump's sundry half-truths and outright deceptions, chose to ignore or more accurately endorse this whopper.

Time to Get Over the Hangover?

How much does such selective remembering and convenient forgetting matter? A lot, in my estimation. Distorting the past distorts the present and sows confusion about the problems we actually face.

For a small illustration of the implications of this particular elision of history we need look no further than the D-Day anniversary–inspired ruminations of *New York Times* columnist Bret Stephens. The purpose of his column, which appeared on June 7, 2019, was to spin the spin. Stephens was intent on reinforcing Trump's carefully edited interpretation of World War II in order to further his own version of a crusading and militarized American foreign policy agenda.

Now, the war against Adolf Hitler occurred a considerable time ago. The war against Iraqi autocrat Saddam Hussein is a far more recent memory. Which should have greater relevance for US policy today? On that score, Stephens is quite clear: it's the "lessons" of World War II, not of the reckless invasion of Iraq, that must pertain, not only today but in perpetuity. Sure, the Iraq War turned out to be a bit of a headache. "But how long," Stephens asks, "should the hangover last?" Time to take an Alka-Seltzer and get back to smiting evildoers, thereby keeping alive the ostensible tradition of the Greatest Generation.

"If we really wanted to honor the sacrifices of D-Day," Stephens writes, "we would do well to learn again what it is the Allies really fought for." According to him, they fought "not to save the United States or even Britain," but to liberate all of Europe; not to defeat Nazi Germany, "but to eradicate a despicable ideology"; and "not to subsume our values under our interests but to define our interests according to our values."

Now, only someone oblivious to the actual experience of war could subscribe to such a noble list of "what the Allies really fought for." Perhaps more to the point, in expounding on what inspired the Allied war effort, Stephens chose to overlook the fact that the ranks of those Allies included the Soviet Union. Winston Churchill, Franklin Roosevelt, and their generals would not have considered this a casual omission. They thanked their lucky stars for the Soviet Union's participation.

Furthermore, Soviet leaders from Joseph Stalin on down entertained their own distinct ideas about the war's purposes. They adhered to and were intent on exporting an ideology hardly less despicable than that of the Nazis. Their purpose was not to liberate Europe, but to absorb large chunks of it into an expanded Soviet sphere of influence. And while correlating interests with values might have appealed to the Soviet dictator, the values to which he subscribed excluded just about every item in the American Bill of Rights. So if we are serious about identifying common war aims, "what the Allies really fought for" focused on one thing only: destroying the Third Reich.

Just like Trump, however, Stephens airbrushes the Soviet Union out of the picture. In doing so, he sanitizes the past. His motive is anything but innocent. Having concocted his own spurious version of "what the Allies really fought for," Stephens pivots to the present moment and discovers—wouldn't you know it—that we are right back in those terrible days of the 1930s when the Western democracies hesitated to confront the rising threat posed by Hitler.

Seventy years after D-Day, the world is in disarray. And the West, Stephens charges, is sitting on its hands. Syria is a mess. So is Venezuela. Kim Jong-un, "the world's most sinister dictator," still rules North Korea. In Cuba, China, Saudi Arabia, and Iran, dissidents languish behind bars. Nobody "other than a few journalists and activists" seems to care. Everywhere indifference prevails.

And we've seen this movie before, he insists. "This is the West almost as it looked in the 1930s: internally divided and inward looking, hesitant in the face of aggression, incanting political pieties in which it no longer believed—and so determined not to repeat the mistakes of the last war that it sleepwalked its way into the next."

Now, in those circles where neoconservatives congregate and call for the United States to embark upon some new crusade, this analysis undoubtedly finds favor. But as a description of actually existing reality, it's about as accurate as Trump's own periodic blathering about the state of the world.

Is the West today "inward looking"? Then how do we explain the presence of Western forces in Afghanistan, of all places, for nigh onto twenty years? Is the West "hesitant in the face of aggression"? How does that charge square with actions taken by the United States and its allies in Iraq, Libya, Somalia, Yemen, and elsewhere? When it comes to war, some might suggest that our problem of late has not been hesitancy, but unending hubris and the absence of even minimal due diligence. More often than not, when it comes to aggressive behavior, we're the ones spoiling for a fight. Take General Kenneth McKenzie, the latest belli-cose head of US Central Command, for example, who is now plugging for "a return to a larger US military presence in the Middle East" with Iran in mind. Don't accuse him of hesitance.

The prescription that Stephens offers reduces to this: just as in June 1944, brave men with guns, preferably speaking English, will put things right and enable freedom and democracy to prevail. We need only gird our loins and make the effort.

It's all very inspiring really. Yet Stephens leaves out something im-portant: this time we won't be able to count on some other nation with a large and willing army to do most of the fighting and dying on our behalf.

8
Reflections on "Peace" in Afghanistan

Leaving a Misguided War and Not Looking Back

September 10, 2019

When the conflict that the Vietnamese refer to as the American War ended in April 1975, I was a US Army captain attending a course at Fort Knox, Kentucky. In those days, the student body at any of our Army's myriad schools typically included officers from the Army of the Republic of Vietnam (ARVN).

Since ARVN's founding two decades earlier, the United States had assigned itself the task of professionalizing that fledgling military establishment. Based on a conviction that the standards, methods, and ethos of our armed forces were universally applicable and readily exportable, the attendance of ARVN personnel at such Army schools was believed to contribute to the professionalizing of the South Vietnamese military.

Evidence that the US military's own professional standards had recently taken a hit—memories of the My Lai massacre were then still fresh—elicited no second thoughts on our part. Association with American officers like me was sure to rub off on our South Vietnamese counterparts in ways that would make them better soldiers. So we professed to believe, even while subjecting that claim to no more scrutiny than we did the question of why most of us had spent a year or more of our lives participating in an obviously misbegotten and misguided war in Indochina.

For serving officers at that time one question in particular remained off-limits (though it had been posed incessantly for years by anti-war

protestors in the streets of America): Why Vietnam? Prizing compliance as a precondition for upward mobility, military service rarely en-
courages critical thinking.

On the day that Saigon, the capital of the Republic of Vietnam, fell
and that country ceased to exist, I approached one of my ARVN class-
mates, also a captain, wanting at least to acknowledge the magnitude of
the disaster that had occurred. "I'm sorry about what happened to your
country," I told him.

I did not know that officer well and no longer recall his name. Let's
call him Captain Nguyen. In my dim recollection, he didn't even bother
to reply. He simply looked at me with an expression both distressed and
mournful. Our encounter lasted no more than a handful of seconds. I
then went on with my life and Captain Nguyen presumably with his.
Although I have no inkling of his fate, I like to think that he is now
retired in Southern California after a successful career in real estate.
But who knows?

All I do know is that today I recall our exchange with a profound
sense of embarrassment and even shame. My pathetic effort to con-
sole Captain Nguyen had been both presumptuous and inadequate. Far
worse was my failure—inability? refusal?—to acknowledge the context
within which that catastrophe was occurring: the United States and its
armed forces had, over years, inflicted horrendous harm on the people
of South Vietnam.

In reality, their defeat was our defeat. Yet while we had decided
that we were done paying, they were going to pay and pay for a long
time to come.

Rather than offering a fatuous expression of regret for the collapse
of his country, I ought to have apologized for having played even a mi-
nuscule role in what was, by any measure, a catastrophe of epic proportions. It's a wonder Captain Nguyen didn't spit in my eye.

I genuinely empathized with Captain Nguyen. Yet the truth is that,
along with most other Americans, soldiers and civilians alike, I was
only too happy to be done with South Vietnam and all its troubles. Dating back to the presidency of Dwight D. Eisenhower, the United States

and its armed forces had made a gargantuan effort to impart legitimacy to the Republic of Vietnam and to coerce the Democratic Republic of Vietnam to its north into giving up its determination to exercise sovereignty over the entirety of the country. In that, we had failed spectacularly and at a staggering cost.

"Our" war in Indochina—the conflict we chose to call the Vietnam War—officially ended in January 1973 with the signing in Paris of the "Agreement on Ending the War and Restoring Peace in Viet Nam." Under the terms of that fraudulent pact, American prisoners of war were freed from captivity in North Vietnam and the last US combat troops in the south left for home, completing a withdrawal begun several years earlier. Primary responsibility for securing the Republic of Vietnam thereby fell to ARVN, long deemed by US commanders incapable of accomplishing that mission.

Meanwhile, despite a nominal cessation of hostilities, approximately 150,000 North Vietnamese regulars still occupied a large swathe of South Vietnamese territory—more or less the equivalent to agreeing to end World War II when there were still several German panzer tank divisions lurking in Belgium's Ardennes Forest. In effect, our message to our enemy *and* our ally was, We're outta here—you guys sort this out. In a bit more than two years, that sorting-out process would extinguish the Republic of Vietnam.

Been There, Done That

The course Captain Nguyen and I were attending in the spring of 1975 paid little attention to fighting wars like the one that, for years, had occupied the attention of my army and his. Our army, in fact, was already moving on. Having had their fill of triple-canopy jungles in Indochina, America's officer corps now turned to defending the Fulda Gap, the region in West Germany deemed most hospitable to a future Soviet invasion. As if by fiat, gearing up to fight those Soviet forces and their Warsaw Pact allies, should they (however improbably) decide to take on NATO and lunge toward the English Channel, suddenly emerged as priority number one. At Fort Knox and throughout the Army's ranks, we were suddenly focused on "high-intensity combined arms operations"—essentially, a replay of World War II–style combat with fancier weaponry. In short, the armed forces of the United States had reverted to "real soldiering."

And so it is again today. At the end of the seventeenth year of what Americans commonly call the Afghanistan War—one wonders what name Afghans will eventually assign it—US military forces are moving on. Pentagon planners are shifting their attention back to Russia and China. Great power competition has become the name of the game. However we might define Washington's evolving purposes in its Afghanistan War—"nation building," "democratization," "pacification"—the likelihood of mission accomplishment is nil. As in the early 1970s, so in 2019, rather than admitting failure, the Pentagon has chosen to change the subject and is once again turning its attention to "real soldiering."

Remember the infatuation with counterinsurgency (commonly known by its acronym COIN) that gripped the national security establishment around 2007 when the Iraq "surge" overseen by General David Petraeus briefly ranked alongside Gettysburg as a historic victory? Well, these days promoting COIN as the new American way of war has become, to put it mildly, a tough sell. Given that few in Washington will openly acknowledge the magnitude of the military failure in Afghanistan, the incentive for identifying new enemies in settings deemed more congenial becomes all but irresistible.

Only one thing is required to validate this reshuffling of military priorities. Washington needs to create the appearance, as in 1973, that it's exiting Afghanistan on its own terms. What's needed, in short, is an updated equivalent of that "Agreement on Ending the War and Restoring Peace in Viet Nam."

Until last weekend, the signing of such an agreement seemed imminent. Donald Trump and his envoy, former ambassador to Afghanistan Zalmay Khalilzad, appeared poised to repeat the trick that President Richard Nixon and National Security Advisor Henry Kissinger pulled off in 1973 in Paris: pause the war and call it peace. Should fighting subsequently resume after a "decent interval," it would no longer be

America's problem. Now, however, to judge by the president's Twitter account—currently the authoritative record of US diplomacy—the proposed deal has been postponed, or perhaps shelved, or even abandoned altogether. If National Security Advisor John Bolton has his way, US forces might just withdraw in any case, without an agreement of any sort being signed.

Based on what we can divine from press reports, the terms of that prospective Afghan deal would mirror those of the 1973 Paris Accords in one important respect. It would, in effect, serve as a ticket home for the remaining US and NATO troops still in that country (though for the present only the first five thousand of them would immediately depart). Beyond that, the Taliban was to promise not to provide sanctuary to anti-American terrorist groups, even though the Afghan branch of ISIS is already firmly lodged there. Still, this proviso would allow the Trump administration to claim that it had averted any possible recurrence of the 9/11 terror attacks that were, of course, planned by Osama bin Laden while residing in Afghanistan in 2001 as a guest of the Taliban-controlled government. Mission accomplished, as it were.

Back in 1973, North Vietnamese forces occupying parts of South Vietnam neither disarmed nor withdrew. Should this new agreement be finalized, Taliban forces currently controlling or influencing significant swaths of Afghan territory will neither disarm nor withdraw. Indeed, their declared intention is to continue fighting.

In 1973, policymakers in Washington were counting on ARVN to hold off communist forces. In 2019, almost no one expects Afghan security forces to hold off a threat consisting of both the Taliban and ISIS. In a final insult, just as the Saigon government was excluded from US negotiations with the North Vietnamese, so, too, has the Western-installed government in Kabul been excluded from US negotiations with its sworn enemy, the Taliban.

A host of uncertainties remain. As with the olive branches that President Trump has ostentatiously offered to Russia, China, and North Korea, this particular peace initiative may come to naught—or, given the approach of the 2020 elections, he may decide that Afghanistan offers his last best hope of claiming at least one foreign policy success. One way or another, in all likelihood, the deathwatch for the US-backed Afghan government has now begun. One thing only is for sure. Having had their fill of Afghanistan, when the Americans finally leave, they won't look back. In that sense, it will be Vietnam all over again.

What Price Peace?

However great my distaste for President Trump, I support his administration's efforts to extricate the United States from Afghanistan. I do so for the same reason I supported the Paris Peace Accords of 1973. Prolonging this folly any longer does not serve US interests. Rule number one of statecraft ought to be, when you're doing something really stupid, stop. To my mind, this rule seems especially applicable when the lives of American soldiers are at stake.

In Vietnam, Washington wasted 58,000 of those lives for nothing. In Afghanistan, we have lost more than 2,300 troops, with another 20,000 wounded, again for next to nothing. Last month, two American Special Forces soldiers were killed in a firefight in Faryab Province. For what?

That said, I'm painfully aware of the fact that, on the long-ago day when I offered Captain Nguyen my feeble condolences, I lacked the imagination to conceive of the trials about to befall his countrymen. In the aftermath of the American War, something on the order of 800,000 Vietnamese took to open and unseaworthy boats to flee their country. According to estimates by the United Nations High Commissioner for Refugees, between 200,000 and 400,000 boat people died at sea. Most of those who survived were destined to spend years in squalid refugee camps scattered throughout Southeast Asia. Back in Vietnam itself, some 300,000 former ARVN officers and South Vietnamese officials were imprisoned in so-called reeducation camps for up to eighteen years. Reconciliation did not rank high on the postwar agenda of the unified country's new leaders.

Meanwhile, for the Vietnamese, north and south, the American War has in certain ways only continued. Mines and unexploded ordnance left from that war have inflicted more than 100,000 casualties since the last American troops departed. Even today, the toll caused by Agent Orange and other herbicides that the US Air Force sprayed with abandon over vast stretches of territory continues to mount. The Red Cross calculates that more than one million Vietnamese have suffered health problems, including serious birth defects and cancers as a direct consequence of the promiscuous use of those poisons as weapons of war.

For anyone caring to calculate the moral responsibility of the United States for its actions in Vietnam, all of those would have to find a place on the final balance sheet. The 1.3 million Vietnamese admitted to the United States as immigrants since the American War formally concluded can hardly be said to make up for the immense damage suffered by the people of Vietnam as a direct or indirect result of US policy.

As to what will follow if Washington does succeed in cutting a deal with the Taliban, well, don't count on President Trump (or his successor for that matter) welcoming anything like 1.3 million Afghan refugees to the United States once a "decent interval" has passed. Yet again, our position will be *we're outta here; you guys sort this out.*

Near the end of his famed novel, *The Great Gatsby*, F. Scott Fitzgerald described two of his privileged characters, Tom and Daisy, as "careless people" who "smashed up things and creatures" and then "retreated back into their money or their vast carelessness" to "let other people clean up the mess they had made." That description applies to the United States as a whole, especially when Americans tire of a misguided war. We are a careless people. In Vietnam, we smashed up things and human beings with abandon, only to retreat into our money, leaving others to clean up the mess in a distinctly bloody fashion.

Count on us, probably sooner rather than later, doing precisely the same thing in Afghanistan.

9

A Report Card on the American Project

The "Revolution of '89" Reassessed

January 7, 2020

Thirty years ago this month, President George H. W. Bush appeared before a joint session of Congress to deliver his first State of the Union Address, the first post–Cold War observance of this annual ritual. Just weeks before, the Berlin Wall had fallen. That event, the president declared, "marks the beginning of a new era in the world's affairs." The Cold War, that "long twilight struggle" (as President John F. Kennedy so famously described it), had just come to an abrupt end. A new day was dawning. President Bush seized the opportunity to explain just what that dawning signified.

"There are singular moments in history, dates that divide all that goes before from all that comes after," the president said. The end of World War II had been just such a moment. In the decades that followed, 1945 provided "the common frame of reference, the compass points of the postwar era we've relied upon to understand ourselves." Yet the hopeful developments of the year just concluded—Bush referred to them collectively as "the Revolution of '89"—had initiated "a new era in the world's affairs."

While many things were certain to change, the president felt sure that one element of continuity would persist: the United States would determine history's onward course. "America, not just the nation but an idea," he emphasized, is and was sure to remain "alive in the minds of people everywhere."

"As this new world takes shape, America stands at the center of a widening circle of freedom—today, tomorrow, and into the next century. Our nation is the enduring dream of every immigrant who ever set foot on these shores and the millions still struggling to be free. This nation, this idea called America, was and always will be a new world— our new world."

Bush had never shown himself to be a particularly original or imaginative thinker. Even so, during a long career in public service, he had at least mastered the art of packaging sentiments deemed appropriate for just about any occasion. The imagery he employed in this instance— America occupying the center of freedom's widening circle—did not stake out a new claim devised for fresh circumstances. That history centered on what Americans professed or did expressed a hallowed proposition, one with which his listeners were both familiar and comfortable. Indeed, Bush's description of America as a perpetually self-renewing enterprise engaged in perfecting freedom summarized the essence of the nation's self-assigned purpose.

In his remarks to Congress, the president was asserting a prerogative that his predecessors had long ago appropriated: interpreting the zeitgeist in such a way as to merge past, present, and future into a seamless, self-congratulatory, and reassuring narrative of American power. He was describing history precisely as Americans—or at least privileged Americans—wished to see it. He was, in other words, speaking a language in which he was fluent: the idiom of the ruling class.

As the year 1990 began, duty—destiny, even—was summoning members of that ruling class to lead not just this country, but the planet itself and not just for a decade or two, or even for an "era," but forever and a day. In January 1990, the way ahead for the last superpower on planet Earth—the Soviet Union would officially implode in 1991 but its fate already seemed obvious enough—was clear indeed.

So, How'd We Do?

Thirty years later, perhaps it's time to assess just how well the United States has fulfilled the expectations President Bush articulated in 1990.

Personally, I would rate the results somewhere between deeply disappointing and flat-out abysmal.

Bush's "circle of freedom" invoked a planet divided between the free and the unfree. During the Cold War, this distinction had proven useful even if it was never particularly accurate. Today, it retains no value whatsoever as a description of the actually existing world, even though in Washington it persists, as does the conviction that the US has a unique responsibility to expand that circle.

Encouraged by ambitious politicians and ideologically driven commentators, many (though not all) Americans bought into a militarized, Manichean, vastly oversimplified conception of the Cold War. Having misconstrued its meaning, they misconstrued the implications of its passing, leaving them ill-prepared to see through the claptrap in President Bush's 1990 State of the Union Address.

Bush depicted the "Revolution of '89" as a transformative moment in world history. In fact, the legacy of that moment has proven far more modest than he imagined. As a turning point in the history of the modern world, the end of the Cold War ranks slightly above the invention of the machine gun (1884), but well below the fall of Russia's Romanov dynasty (1917) or the discovery of penicillin (1928). Among the factors shaping the world in which we now live, the outcome of the Cold War barely registers.

Fairness obliges me to acknowledge two exceptions to that broad claim, one pertaining to Europe and the other to the United States.

First, the end of the Cold War led almost immediately to a Europe made "whole and free" thanks to the collapse of the Soviet empire. Yet while Poles, Lithuanians, the former citizens of the German Democratic Republic, and other Eastern Europeans are certainly better off today than they were under the Kremlin's boot, Europe itself plays a significantly diminished role in world affairs. In healing its divisions, it shrank, losing political clout. Meanwhile, in very short order, new cleavages erupted in the Balkans, Spain, and even the United Kingdom, with the emergence of a populist right calling into question Europe's assumed commitment to multicultural liberalism.

In many respects, the Cold War began as an argument over who would determine Europe's destiny. In 1989, our side won that argument. Yet, by then, the payoff to which the United States laid claim had largely been depleted. Europe's traditional great powers were no longer especially great. After several centuries in which global politics had centered on that continent, Europe had suddenly slipped to the periphery. In practice, "whole and free" turned out to mean "preoccupied and anemic," with Europeans now engaging in their own acts of folly. Three decades after the "Revolution of '89," Europe remains an attractive tourist destination. Yet, from a geopolitical perspective, the action has long since moved elsewhere.

The second exception to the Cold War's less than momentous results relates to US attitudes toward military power. For the first time in its history, the onset of the Cold War had prompted the United States to create and maintain a powerful peacetime military establishment. The principal mission of that military was to defend, deter, and contain. While it would fight bitter wars in Korea and Vietnam, its advertised aim was to avert armed conflicts or, at least, keep them from getting out of hand. In that spirit, the billboard at the entrance to the headquarters of the Strategic Air Command, the Pentagon's principal Cold War nuclear strike force (which possessed the means to extinguish humankind), reassuringly announced that "peace is our profession."

When the Cold War ended, however, despite the absence of any real threats to US security, Washington policymakers decided to maintain the mightiest armed forces on the planet in perpetuity. Negligible debate preceded this decision, which even today remains minimally controversial. That the United States should retain military capabilities far greater than those of any other nation or even combination of numerous other nations seemed eminently sensible.

In appearance or configuration, the post–Cold War military differed little from what it had looked like between the 1950s and 1989. Yet the armed forces of the United States now took on a radically different, far more ambitious mission: to impose order and spread American values globally, while eliminating obstacles deemed to impede those efforts. During the Cold War, policymakers had placed a premium on holding US forces in readiness. Now, the idea was to put "the troops" to work. Power projection became the name of the game.

Just a month prior to his State of the Union Address, President Bush himself had given this approach a test run, ordering US forces to intervene in Panama, overthrow the existing government there, and install in its place one expected to be more compliant. The president now neatly summarized the outcome of that action in three crisp sentences. "One year ago," he announced, "the people of Panama lived in fear, under the thumb of a dictator. Today democracy is restored; Panama is free. Operation Just Cause has achieved its objective." Mission accomplished; end of story. Here, it seemed, was a template for further application globally.

As it happened, however, Operation Just Cause proved to be the exception rather than the rule. Intervention in Panama did inaugurate a period of unprecedented American military activism. In the years that followed, US forces invaded, occupied, bombed, or raided an astonishing array of countries. Rarely, however, was the outcome as tidy as it had been in Panama, where the fighting lasted a mere five days. Untidy and protracted conflicts proved more typical of the post–Cold War US experience, with the Afghanistan War, a futile undertaking now in its nineteenth year, a notable example. The present-day US military qualifies by any measure as highly professional, much more so than its Cold War predecessor. Yet the purpose of today's professionals is not to preserve peace but to fight unending wars in distant places.

Intoxicated by a post–Cold War belief in its own omnipotence, the United States allowed itself to be drawn into a long series of armed conflicts, almost all of them yielding unintended consequences and imposing greater than anticipated costs. Since the end of the Cold War, US forces have destroyed many targets and killed many people. Only rarely, however, have they succeeded in accomplishing their assigned political purposes. From a military perspective—except perhaps in the eyes of the military-industrial complex—the legacy of the "Revolution of '89" turned out to be almost entirely negative.

A Broken Compass

So, contrary to President Bush's prediction, the fall of the Berlin Wall did not inaugurate a "new era in world affairs" governed by "this idea called America." It did, however, accelerate Europe's drift toward geopolitical insignificance and induced in Washington a sharp turn toward reckless militarism—neither of which qualifies as cause for celebration.

Yet today, thirty years after Bush's 1990 State of the Union, a "new era of world affairs" is indeed upon us, even if it bears scant resemblance to the order Bush expected to emerge. If his "idea called America" did not shape the contours of this new age, then what has? Answer: all the things post–Cold War Washington policy elites misunderstood or relegated to the status of afterthought. Here are three examples of key factors that actually shaped the present era. Notably, each had its point of origin *prior to* the end of the Cold War. Each came to maturity while US policymakers, hypnotized by the "Revolution of '89," were busily trying to reap the benefits they fancied to be this country's for the taking. Each far surpasses in significance the fall of the Berlin Wall.

The "rise" of China: The China that we know today emerged from reforms instituted by Communist Party leader Deng Xiaoping, reforms that transformed the People's Republic into an economic powerhouse. No nation in history, including the United States, has ever come close to matching China's spectacular ascent. In just three decades, its per capita gross domestic product skyrocketed from $156 in 1978 to $9,771 in 2017.

The post–Cold War assumption common among American elites that economic development would necessarily prompt political liberalization turned out to be wishful thinking. In Beijing today, the Communist Party remains firmly in control. Meanwhile, as illustrated by its Belt and Road Initiative, China has begun to assert itself globally, while simultaneously enhancing the capabilities of the People's Liberation Army. In all of this, the United States—apart from borrowing from China to pay for an abundance of its imported products (now well over a half-trillion dollars of them annually)—has figured as little more than a bystander. As China radically alters the balance of power in twenty-first-century East Asia, the outcome of the Cold War has no more relevance than does Napoleon's late-eighteenth-century expedition to Egypt.

A resurgence of religious extremism: Like the poor, religious fanatics will always be with us. They come in all stripes: Christians, Hindus, Jews, Muslims. Yet implicit in the American idea that lay at the heart of Bush's State of the Union Address was an expectation of modernity removing religion from politics. That the global advance of secularization would lead to the privatization of faith was accepted as a given in elite circles. After all, the end of the Cold War ostensibly left little to fight about. With the collapse of communism and the triumph of democratic capitalism, all the really big questions had been settled. That religiously inspired political violence would become a crucial factor in global politics therefore seemed inconceivable.

Yet a full decade before the "Revolution of '89," events were already shredding that expectation. In November 1979, radical Islamists shocked the House of Saud by seizing the Masjid al-Haram, or Grand Mosque, in Mecca. Although local security forces regained control after a bloody gun battle, the Saudi royal family resolved to prevent any recurrence of such a disaster by demonstrating beyond the shadow of a doubt its own fealty to the teachings of Allah. It did so by expending staggering sums throughout the *ummah* to promote a puritanical form of Islam known as Wahhabism.

In effect, Saudi Arabia became the principal underwriter of what would morph into Islamist terror. For Osama bin Laden and his militant followers, the American idea to which President Bush paid tribute that January in 1990 was blasphemous, intolerable, and a justification for war. Lulled by a belief that the end of the Cold War had yielded a definitive victory, the entire US national security apparatus would be caught unawares in September 2001 when religious warriors assaulted New York and Washington. Nor was the political establishment prepared for the appearance of violence perpetrated by domestic religious extremists. During the Cold War, it had become fashionable to declare God dead. That verdict turned out to be premature.

The assault on nature: From its inception, the American idea so lavishly praised by President Bush in 1990 had allowed, even fostered, the exploitation of the natural world based on a belief in Planet Earth's infinite capacity to absorb punishment. During the Cold War, critics like Rachel Carson, author of the pioneering environmental book *Silent Spring*, had warned against just such an assumption. While their warnings received respectful hearings, they elicited only modest corrective action.

Then, in 1988, a year prior to the fall of the Berlin Wall, in testimony before Congress, NASA scientist James Hansen issued a far more alarming warning: human activity, particularly the burning of fossil fuels, was inducing profound changes in the global climate with potentially catastrophic consequences. (Of course, a prestigious scientific advisory committee had offered just such a warning to President Lyndon Johnson more than two decades earlier, predicting the early twenty-first-century effects of climate change, to no effect whatsoever.)

To put it mildly, President Bush and other members of the political establishment did not welcome Hansen's analysis. After all, to take him seriously meant admitting to the necessity of modifying a way of life centered on self-indulgence, rather than self-restraint. At some level, perpetuating the American penchant for material consumption and personal mobility had described the ultimate purpose of the Cold War. Bush could no more tell Americans to settle for less than he could imagine a world order in which the United States no longer occupied "the center of a widening circle of freedom."

Some things were sacrosanct. As he put it on another occasion, "The American way of life is not up for negotiations. Period."

So while President Bush was not an outright climate-change denier, he temporized. Talk took precedence over action. He thereby set a pattern to which his successors would adhere, at least until the Trump years. To thwart communism during the Cold War, Americans might have been willing to "pay any price, bear any burden." Not so when it came to climate change. The Cold War itself had seemingly exhausted the nation's capacity for collective sacrifice. So, on several fronts, the assault on nature continues and shows signs of becoming dire.

In sum, from our present vantage point, it becomes apparent that the "Revolution of '89" did not initiate a new era of history. At most, the events of that year fostered various unhelpful illusions that impeded our capacity to recognize and respond to the forces of change that actually matter.

Restoring the American compass to working order won't occur until we recognize those illusions for what they are. Step one might be to revise what "this idea called America" truly signifies.

10
How "Historic" Are We?

Or, Going Off-Script in the Age of Trump

February 23, 2020

The impeachment of the president of the United States! Surely such a mega-historic event would reverberate for weeks or months, leaving in its wake no end of consequences, large and small. Wouldn't it? Shouldn't it?

Truth to tell, the word *historic* does get tossed around rather loosely these days. Just about anything that happens at the White House, for example, is deemed historic. Watch the cable news networks and you'll hear the term employed regularly to describe everything from Oval Office addresses to Rose Garden pronouncements to press conferences in which foreign dignitaries listen passively while their presidential host pontificates about subjects that have nothing to do with them and everything to do with him.

Of course, almost all of these are carefully scripted performances that are devoid of authenticity. In short, they're fraudulent. The politicians who participate in such performances know that it's all a sham. So, too, do the reporters and commentators paid to "interpret" the news. So, too, does any semi-attentive, semi-informed citizen.

Yet on it goes, day in, day out, as politicians, journalists, and ordinary folk collaborate in manufacturing, propagating, and consuming a vast panoply of staged incidents, which together comprise what Americans choose to treat as the very stuff of contemporary history. "Pseudo-events" was the term that historian Daniel Boorstin coined to describe them in his classic 1961 book *The Image: A Guide to Pseudo-Events in America.* The accumulation of such incidents creates a make-believe world. As Boorstin put it, they give rise to a "thicket of unreality that stands between us and the facts of life."

As substitutes for reality, pseudo-events, he claimed, breed "extravagant expectations" that can never be met, with disappointment, confusion, and anger among the inevitable results. Writing decades before the advent of CNN, Fox News, Google, Facebook, and Twitter, Boorstin observed that "we are deceived and obstructed by the very machines we make to enlarge our vision." So it was back then during the presidency of John F. Kennedy, a master of pseudo-events in the still relatively early days of television. And so our world remains today during the presidency of Donald Trump who achieved high office by unmasking the extravagant post–Cold War/sole superpower/indispensable nation/end of history expectations of the political class, only to weave his own in their place.

As Trump so skillfully demonstrates, even as they deceive, pseudo-events also seduce, inducing what Boorstin referred to as a form of "national self-hypnosis." With enough wishful thinking, reality becomes entirely optional. So the thousands of Trump loyalists attending MAGA rallies implicitly attest as they count on their hero to make their dreams come true and their nightmares go away.

Yet when it comes to extravagant expectations, few pseudo-events can match the recently completed presidential impeachment and trial. Even before his inauguration, the multitudes who despise Trump longed to see him thrown out of office. To ensure the survival of the republic, Trump's removal *needed* to happen. And when the impeachment process did finally begin to unfold, feverish reporters and commentators could find little else to talk about.

With the integrity of the Constitution itself said to be at stake, the enduringly historic significance of each day's developments appeared self-evident. Or so we were told anyway.

Yet while all parties involved dutifully recited their prescribed lines—no one with greater relish than Trump himself—the final outcome was never in doubt. The Republican Senate was no more likely to

convict the president than he was to play golf without cheating. So no
sooner did the Senate let Trump off the hook than the fever broke. In
an instant, the farcical nature of the entire process became blindingly
apparent. Rarely has the gap between hype and actual historical substance been so vast.

The effort to oust the president from office had unleashed a tidal
wave of angst, anxiety, anger, and hope. Yet a mere handful of weeks
after its conclusion, the impeachment of Donald Trump retains about
as much salience as the impeachment of Andrew Johnson, which concluded in 1868.

What does the instantaneous deflation of this ostensibly historic event
signify? Among other things, it shows that we still live in the world of
pseudo-events that Boorstin described nearly sixty years ago. The American susceptibility to contrived and scripted versions of reality persists,
revealing an emptiness at the core of our national politics. Arguably, in
our age of social media, that emptiness is greater still. To look past the
pseudo-events staged to capture our attention is to confront a void.

Pseudo-events Gone Wrong

Yet in this dismal situation, flickering bits of truth occasionally do appear in moments when pseudo-events inadvertently expose realities
they are meant to conceal. Boorstin posited that "pseudo-events produce more pseudo-events." While that might be broadly correct, let
me offer a caveat: given the right conditions, pseudo-events can also be
self-subverting, their cumulative absurdity undermining their cumulative authority. Every now and then, in other words, we get the sneaking
suspicion that much of what in Washington gets advertised as historic
just might be a load of bullshit.

As it happens, the season of Trump's impeachment offered three
encouraging instances of a prominent pseudo-event being exposed as
delightfully bogus: the Iowa caucuses, the State of the Union Address,
and the National Prayer Breakfast.

According to custom, every four years the Iowa caucuses initiate
what is said to be a fair, methodical, and democratic process of selecting

the presidential nominees of the two principal political parties. According to custom and in accordance with a constitutional requirement, the State of the Union Address offers presidents an annual opportunity to appear before Congress and the American people to assess the nation's condition and describe administration plans for the year ahead. Pursuant to a tradition dating from the early years of the Cold War, the National Prayer Breakfast, held annually in Washington, invites members of the political establishment to bear witness to the assertion that we remain a people "under God," united in all our wondrous diversity by a shared faith in the Almighty.

This year all three went haywire, each in a different way, but together hinting at the vulnerability of other pseudo-events assumed to be fixed and permanent. By offering a peek at previously hidden truths, the trio of usually forgettable events just might merit celebration.

First, on February 3, came the long-awaited Iowa caucuses. Commentators grasping for something to write about in advance of caucus night entertained themselves by lamenting the fact that the Hawkeye State is too darn white, implying, in effect, that Iowans aren't sufficiently American. As it happened, the problem turned out to be not a lack of diversity, but a staggering lack of competence, as the state's Democratic Party thoroughly botched the one and only event that allows Iowa to claim a modicum of national political significance. To tally caucus results, it employed an ill-tested and deficient smartphone app created by party insiders who were clearly out of their depth.

The result was an epic cock-up, a pseudo-event exposed as political burlesque. The people of Iowa had spoken—the people defined in this instance as registered Democrats who bothered to show up—but no one quite knew what they had said. By the time the counting and recounting were over, the results no longer mattered. Iowa was supposed to set in motion an orderly sorting-out process for the party and its candidates. Instead, it sowed confusion and then more confusion. Yet in doing so, the foul-up in Iowa suggested that maybe, just maybe, the entire process of selecting presidential candidates is in need of a complete overhaul, with the present quadrennial circus replaced by an approach that might yield an outcome more expeditiously, while wasting less money and, yes, also taking diversity into account.

Next, on February 4, came the State of the Union Address. Resplendent with ritual and ceremony, this event certainly deserves an honored place in the pseudo-event Hall of Fame. This year's performance was no exception. President Trump bragged shamelessly about his administration's many accomplishments, planted compliant live mannequins in the gallery of the House of Representatives to curry favor with various constituencies—hate-mongering radio host Rush Limbaugh received the Medal of Freedom from the First Lady!—even as he otherwise kept pretty much to the model employed by every president since Ronald Reagan. It was, in other words, a pseudo-event par excellence.

The sole revelatory moment came just after Trump finished speaking. In an endearing and entirely salutary gesture, House Speaker Nancy Pelosi, standing behind the president, promptly rendered her verdict on the entire occasion. Like a thoroughly miffed schoolteacher rejecting unsatisfactory homework from a delinquent pupil, she tore the text of Trump's remarks in two. In effect, Pelosi thereby announced that the entire evening had consisted of pure, unadulterated nonsense, as indeed it had and as has every other State of the Union Address in recent memory.

Blessings upon Speaker Pelosi. Next year, we must hope that she will skip the occasion entirely as not worthy of her time. Other members of Congress, preferably from both parties, may then follow her example, finding better things to do. Within a few years, presidents could find themselves speaking in an empty chamber. The networks will then lose interest. At that juncture, the practice that prevailed from the early days of the republic until the administration of Woodrow Wilson might be restored. Every year or so, presidents can simply send a letter to Congress ruminating about the state of the nation, with members choosing to attend to or ignore it as it pleases them. And the nation's calendar will therefore be purged altogether of one prominent pseudo-event.

The National Prayer Breakfast, which occurred on February 6, completes our trifecta of recent pseudo-events gone unexpectedly awry.

Here the credit belongs entirely to President Trump, who used his time at the dais during this nominally religious event as an opportunity to whine about the "terrible ordeal" he had just endured at the hands of "some very dishonest and corrupt people." Alluding specifically to Pelosi (and perhaps with Mitt Romney also in mind), Trump denounced his critics as hypocrites. "I don't like people who use their faith as justification for doing what they know is wrong," he said. "Nor do I like people who say, 'I pray for you,' when they know that that's not so."

Jesus might have forgiven his tormentors, but Donald Trump, a self-described Christian, is not given to following the Lord's example. So instead of an occasion for faux displays of brotherly ecumenism, this year's National Prayer Breakfast became one more exhibition of petty partisanship—relieving the rest of us (and the media) of any further need to pretend that it ever possessed anything approximating a serious religious motivation.

So if only in an ironic sense, the first week of February 2020 did end up qualifying as a genuinely historic occasion. Granted, those who claim the authority to instruct the rest of us on what deserves that encomium missed its true significance. They had wasted no time in moving on to the next pseudo-event, this one in New Hampshire. Yet over the course of a handful of days, Americans had been granted a glimpse of the reality that pseudo-events are designed to camouflage.

A few more such glimpses and something like "the facts of life" to which Boorstin alluded so long ago might become impossible to hide any longer. Imagine: no more bullshit. In these dark and discouraging times, aren't we at least entitled to such a hope?

11
V-E Day Plus Seventy-Five

From a Moment of Victory to a Time of Pandemic

May 5, 2020

The seventy-fifth anniversary of Nazi Germany's surrender in May 1945 ought to prompt thoughtful reflection. For Americans, V-E Day, as it was then commonly called, marked the beginning of "our times." The COVID-19 pandemic may signal that our times are now coming to an end.

Tom Engelhardt, editor and proprietor of *TomDispatch*, was born less than a year prior to V-E Day. I was born less than two years after its counterpart V-J Day, marking the surrender of Imperial Japan in August 1945.

Tom is a New Yorker, born and bred. I was born and raised in the Midwest.

Tom is Jewish, although nonobservant. I am a mostly observant Catholic.

Tom is a progressive who as a young man protested against the Vietnam War. I am, so I persist in claiming, a conservative. As a young man, I served in Vietnam.

Yet let me suggest that these various differences matter less than the fact that we both came of age in the shadow of World War II—or more specifically in a time when the specter of Nazi Germany haunted the American intellectual landscape. Over the years, that haunting would become the underlying rationale for the US exercise of global power, with consequences that undermined the nation's capacity to deal with the menace that it now faces.

Tom and I both belong to what came to be known as the baby boom generation (though including him means ever so slightly backing up the official generational start date). As a group, boomers are generally associated with having had a pampered upbringing before embarking upon a rebellious youth (Tom more than I), and then as adults helping ourselves to more than our fair share of all that life, liberty, and happiness had on offer. Now, preparing to exit the stage, we boomers are passing on to those who follow us a badly damaged planet and a nation increasingly divided, adrift, and quite literally sick. A Greatest Generation we are not.

How did all this happen? Let me suggest that, to unpack American history during the decades when we baby boomers sashayed across the world stage, you have to begin with World War II, or more specifically, with how that war ended and became enshrined in American memory.

Of course, we boomers never experienced the war directly. Our parents did. Tom's father and both of my parents served in World War II. Yet neither were we boomers ever truly able to put that war behind us. For better or worse, members of our generation remain the children of V-E Day, when—so we tell ourselves—evil was finally vanquished and good prevailed.

Never Forget

For Tom, for me, and for our contemporaries, World War II as history and as metaphor centers specifically on the Nazis and their handiwork: swastikas, mammoth staged rallies, the gestapo and the SS, the cowardice of surrender at Munich, the lightning offensive campaigns known as blitzkrieg, London burning, the Warsaw Ghetto, slave labor, and, of course, a vast network of death camps leading to the Holocaust, all documented in film, photographs, archives, and eyewitness accounts.

And then there was *der Führer* himself, Adolf Hitler, the subject of a fascination that, over the decades, proved bottomless and more than slightly disturbing. (If your local library ever reopens, compare the number of books about Hitler to those about Italian fascist leader Benito Mussolini or wartime Japanese emperor Hirohito.) Seventy-five years after his death, Hitler remains among us, the supreme villain routinely pressed into service by politicians and media pundits alike intent on raising the alarm about some imminent danger. If ever there were a man for all seasons, it is Adolf Hitler.

Hitler's centrality helps explain why Americans typically date the opening of World War II to September 1939 when the *Wehrmacht* invaded Poland. Only in December 1941 did the United States (belatedly) join the conflict, the Imperial Japanese Navy's attack on Pearl Harbor and other American installations in the Pacific forcing Washington's hand. In fact, however, a full decade earlier Japan had already set out to create what it would eventually call its Greater East Asia Co-prosperity Sphere. In September 1931, its forces invaded then Chinese-controlled Manchuria, an undertaking that soon enough morphed into a very large and brutal armed conflict with China proper in which the United States participated on a proxy basis. (Remember the Flying Tigers?) In other words, World War II actually began in Asia rather than Europe, with the first shots fired years before the Nazi attack on Poland.

Yet launching the narrative in September 1939 has the effect of keeping the primary focus on Germany. From a moral perspective, there are ample reasons for doing this: even in a century of horrendous crimes—the Armenian genocide, Stalin's extermination of Ukraine's Kulaks, and Mao Zedong's murderous campaign against his own people—the sheer unadulterated evil of the Nazi regime stands apart.

From a political perspective, however, intense preoccupation with one example of iniquity, however horrific, induces a skewed perspective. So it proved to be with the United States during the decades that followed V-E Day. Subsumed within the advertised purposes of postwar US policy, whether called "defense," "deterrence," "containment," "liberation," or "the protection of human rights," has been this transcendent theme: "Never Again." That is, never again will the United States ignore or appease or fail to confront a regime that compares to—or even vaguely resembles—Nazi Germany. Never again will it slumber until rudely awakened by a Pearl Harbor–like surprise. Never again will it allow its capacity for projecting power against distant threats to dissipate. Never again will it fail to lead.

Of all Donald Trump's myriad deficiencies, large and small, this may be the one that his establishment critics find most difficult to stomach: his resurrection of "America First" as a primary principle of statecraft suggests a de facto nullification of "Never Again."

To Trump's critics, it hardly matters that "America First" in no way describes actual administration policy. After all, more than three years into the Trump presidency, our endless wars persist (and in some cases have even intensified); the nation's various alliances and its empire of overseas bases remain intact; US troops are still present in something like 140 countries; Pentagon and national security state spending continues to increase astronomically. Even so, the president does appear oblivious to the historical antecedent—that is, the imperative of standing ready to deal with the next Hitler—that finds concrete expression in these several manifestations of US national security policy. No one has ever accused Trump of possessing a profound grasp of history. Yet here his apparent cluelessness is especially telling.

Not least among the unofficial duties of any president is to serve as the authoritative curator of public memory. Through speeches, proclamations, and the laying of wreaths, presidents tell us what we should remember and how. Through their silence, they give us permission to forget the parts of our past that we prefer to forget. Himself born barely a year after V-E Day, Trump seems to have forgotten World War II.

New Signs for a New Time?
Yet let's consider this admittedly uncongenial possibility: Perhaps Trump is onto something. What if V-E Day is no more relevant to the present than the Treaty of Ghent, which ended the War of 1812? What if, as a basis for policy, "Never Again" is today just as outmoded as "America First"? What if clinging to the canonical lessons of the war against Hitler impedes efforts to repair our nation and our planet?

An abiding problem with "Never Again" is that US policymakers have never applied it to the United States. Since V-E Day, individuals and regimes deemed in Washington to be the spawn of Hitler and the Nazis have provided justification for successive administrations to accumulate arms, impose punishments, underwrite coups and assassination plots, and, of course, wage war endlessly. Beginning with Soviet dictator Joseph Stalin and China's Mao Zedong, the list of malefactors that US officials and militant journalists have likened to Hitler is a long one. They've ranged from North Korea's Kim Il-sung in the 1950s to Cuba's Fidel Castro in the 1960s to Iraq's Saddam Hussein in the 1990s. And just to bring things up to date, let's not overlook the ayatollahs governing present-day Iran.

Two decades after V-E Day, a succession of presidents deployed lessons ostensibly derived from the war against Hitler to justify the Vietnam War. John F. Kennedy described South Vietnam as "the cornerstone of the Free World in Southeast Asia, the keystone of the arch, the finger in the dike." Failing to defend that country would allow "the red tide of Communism," as he put it, to sweep across the region much as appeasers had allowed the Nazi tide to sweep across Europe. "Everything I knew about history," Lyndon Johnson reflected, "told me that if I got out of Vietnam and let Ho Chi Minh run through the streets of Saigon, then I'd be doing exactly what [Neville] Chamberlain did in World War II," a reference, of course, to the Munich Agreement with Hitler, which that British prime minister so infamously labeled "peace in our time." Even as late as 1972, Nixon was assuring the public that "an American defeat" in Vietnam "would encourage this kind of aggression all over the world."

Vietnam provides but one example among many of how viewing problems through the lens of World War II in Europe has obscured real situations and actual stakes on this planet. In short, the promiscuous use of the Hitler analogy has produced deeply flawed policy decisions, while also deceiving the American people. This has inhibited our ability to see the world as it actually is.

Overall, the approach to statecraft that grew out of V-E Day defined the ultimate purpose of US policy in terms of resisting evil. That, in turn, provided all the justification needed for building up American military capabilities beyond compare and engaging in military action on a planetary scale.

In Washington, policymakers have shown little inclination to consider the possibility that the United States itself might be guilty of doing evil. In effect, the virtuous intentions implicit in "Never Again" inoculated the United States against the virus to which ordinary nations were susceptible. V-E Day seemingly affirmed that America was anything but ordinary.

Here, then, we arrive at one explanation for the predicament in which the United States now finds itself. In a recent article in the *New York Times*, journalist Katrin Bennhold wondered how it could be that, when it came to dealing with COVID-19, "the country that defeated fascism in Europe 75 years ago" now finds itself "doing a worse job protecting its citizens than many autocracies and democracies" globally.

Yet it might just be that events that occurred seventy-five years ago in Europe no longer have much bearing on the present. The country that defeated Hitler's version of fascism (albeit with considerable help from others) has since allowed its preoccupation with fascists, quasi-fascists, and other ne'er-do-wells to serve as an excuse for letting other things slip, particularly here in the homeland.

The United States is fully capable of protecting its citizens. Yet the present pandemic drives home that doing so, while also creating an environment in which all citizens can flourish, is going to require a radical revision of what we still, however inaccurately, call "national security" priorities. This does not mean turning a blind eye to mass murder. Yet the militarization of US policy that occurred in the wake of V-E Day has for too long distracted attention from more pressing matters, not least among them creating a way of life that is equitable and sustainable. This perversion of priorities must now cease.

So, yes, let's mark this V-E Day anniversary with all due solemnity. Yet seventy-five years after the collapse of the Third Reich, the challenge facing the United States is not "Never Again." It's "What Now?"

For the moment at least, Tom and I are still around. Yet "our times"—the period that began when World War II ended—have run their course. The "new times" upon which the nation has now embarked will pose their own distinctive challenges, as the COVID-19 pandemic makes unmistakably clear. Addressing those challenges will require leaders able to free themselves from a past that has become increasingly irrelevant.

❯

12
Martin Luther King's Giant Triplets

Racism, Yes, but What about Militarism and Materialism?

June 23, 2020

In the wake of the police killing of George Floyd, Americans are finally—or is it once again?—confronting the racism that afflicts this country and extends into just about every corner of our national life. Something fundamental just might be happening.

Yet to state the obvious, we've been here before. Mass protests in response to racial inequality and discrimination, including police brutality, have been anything but unknown in the United States. Much the same can be said of riots targeting Black Americans, fomented and exploited by white racists, often actively or passively abetted by local law enforcement officials. If Jamil Abdullah Al-Amin, formerly known as H. Rap Brown, was correct in calling violence "as American as cherry pie," then race-related urban unrest is the apple-filled equivalent.

The optimists among us believe that "this time is different." I hope events will prove them right. Yet recalling expectations that Barack Obama's election in 2008 signaled the dawn of a "post-racial America," I see no reason to expect it to be so. A yawning gap, I fear, separates hope from reality.

Let me suggest, however, that the nation's current preoccupation with race, as honorable and necessary as it may be, falls well short of adequately responding to the situation confronting Americans as they enter the third decade of the twenty-first century. Racism is a massive problem, but hardly our only one. Indeed, as Martin Luther King sought to remind us many years ago, there are at least two others of comparable magnitude.

MLK Defines the Problem

In April 1967, at New York City's Riverside Church, Dr. King delivered a sermon that offered a profound diagnosis of the illnesses afflicting the nation. His analysis remains as timely today as it was then, perhaps more so.

Americans remember King primarily as a great civil rights leader and indeed he was that. In his Riverside Church address, however, he turned to matters that went far beyond race. In an immediate sense, his focus was the ongoing Vietnam War, which he denounced as "madness" that "must cease." Yet King also used the occasion to summon the nation to "undergo a radical revolution of values" that would transform the United States "from a thing-oriented society to a person-oriented society." Only through such a revolution, he declared, would we be able to overcome "the giant triplets of racism, extreme materialism, and militarism."

The challenge confronting Americans was to dismantle what King referred to as the "edifice" that produced and sustained each of those giant triplets. Today's protesters, crusading journalists, and engaged intellectuals make no bones about their determination to eliminate the first of those giant triplets. Yet they generally treat the other two as, at best, mere afterthoughts, while the edifice itself, resting on a perverse understanding of freedom, goes almost entirely ignored.

I'm not suggesting that members of the grand coalition of Americans today fervently campaigning against racism favor extreme materialism. Many of them merely accept its reality and move on. Nor am I suggesting that they consciously endorse militarism, although in confusing "support" for the troops with genuine patriotism some of them do so implicitly. What I am suggesting is that those calling for fundamental change will go badly astray if they ignore Dr. King's insistence that each of the giant triplets is intimately tied to the other two.

Defund the Pentagon?

The protests triggered by the recent murders of George Floyd and other Black Americans have produced widespread demands to "defund the police." Those demands don't come out of nowhere. While "reform" programs undertaken in innumerable American cities over the course of many years have demonstrably enhanced police firepower, they have done little, if anything, to repair relations between police departments and communities of color.

As an aging middle-class white male, I don't fear cops. I respect the fact that theirs is a tough job, which I would not want. Yet I realize that my attitude is one more expression of white privilege, which Black people, regardless of their age, gender, and economic status, can ill afford to indulge. So I fully accept the need for radical changes in policing—that's what "defund" appears to imply—if American cities are ever to have law enforcement agencies that are effective, humane, and themselves law-abiding.

What I can't fathom is why a similar logic doesn't apply to the armed forces that we employ to police huge chunks of the world beyond our borders. If Americans have reason to question the nation's increasingly militarized approach to law enforcement, then shouldn't they have equal reason to question this country's thoroughly militarized approach to statecraft?

Consider that on an annual basis, police officers in the United States kill approximately one thousand Americans, with Blacks two-and-a-half times more likely than whites to be victimized. Those are appalling figures, indicative of basic policy gone fundamentally awry. So the outpouring of protest over the police and demands for change are understandable and justified.

Still, the question must be asked: why have the nation's post-9/11 wars not prompted similar expressions of outrage? The unjustified killing of Black Americans rightly finds thousands upon thousands of protesters flooding the streets of major cities. Yet the loss of thousands of American soldiers and the physical and psychological wounds sustained by tens of thousands more in foolhardy wars elicits, at best, shrugs. Throw in the hundreds of thousands of non-American lives taken in those military campaigns and the trillions of taxpayer dollars they have consumed and you have a catastrophe that easily exceeds in scale the myriad race-related protests and riots that have roiled American cities in the recent past.

With their eyes fixed on elections that are now just months away, politicians of all stripes spare no effort to show that they "get it" on the issue of race and policing. Race may well play a large role in determining who wins the White House this November and which party controls Congress. It should. Yet while the election's final outcome may be uncertain, this much is not: neither the American propensity for war, nor the bloated size of the Pentagon budget, nor the dubious habit of maintaining a sprawling network of military bases across much of the planet will receive serious scrutiny during the political season now underway. Militarism will escape unscathed.

At Riverside Church, King described the US government as "the greatest purveyor of violence in the world today." So it unquestionably remains, perpetrating immeasurably more violence than any other great power and with remarkably little to show in return. Why, then, except on the easily ignored fringes of American politics, are there no demands to "defund" the Pentagon?

King considered the Vietnam War an abomination. At that time, more than a few Americans agreed with him and vigorously demonstrated against the conflict's continuation. That today's demonstrators have seemingly chosen to file away our post-9/11 military misadventures under the heading of regrettable but forgettable is itself an abomination. While their sensitivity to racism is admirable, their indifference to war is nothing short of disheartening.

In 1967, Dr. King warned that "a nation that continues year after year to spend more money on military defense than on programs of social uplift is approaching spiritual death." During the intervening decades, his charge has lost none of its sting or aptness.

America's National Signature

Given their size and duration, the protests occurring in the wake of the murder of George Floyd have been remarkably peaceful. That said, some of them did, early on, include rioters who resorted to looting.

Smashing windows and ransacking stores, they walked off not with milk and bread for the hungry, but with shopping bags filled with high-end swag—designer shoes and sneakers, purses, clothing, and jewelry lifted from stores like Prada and Alexander McQueen. Also stolen were smartphones, handguns, even automobiles. In-store surveillance systems recorded scenes reminiscent of Black Friday doorbuster sales, though without anyone bothering to pass through a checkout counter. Some looters quickly attempted to monetize their hauls by offering to sell purloined items online.

Certain right-wing commentators wasted no time in using the looting to tar the protest movement as little more than an expression of nihilism. Tucker Carlson of Fox News was particularly emphatic on this point. Americans taking to the streets in response to Floyd's murder, he said, "reject society itself."

"Reason and process and precedent mean nothing to them. They use violence to get what they want immediately. People like this don't bother to work. They don't volunteer or pay taxes to help other people. They live for themselves. They do exactly what they feel like doing . . . On television, hour by hour, we watch these people—criminal mobs—destroy what the rest of us have built . . ."

To explain such selfish and destructive misconduct, Carlson had an answer readily at hand: "The ideologues will tell you that the problem is race relations, or capitalism, or police brutality, or global warming. But only on the surface. The real cause is deeper than that and it's far darker. What you're watching is the ancient battle between those who have a stake in society, and would like to preserve it, and those who don't, and seek to destroy it."

This is vile, hateful stuff, and entirely wrong—except perhaps on one point. In attributing the looting to a deeper cause, Carlson was onto something, even if his effort to pinpoint that cause was wildly off the mark.

I won't try to unravel the specific motives of those who saw an opportunity in the protests against racism to help themselves to goods that were not theirs. How much was righteous anger turned to rage and how much cynical opportunism is beyond my ability to know.

This much, however, can be said for certain: the grab-all-you-can-get impulse so vividly on display was as all-American as fireworks on the Fourth of July. Those looters, after all, merely wanted more stuff. What could be more American than that? In this country, after all, stuff carries with it the possibility of personal fulfillment, of achieving some version of happiness or status.

The looters that Tucker Carlson targeted with his ire were doing anything but "rejecting society itself." They were merely helping themselves to what this society today has on offer for those with sufficient cash and credit cards in their wallets. In a sense, they were treating themselves to a tiny sip of what passes these days for the American Dream.

With the exception of cloistered nuns, hippies, and other vanishing breeds, virtually all Americans have been conditioned to buy into the proposition that stuff correlates with the good life. Unconvinced? Check out the videos from last year's Black Friday and then consider the intense, if unsurprising, interest of economists and journalists in tracking the latest consumer spending trends. At least until COVID-19 came along, consumer spending served as the authoritative measure of the nation's overall health.

The primary civic obligation of US citizens today is not to vote or pay taxes. And it's certainly not to defend the country, a task offloaded onto those who can be enticed to enlist (with minorities vastly overrepresented) in the so-called all-volunteer military. No, the primary obligation of citizenship is to spend.

Ours is not a nation of mystics, philosophers, poets, artisans, or Thomas Jefferson's yeomen farmers. We are now a nation of citizen-consumers, held in thrall to the extreme materialism that Dr. King decried. This, not a commitment to liberty or democracy, has become our true national signature and our chief contribution to late modernity.

Tearing Down the Edifice

At Riverside Church, King reminded his listeners that the Southern Christian Leadership Conference, which he had helped to found a decade earlier, had chosen "To save the soul of America" as its motto. The soul of a nation corrupted by racism, militarism, and extreme materialism represented King's ultimate concern. Vietnam, he said, was "but a symptom of a far deeper malady within the American spirit."

In a tone-deaf editorial criticizing his Riverside Church sermon, the *New York Times* chastised King for "fusing two public problems"— racism and the Vietnam War—"that are distinct and separate." Yet part of King's genius lay in his ability to recognize the interconnectedness of matters that *Times* editors, as oblivious to deeper maladies then as they are today, wish to keep separate. King sought to tear down the edifice that sustained all three of those giant triplets. Indeed, it is all but certain that, were he alive now, he would call similar attention to a fourth related factor: climate change denial. The refusal to treat seriously the threat posed by climate change underwrites the persistence of racism, militarism, and extreme materialism.

During the course of his sermon, King quoted this sentence from the statement of a group that called itself the Clergy and Laymen Concerned About Vietnam: "A time comes when silence is betrayal." Regarding race, it appears that the great majority of Americans have now rejected such silence. This is good. It remains an open question, however, when their silent acceptance of militarism, materialism, and the abuse of Planet Earth will end.

13

Patton and Westy Meet in a Bar

A Play of Many Parts in One Act

September 10, 2020

It's only midafternoon and Army Lieutenant General Victor Constant has already had a bad day. Soon after he arrived at the office at 0700, the chief had called. "Come see me. We need to talk."

The call was not unexpected. Any day now, POTUS will announce the next four-star to command the war effort in Afghanistan—how many have there been?—and Constant felt certain that he'd be tapped for the job. He'd certainly earned it. Multiple tours in Iraq *and* Afghanistan *and*, worse still, at the Pentagon. If anyone deserved that fourth star, he did.

Unfortunately, the chief sees things differently. "Time's up, Vic. I need you to retire."

Thirty-three years of service and this is what you get: your walking papers, with maybe a medal thrown in.

Constant returns to his office, then abruptly tells his staff that he needs some personal time. A ten-minute drive and he's at the O-Club, where the bar is just opening. "Barkeep," he growls. "Bourbon. Double. Rocks."

On the job long enough to have seen more than a few senior officers get the axe, the bartender quietly complies.

Constant has some thinking to do. For the first time in his adult life, he's about to become unemployed. Alimony payments and college tuition bills are already killing him. When he and Sally have to move out of quarters, she's going to expect that fancy house in McLean or Potomac that he had hinted at when they were dating. But where's the money going to come from?

He needs a plan. "Barkeep. Another."

Lost in thought, Constant doesn't notice that he's no longer alone. Two soldiers—one boisterous, the other melancholy—have arrived and are occupying adjacent bar stools. The first of them smells of horses. To judge by his jodhpurs and riding crop, he's just returned from playing polo. He has thinning gray hair, small uneven teeth, a high-pitched voice, and a grin that says *I know things you never will, you dumb sonofa-bitch.* He exudes arrogance and charisma. He is George S. Patton. He orders whiskey with a beer chaser.

The second wears Vietnam-era jungle fatigues, starched. His jump boots glisten. On his ballcap, which he carefully sets aside, are four embroidered silver stars. He is impeccably groomed and manicured. The name tape over his breast pocket reads WESTMORELAND. He exudes the resentment of someone who has been treated unfairly—or thinks he has.

"Westy! Damned if you still don't look like *TIME*'s Man of the Year back in '65! Ease up, man! Have a drink. What'll it be?"

"Just water for me, General. It's a bit early in the day."

"Shit. Water? You think my guys beat the Nazis by filling their canteens with water?"

Westmoreland sniffs. "Alcohol consumption does not correlate with battlefield performance—although my troops did not suffer from a shortage of drink. They never suffered from shortages of anything."

Patton guffaws. "But you lost! That's the point, ain't it? You lost!"

The bickering draws Victor Constant out of his reverie. "Gentlemen, please."

"Who are you, bucko?" asks Patton.

"I am Lieutenant General Victor Constant, US Army. To my friends, I'm VC."

"VC!" Westy nearly falls off of his stool. "My army has generals named after the Vietcong?"

Patton intervenes. "Well, VC, tell us old-timers what you're famous for and why you're here, drinking in uniform during duty hours."

"Well, sir, first of all, I'm a warrior. I commanded a company in combat, then a battalion, then a brigade, then a division. But I'm here now because the chief just told me that I need to retire. That came as a bit of a blow. I don't know what Sally is going to say." He stares at his drink.

Patton snorts. "Well, my young friend, sounds like you've seen plenty of action. All that fighting translates into how many wins?"

"Wins?" VC doesn't quite grasp the question.

"Wins," Patton says again. "You know, victories. The enemy surrenders. Their flag comes down and ours goes up. The troops go home to a heroes' welcome. Polo resumes."

Westy interjects. "Wins? Are you that out of touch, George? The answer is: none. These so-called warriors haven't won anything."

"With all due respect, sir, I don't think that's fair. Everyone agrees that, back in '91, Operation Desert Storm was a historic victory. I know. I was there, fresh out of West Point."

Patton smirks. "Then why did you have to go back and do it again in 2003? And why has your army been stuck in Iraq ever since? Not to mention Syria! And don't get me started on Afghanistan or Somalia! The truth is your record isn't any better than Westy's."

"Now, see here, George. You're being unreasonable. We never lost a fight in Vietnam." He pauses and corrects himself. "Well, maybe not never, but very rarely."

"Rarely lost a fight!" Patton roars. "What does that have to do with anything? That's like you and your thing with body counts! Dammit, Westy, don't you know anything about war?"

VC ventures an opinion. "General Westmoreland, sir, I'm going to have to agree with General Patton on this one. You picked the wrong metric to measure progress. We don't do body counts anymore."

"Well, what's your metric, sonny?"

VC squirms and falls silent.

His hackles up, Westy continues. "First of all, the whole body-count business was the fault of the politicians. We knew exactly how to defeat

North Vietnam. Invade the country, destroy the NVA, occupy Hanoi. Just like World War II: Mission accomplished. Not complicated.",

He pauses to take a breath. "But LBJ and that arrogant fool McNamara wouldn't let us. They imposed limits. They wouldn't even mobilize the reserves. They set restrictions on where we could go, what we could attack. General Patton here had none of those problems in '44–45. And then the press turned on us. And the smartass college kids who should have been fighting communists started protesting. Nothing like it before or since—the home front collaborating with the enemy."

Westy changes his mind about having a drink. "Give me a gin martini," he barks. "Straight up. Twist of lemon. And give VC here"—his voice drips with contempt—"another of whatever he's having."

The bartender, who has been eavesdropping while pretending to polish glassware, grabs a bottle and pours.

"Hearts and minds, Westy, hearts and minds." Patton taunts, obviously enjoying himself.

"Yes, hearts and minds. Don't you think, George, that we understood the importance of winning over the South Vietnamese? But after Diem's assassination, the Republic of Vietnam consisted of little more than a flag. After D-Day, you didn't need to create France. You just needed to kick out the Germans and hand matters over to de Gaulle."

Westmoreland is becoming increasingly animated. "And you fought alongside the Brits. We were shackled to a Vietnamese army that was miserably led and not eager to fight either."

"Monty was a horse's ass," Patton interjects, apropos of nothing.

"The point is," Westmoreland continues, "liberating Europe was politically simple. Defending South Vietnam came with complications you could never have dreamed of. Did the *New York Times* pester you about killing civilians? All you had to do to keep the press on your side was not to get caught slapping your own soldiers."

"That was an isolated incident and I apologized," Patton replies, with a tight smile. "But the fact is, Westy, all your talk about 'firepower and mobility' didn't work. 'Search and destroy'? Hell, you damn near destroyed the whole US Army. And the war ended with the North Vietnamese sitting in Saigon."

"Ho Chi Minh City," Victor Constant offers by way of correction.

"Oh, shut up," Patton and Westmoreland respond simultaneously.

Patton leans menacingly toward Victor Constant and looks him right in the eye. "Have you seen my movie, son?"

"Yes, of course, sir. Several times."

"Then you should understand what war is all about. You 'hold onto him by the nose' and you 'kick him in the ass.' That's what I said in the movie. Why is that so hard to understand? How is it that my soldiers could defeat those Hun bastards and you and your crew can't manage to take care of a few thousand 'militants' who don't have tanks or an air force or even decent uniforms, for God's sake?"

"Hearts and minds, George, hearts and minds."

"What's that supposed to mean, Westy?"

"Your kick-them-in-the-ass approach isn't good enough these days. You studied Clausewitz—war is politics with guns. Now, I'll give you this much: In Vietnam, we never got the politics right. We couldn't solve the puzzle of making war work politically. Maybe there wasn't a solution. Maybe the war was already lost the day I showed up. So we just killed to no purpose. That's a failure I took to my grave."

A bead of perspiration is forming on Westmoreland's lip. "But these guys"—he nods toward Constant—"now, we've got a generation of generals who think they've seen a lot of war but don't know squat about politics—and don't even want to know. And we've got a generation of politicians who don't know squat about war, but keep doling out the money. There's no dialogue, no strategy, no connecting war and politics."

Victor Constant is mystified. Dialogue? He rouses himself to defend his service. "Gentlemen, let me remind you that the United States Army today is far and away the world's finest military force. No one else comes close."

Westy just presses on. "So what has your experience in war taught you? What have you learned?"

Patton repeats the question. "What have you learned, Mr. Warrior? Tell us."

Learned? After several drinks, Victor Constant is not at his best. "Well, I've learned a lot. The whole army has."

He struggles to recall recent PowerPoint briefings that he's dozed through. Random phrases come to mind. "Leap-ahead technology. Dominant maneuver in an ever-enlarging battlespace. Simultaneous and sequential operations. Artificial Intelligence. Quantum computing. Remote sensing. Machine learning. Big data analytics. 5G technology. High-fidelity, multi-domain training."

However dimly, VC realizes he's babbling. He pauses to catch his breath. "It's all coming, if they'll just give us the money."

Patton stares at him silently. Victor Constant senses that it's time to go home.

"Can I call you a taxi?" Westmoreland asks.

"No, sir. Thank you." With as much dignity as he can muster, Victor Constant straightens his tie, finds his headgear, and walks unsteadily toward the door.

What have I learned? What did they even mean? He was a general officer in the best army in the world. Maybe the best army ever. Wasn't that enough? He needed to ask Sally.

14

Reframing America's Role in the World

The Specter of Isolationism

October 18, 2020

T he so-called Age of Trump is also an age of instantly forgotten best-selling books, especially ones purporting to provide the inside scoop on what goes on within Trump's haphazard and continuously shifting orbit. With metronomic regularity, such gossipy volumes appear, make a splash, and almost as quickly vanish, leaving a mark no more lasting than a trout breaking the surface in a pond.

Remember when Michael Wolff's *Fire and Fury: Inside the Trump White House* was all the rage? It's now available in hardcover for $0.99 from online used booksellers. James Comey's *A Higher Loyalty* also sells for a penny less than a buck.

An additional forty-six cents will get you Omarosa Manigault Newman's "insider's account" of her short-lived tenure in that very White House. For the same price, you can acquire Sean Spicer's memoir as Trump's press secretary, Anthony Scaramucci's rendering of his tumultuous eleven-day stint as White House communications director, and Corey Lewandowski's "inside story" of the 2016 presidential campaign.

Bibliophiles intent on assembling a complete library of Trumpiana will not have long to wait before the tell-all accounts of John Bolton, Michael Cohen, Mary Trump, and that journalistic amanuensis Bob Woodward will surely be available at similar bargain basement prices.

All that said, even in these dismal times genuinely important books do occasionally make their appearance. My friend and colleague Stephen Wertheim is about to publish one. It's called *Tomorrow, the World: The Birth of U.S. Global Supremacy*, and if you'll forgive me for being direct, you really ought to read it. Let me explain why.

The "Turn"

Wertheim and I are cofounders of the Quincy Institute for Responsible Statecraft, a small Washington, DC-based think tank. That *Quincy* refers to John Quincy Adams, who, as secretary of state nearly two centuries ago, warned his fellow citizens against venturing abroad "in search of monsters to destroy." Were the United States to do so, Adams predicted, its defining trait—its very essence—"would insensibly change from *liberty* to *force*." By resorting to force, America "might become the dictatress of the world," he wrote, but "she would be no longer the ruler of her own spirit." While his gendered punchline might rankle contemporary sensibilities, it remains apt.

A privileged man of his times, Adams took it for granted that a WASP male elite was meant to run the country. Women were to occupy their own separate sphere. And while he would eventually become an ardent opponent of slavery, in 1821 race did not rank high on his agenda either. His immediate priority as secretary of state was to situate the young republic globally so that Americans might enjoy both safety and prosperity. That meant avoiding unnecessary trouble. We had already had our revolution. In his view, it wasn't this country's purpose to promote revolution elsewhere or to dictate history's future course.

Adams was to secretaries of state what Tom Brady is to NFL quarterbacks: the Greatest Of All Time. As the consensus GOAT in the estimation of diplomatic historians, he brought to maturity a pragmatic tradition of statecraft originated by a prior generation of New Englanders and various slaveholding Virginians with names like Washington, Jefferson, and Madison. That tradition emphasized opportunistically ruthless expansionism on this continent, avid commercial engagement, and the avoidance of great power rivalries abroad. Adhering to such a template, the United States had, by the beginning of the twentieth century, become the wealthiest, most secure nation on the planet—at which point Europeans spoiled the party.

The disastrous consequences of one European world war fought between 1914 and 1918 and the onset of a second in 1939 rendered that pragmatic tradition untenable—so at least a subsequent generation of WASPs concluded. This is where Wertheim takes up the story.

Prompted by the German army's lightning victory in the Battle of France in May and June 1940, members of that WASP elite set about creating—and promoting—an alternative policy paradigm, one Wertheim describes as pursuing "dominance in the name of internationalism," with US military supremacy deemed "the prerequisite of a decent world."

The new elite that devised this paradigm did not consist of lawyers from Massachusetts or planters from Virginia. Its key members held tenured positions at Yale and Princeton, wrote columns for leading New York newspapers, staffed Henry Luce's *Time–Life* press empire, and distributed philanthropic largesse to fund worthy causes (grasping the baton of global primacy being anything but least among them). Most importantly, just about every member of this Eastern establishment cadre was also a member of the Council on Foreign Relations (CFR). As such, they had a direct line to the State Department, which in those days actually played a large role in formulating basic foreign policy.

While *Tomorrow, The World* is not a long book—fewer than two hundred pages of text—it is a tour de force. In it, Wertheim describes the new narrative framework that the foreign policy elite formulated in the months following the fall of France. He shows how Americans with an antipathy for war now found themselves castigated as "isolationists," a derogatory term created to suggest provincialism or selfishness. Those favoring armed intervention, meanwhile, became "internationalists," a term connoting enlightenment and generosity. Even today, members of the foreign policy establishment pledge undying fealty to the same narrative framework, which still warns against the bugaboo of "isolationism" that threatens to prevent high-minded policymakers from exercising "global leadership."

Wertheim persuasively describes the "turn" toward militarized globalism engineered from above by that self-selected, unelected crew. Crucially, their efforts achieved success *prior to* Pearl Harbor. The Japanese attack of December 7, 1941, may have thrust the United States into the ongoing world war, but the essential transformation of policy had already occurred, even if ordinary Americans had yet to be notified as to what it meant. Its future implications—permanently high levels of military spending, a vast network of foreign bases stretching across the globe, a penchant for armed intervention abroad, a sprawling "national security" apparatus, and a politically subversive arms industry—would only become apparent in the years ahead.

While Wertheim is not the first to expose isolationism as a carefully constructed myth, he does so with devastating effect. Most of all, he helps his readers understand that "so long as the phantom of isolationism is held to be the most grievous sin, all is permitted."

Contained within that *all* is a cavalcade of forceful actions and grotesque miscalculations, successes and failures, notable achievements and immense tragedies both during World War II and in the decades that followed. While beyond the scope of Wertheim's book, casting the Cold War as a de facto extension of the war against Nazi Germany, with Soviet dictator Joseph Stalin as a stand-in for Adolf Hitler, represented an equally significant triumph for the foreign policy establishment.

At the outset of World War II, ominous changes in the global distribution of power prompted a basic reorientation of US policy. Today, fundamental alterations in the global distribution of power—did someone say "the rise of China"?—are once again occurring right before our eyes. Yet the foreign policy establishment's response is simply to double down.

So, even now, staggering levels of military spending, a vast network of foreign bases, a penchant for armed intervention abroad, a sprawling "national security" apparatus, and a politically subversive arms industry remain the taken-for-granted signatures of US policy. And even now, the establishment employs the specter of isolationism as a convenient mechanism for self-forgiveness and expedient amnesia, as well as a means to enforce discipline.

Frozen Compass

The fall of France was indeed an epic disaster. Yet implicit in *Tomorrow, The World* is this question: if the disaster that befell Europe in 1940 could prompt the United States to abandon a hitherto successful policy paradigm, then why have the serial disasters befalling the nation in the present century not produced a comparable willingness to reexamine an approach to policy that is obviously failing today?

To pose that question is to posit an equivalence between the French army's sudden collapse in the face of the *Wehrmacht*'s assault and the accumulation of US military disappointments dating from 9/11. From a tactical or operational perspective, many will find such a comparison unpersuasive. After all, the present-day armed forces of the United States have not succumbed to outright defeat, nor is the government of the United States petitioning for a cessation of hostilities as the French authorities did in 1940.

Yet what matters in war are political outcomes. Time and again since 9/11, whether in Afghanistan, Iraq, or lesser theaters of conflict, the United States has failed to achieve the political purposes for which it went to war. From a strategic and political perspective, therefore, the comparison with France is instructive, even if failure need not entail abject surrender.

The French people and other supporters of the 1930s European status quo (including Americans who bothered to pay attention) were counting on that country's soldiers to thwart further Nazi aggression once and for all. Defeat came as a profound shock. Similarly, after the Cold War, most Americans (and various beneficiaries of a supposed Pax Americana) counted on US troops to maintain an agreeable and orderly global status quo. Instead, the profound shock of 9/11 induced Washington to embark upon what became a series of "endless wars" that US forces proved incapable of bringing to a successful conclusion.

Crucially, however, no reevaluation of US policy comparable to the "turn" that Wertheim describes has occurred. An exceedingly generous reading of President Trump's promise to put "America First" might credit him with attempting such a turn. In practice, however, his incompetence and inconsistency, not to mention his naked dishonesty, produced a series of bizarre and random zigzags. Threats of "fire and fury" alternated with expressions of high regard for dictators ("we fell in love"). Troop withdrawals were announced and then modified or forgotten. Trump abandoned a global environmental agreement, massively rolled back environmental regulations domestically, and then took credit for providing Americans with "the very cleanest air and cleanest water on the planet." Little of this was to be taken seriously.

Trump's legacy as a statesman will undoubtedly amount to the diplomatic equivalent of Mulligan stew. Examine the contents closely enough and you'll be able to find just about anything. Yet taken as a whole, the concoction falls well short of being nutritious, much less appetizing.

On the eve of the upcoming presidential election, the entire national security apparatus and its supporters assume that Trump's departure from office will restore some version of normalcy. Every component of that apparatus from the Pentagon and the State Department to the CIA and the Council on Foreign Relations to the editorial boards of the *New York Times* and *Washington Post* yearns for that moment.

To a very considerable degree, a Biden presidency will satisfy that yearning. Nothing if not a creature of the establishment, Biden himself will conform to its requirements. For proof, look no further than his vote in favor of invading Iraq in 2003. (No isolationist he.) Count on a Biden administration, therefore, to perpetuate the entire obsolete retinue of standard practices.

As Peter Beinart puts it, "When it comes to defense, a Biden presidency is likely to look very much like an Obama presidency, and that's going to look not so different from a Trump presidency when you really look at the numbers." Biden will increase the Pentagon budget, keep US troops in the Middle East, and get tough with China. The United States will remain the world's number-one arms merchant, accelerate efforts to militarize outer space, and continue the ongoing modernization of the entire US nuclear strike force. Biden will stack his team with CFR notables looking for jobs on the "inside."

Above all, Biden will recite with practiced sincerity the mantras of American exceptionalism as a summons to exercise global leadership.

"The triumph of democracy and liberalism over fascism and autocracy created the free world. But this contest does not just define our past. It will define our future, as well." Those uplifting sentiments are, of course, his from a recent *Foreign Affairs* essay.

So if you liked US national security policy before Trump mucked things up, then Biden is probably your kind of guy. Install him in the Oval Office and the mindless pursuit of "dominance in the name of internationalism" will resume. And the United States will revert to the policies that prevailed during the presidencies of Bill Clinton, George W. Bush, and Barack Obama—policies, we should note, that paved the way for Donald Trump to win the White House.

The Voices That Count

What explains the persistence of this pattern despite an abundance of evidence showing that it's not working to the benefit of the American people? Why is it so difficult to shed a policy paradigm that dates from Hitler's assault on France, now a full eighty years in the past?

I hope that in a subsequent book Stephen Wertheim will address that essential question. In the meantime, however, allow me to make a stab at offering the most preliminary of answers.

Setting aside factors like bureaucratic inertia and the machinations of the military-industrial complex—the Pentagon, arms manufacturers, and their advocates in Congress share an obvious interest in discovering new "threats"—one likely explanation relates to a policy elite increasingly unable to distinguish between self-interest and the national interest. As secretary of state, John Quincy Adams never confused the two. His latter-day successors have done far less well.

As an actual basis for policy, the turn that Wertheim describes in *Tomorrow, The World* has proven to be nowhere near as enlightened or farseeing as its architects imagined or its latter-day proponents still purport to believe it to be. The paradigm produced in 1940–1941 was, at best, merely serviceable. It responded to the nightmarish needs of that moment. It justified US participation in efforts to defeat Nazi Germany, a necessary undertaking.

After 1945, except as a device for affirming the authority of foreign policy elites, the pursuit of "dominance in the name of internationalism" proved to be problematic. Yet even as conditions changed, the essentials of US policy remained stubbornly—even intractably—fixed in place: high levels of military spending, a network of foreign bases, a penchant for armed intervention abroad, a sprawling "national security" apparatus, and a politically subversive arms industry. Even after the Cold War and 9/11, these remain remarkably sacrosanct.

My own retrospective judgment of the Cold War tends toward an attitude of *well, I guess it could have been worse*. When it comes to the US response to 9/11, however, it's difficult to imagine what "worse" could have been.

Within the present-day foreign policy establishment, however, a different interpretation prevails. The long, twilight struggle of the Cold War ended in a world historic victory, unsullied by any unfortunate post-9/11 missteps. The effect of this perspective is to affirm the wisdom of American statecraft now eight decades old and therefore justify its perpetuation long after both Hitler and Stalin, not to mention Saddam Hussein and Osama bin Laden, are dead and gone.

This paradigm persists for the sole reason that it ensures that statecraft will remain a realm that resolutely excludes the popular will. Elites decide, while the job of ordinary Americans is to foot the bill. In that regard, the allocation of privileges and obligations now eighty years old still prevails today.

Only by genuinely democratizing the formulation of foreign policy will real change become possible. The turn in US policy described in *Tomorrow, The World* came from the top. The turn needed today will have to come from below and will require Americans to rid themselves of their habit of deference when it comes to determining what this nation's role in the world will be. Those on top will do all in their power to avert any such loss of status.

The United States today suffers from illnesses both literal and metaphorical. Restoring the nation to good health and repairing our democracy must necessarily rate as paramount concerns. While Americans cannot ignore the world beyond their borders, the last thing they need is to embark upon a fresh round of searching for distant monsters to destroy. Heeding the counsel of John Quincy Adams might just offer an essential first step toward recovery.

15
Reflections on Vietnam and Iraq

The Lessons of Two Failed Wars

December 22, 2020

In choosing a title for his final, posthumously published book, the prominent public intellectual Tony Judt turned to a poem by Oliver Goldsmith, "The Deserted Village," published in 1770. Judt found his book's title in the first words of this couplet:

> Ill fares the land, to hastening ills a prey,
> Where wealth accumulates, and men decay

A poignant sentiment but let me acknowledge that I'm not a big Goldsmith fan. My own preferences in verse run more toward Merle Haggard, whose country music hits include the following lyric from his 1982 song "Are the Good Times Really Over":

> Is the best of the free life behind us now?
> And are the good times really over for good?

I wonder, though: is it possible that the insights of an eighteenth-century Anglo-Irish novelist-poet and a twentieth-century American singer-songwriter, each reflecting on a common theme of decadence and each served up with a dollop of nostalgia, just might intersect?

Allow me to try the reader's patience with a bit more of Goldsmith:

> O luxury! thou curst by Heaven's decree,
> How ill exchanged are things like these for thee!
> How do thy potions, with insidious joy,
> Diffuse their pleasures only to destroy!
> Kingdoms, by thee, to sickly greatness grown,
> Boast of a florid vigour not their own;
> At every draught more large and large they grow,
> A bloated mass of rank unwieldy woe;
>
> Till sapped their strength, and every part unsound,
> Down, down they sink, and spread a ruin round.

Powerful stuff, but here's Haggard making a similar point without frills:

> I wish a buck was still silver
> It was back when the country was strong
> Back before Elvis
> And before the Vietnam War came along
>
> . . . .
> Are we rolling downhill
> Like a snowball headed for hell?
> With no kind of chance
> For the flag or the Liberty Bell

Let me concede from the outset that these laments emerge directly from the heart of the patriarchy. In our present moment, some will discount the complaints of Messrs. Goldsmith and Haggard as not to be taken seriously. As the second decade of the twenty-first century draws to a close, bellyaching white guys tend not to command a lot of sympathy.

Still, with this abysmal year finally ending, the melancholy notes sounded by Goldsmith and Haggard strike me as apt. The Age of Biden—or given our preference for faux intimacy, the Age of Joe and

Kamala—beckons. Yet I'm anything but certain that 2021 will inaugurate a happier time.

That said, for those who believe history has its own rhymes and rhythms, the election of Biden and Harris just might herald a turning point of sorts. After all, for more than a century now, presidential elections occurring in even numbered years ending in zero have resulted in big changes.

Don't take my word for it. Check the record.

Thanks to the assassin who prematurely terminated William McKinley's presidency, the election of 1900 inaugurated the reformist Progressive Era. Two decades later, Americans yearning for a return to "normalcy" voted for Warren G. Harding. Instead of normalcy, they got the splashy upheaval of the twenties and the ensuing Great Depression.

Once the balloting in 1940 handed Franklin Roosevelt an unprecedented third term, hopes entertained by some Americans of staying out of World War II were doomed. Global war vaulted the United States to a position of global primacy—and soon gave rise to new challenges. John F. Kennedy's election in 1960 empowered a generation "born in this century, tempered by war, disciplined by a hard and bitter peace" to address those challenges. Unanticipated complications ensued, as they did again in 1980 and 2000, the former initiating the Reagan Revolution, the latter election of George W. Bush setting the stage for the Global War on Terrorism and, by extension, Donald Trump.

The challenges awaiting Biden and Harris arguably outweigh those that confronted any of those past administrations, Roosevelt's excepted. In a recent *New York Times* column, the man who lost that disputed 2000 election, Al Gore, inventoried the most pressing problems that Biden's team will confront. In addition to the coronavirus pandemic, they include forty years of economic stagnation for middle-income families; hyper-inequality of incomes and wealth, with high levels of poverty; horrific structural racism; toxic partisanship; the impending collapse of nuclear arms control agreements; an epistemological crisis undermining the authority of knowledge; recklessly unprincipled behavior by social media companies; and, most dangerous of all, the climate crisis.

That makes for quite a daunting catalog. Yet note this one striking omission: Gore makes no mention of America's seemingly never-ending penchant for war and military adventurism.

Before the Vietnam War Came Along

Surely, though, war has contributed in no small way to "the bloated mass of rank unwieldy woe" besetting our nation today. And were Merle Haggard to update "Are the Good Times Really Over" he would doubtless include the 2003 invasion and occupation of Iraq alongside Vietnam as prominent among the factors that have sent this country caroming downward.

In the evening of my life, as I reflect on the events of our time that ended up mattering most, the wars in Vietnam and Iraq top my list. Together, they define the poles around which much of my professional life has revolved, whether as a soldier, teacher, or writer. It would be fair to say that I'm haunted by those two conflicts.

I could write pages and pages on how Vietnam and Iraq differ from each other, beginning with the fact that they are separated in time by nearly a half-century. Locale, the contours of the battlefields, the character of combat, the casualties inflicted and sustained, the sheer quantity of ordnance expended—when it comes to such measures and others, Vietnam and Iraq differ greatly. Yet while those differences are worth noting, it's the unappreciated similarities between them that are truly instructive.

Seven such similarities stand out:

- First, Vietnam and Iraq were both avoidable. For the United States, they were wars of choice. No one pushed us. We dove in headfirst.
- Second, both turned out to be superfluous, undertaken in response to threats—monolithic communism and Iraqi weapons of mass destruction—that were figments of fevered imaginations. In both cases, cynicism and moral cowardice played a role in paving the way toward war. Dissenting voices were ignored.

- Third, both conflicts proved to be costly distractions. Each devoured on a prodigious scale resources that might have been used so much more productively elsewhere. Each diverted attention from matters of far more immediate importance to Americans. Each, in other words, triggered a massive hemorrhage of blood, treasure, and influence to no purpose whatsoever.

- Fourth, in each instance, political leaders in Washington and senior commanders in the field collaborated in committing grievous blunders. War is complicated. All wars see their share of mistakes and misjudgments. But those two featured a level of incompetence unmatched since Custer's Last Stand.

- Fifth, thanks to that incompetence, both devolved into self-inflicted quagmires. In Washington, in Saigon, and in Baghdad's "Green Zone," baffled authorities watched as the control of events slipped from their grasp. Meanwhile, in the field, US troops flailed about for years in futile pursuit of a satisfactory outcome.

- Sixth, on the home front, both conflicts left behind a poisonous legacy of unrest, rancor, and bitterness. Members of the baby boom generation (to which I belong) have chosen to enshrine Vietnam-era protest as high-minded and admirable. Many Americans then held and still hold a different opinion. As for the Iraq War, it contributed mightily to yawning political cleavages that appear unlikely to heal anytime soon.

- And finally, with both political and military elites alike preferring simply to move on, neither war has received a proper accounting.

Their place in the larger narrative of American history is still unsettled. This may be the most important similarity of all. Both Vietnam and Iraq remain bizarrely undigested, their true meaning yet to be discerned and acknowledged. Too recent to forget, too confounding to ignore, they remain anomalous.

The American wars in Vietnam and Iraq are contradictions that await resolution.

Jaw, Jaw, Not War, War

For that very reason, when politicians (including Biden) talk about war, they talk about others, their all-time favorite being the one fought against Nazi Germany between December 1941 and May 1945. There— and not in Vietnam or Iraq—do members of the establishment find the lessons that they have enshrined as permanently relevant.

The first American war against Germany in 1917–1918 doesn't carry much weight at all. Just a couple of years ago, its centennial came and went virtually unnoticed. Likewise, the war against Japan that occurred in tandem with the second war against Germany seldom gets much attention either. We "remember Pearl Harbor," and that's about it.

The war against the Nazis, however, is a gift that never stops giving. It yields a great bounty of lessons, such as never appease; never hesitate to call evil by its name; never back down; and never flinch from the challenges of leadership, which necessarily implies a willingness to use force. And in moments of distress, channel your inner Winston Churchill circa 1940: "Never surrender!"

The problem with clinging to such ostensibly canonical lessons today is that we are no longer the nation that defeated Nazi Germany. The United States was establishing itself as the dominant industrial power on the planet then, while Washington still had the capacity to mobilize the American people pursuant to what was described at the time as a "Great Crusade." A taken-for-granted tradition of white supremacy underwrote a cultural unity that lent more than a modicum of substance to the claims of e pluribus unum. None of this remains faintly relevant today.

When it comes to present-day policy, the relevant fact is that we are the nation that failed in both Vietnam and Iraq. Along the way, we lost our status as the planet's dominant industrial power. Meanwhile, Washington forfeited its authority to mobilize the American people for war. More recently, cleavages stemming from class, race, religion, gender, and ethnicity split the country into antagonistic factions. Gore was merely premature when, as vice president, he famously mistranslated the nation's motto as "out of one, many."

Now, if you prioritize Vietnam and Iraq over the war against Nazi Germany, you'll come face-to-face with a very different set of lessons. Here are four that the Biden administration might do well to contemplate:

First, situating the United States within a larger entity called the West—a notion dating from the time when America and Great Britain (with plentiful help from the Soviet Union) rallied to defeat Hitler—no longer works. The West doesn't exist. These days when the United States opts for war, it must expect to fight alone or with only nominal allied assistance. This was true in Vietnam and again in Iraq. No grand coalition will form.

Second, however gussied up or camouflaged, imperialism no longer retains the slightest legitimacy. Peoples once classified as inferior, usually on the basis of skin color, no longer tolerate outsiders telling them how to govern themselves. Few Americans are willing to acknowledge the imperial motives that have long shaped this country's global policies. The Vietnamese and Iraqis opposing the US military presence in their midst entertained few doubts on that score; hence, the fierceness with which they defended their right to self-determination.

Third, if the United States remains intent on exporting its version of freedom and democracy, it will have to devise far less coercive ways of doing so. Rather than using armed force to alter the political landscape in faraway places, elites should acknowledge the limited utility of military power. Calling on the troops to defend, deter, and contain works far better than charging them to invade, occupy, and transform.

Fourth, dumb wars deplete. Vietnam and Iraq both inflicted untold damage on the American economy. With the US government currently running an annual deficit of some $3 trillion, we can't afford to squander any more money on ill-advised military campaigns. A less known quote attributed to Churchill commends itself in our present situation: "Jaw, jaw, jaw is better than war, war, war."

As it enters the third decade of the twenty-first century, the United States is badly in need of more jaw, jaw and less war, war—more fix, fix and less fight, fight.

Over to You, Joe

I am not enamored of presidents. I'm even less of a fan of "presidentialism"—the belief, firmly held by American elites, that the fate of the planet turns on what the president of the United States says or does (or doesn't do). For that reason, I have learned not to expect much of whoever happens to occupy the Oval Office.

In practice, the Most Powerful Man in the World usually turns out to be not all that powerful. Rather than directing History with a capital H, he (not yet she), like the rest of us, is pretty much just along for the ride. In their own ways, Goldsmith and Haggard implicitly endorsed such a fatalistic perspective.

In political circles, a different view tends to prevail. Today, virtually all Democrats and many in the media ascribe to Trump full blame for the mess in which this country finds itself. Yet Americans would do well to temper their expectations of what supplanting Trumpism with Bidenism is likely to produce.

On January 20, 2021, the "torch" to which Kennedy memorably referred in his inaugural address will once again be passed. Let's hope that, in grasping it, Biden and Harris will heed one of the principal lessons of the Kennedy era: no more Vietnams. To which I would simply add: no more Iraqs (or Afghanistans, or Yemens, or . . . well, you know the list). Only then might it become possible to undertake the daunting task of repairing our country.

Good luck, Joe. You, too, Kamala. In the coming days, you're both going to need a truckful of it.

II
THE BLOB GOES HAYWIRE

16
Out of Bounds, Off-Limits, or Just Plain Ignored

Six Questions Hillary, Donald, Ted, Marco, et al. Don't
Want to Answer and Won't Even Be Asked

January 26, 2016

To judge by the early returns, the presidential race of 2016 is shaping up as the most disheartening in recent memory. Other than as a form of low entertainment, the speeches, debates, campaign events, and slick TV ads already inundating the public sphere offer little of value. Rather than exhibiting the vitality of American democracy, they testify to its hollowness.

Present-day Iranian politics may actually possess considerably more substance than our own. There, the parties involved, whether favoring change or opposing it, understand that the issues at stake have momentous implications. Here, what passes for national politics is a form of exhibitionism about as genuine as pro wrestling.

A presidential election campaign ought to involve more than competing coalitions of interest groups or bevies of investment banks and billionaires vying to install their preferred candidate in the White House. It should engage and educate citizens, illuminating issues and subjecting alternative solutions to careful scrutiny.

That this one won't even come close we can ascribe as much to the media as to those running for office, something the recent set of "debates" and the accompanying commentary have made painfully clear. With certain honorable exceptions such as NBC's estimable Lester

Holt, representatives of the press are less interested in fulfilling their civic duty than promoting themselves as active participants in the spectacle. They bait, tease, and strut. Then they subject the candidates' statements and misstatements to minute deconstruction. The effect is to inflate their own importance while trivializing the proceedings they are purportedly covering.

Above all in the realm of national security, election 2016 promises to be not just a missed opportunity but a complete bust. Recent efforts to exercise what people in Washington like to call "global leadership" have met with many more failures and disappointments than clearcut successes. So you might imagine that reviewing the scorecard would give the current raft of candidates, Republican and Democratic alike, plenty to talk about.

But if you thought that, you'd be mistaken. Instead of considered discussion of first-order security concerns, the candidates have regularly opted for bluff and bluster, their chief aim being to remove all doubts regarding their hawkish bona fides.

In that regard, nothing tops rhetorically beating up on the so-called Islamic State. So, for example, Hillary Clinton promises to "smash the would-be caliphate," Jeb Bush to "defeat ISIS for good," Ted Cruz to "carpet bomb them into oblivion," and Donald Trump to "bomb the shit out of them." For his part, having recently acquired a gun as the "last line of defense between ISIS and my family," Marco Rubio insists that when he becomes president, "the most powerful intelligence agency in the world is going to tell us where [ISIS militants] are; the most powerful military in the world is going to destroy them; and if we capture any of them alive, they are getting a one-way ticket to Guantanamo Bay."

These carefully scripted lines perform their intended twofold function. First, they elicit applause and certify the candidate as plenty tough. Second, they spare the candidate from having to address matters far more deserving of presidential attention than managing the fight against the Islamic State.

In the hierarchy of challenges facing the United States today, ISIS ranks about on a par with Sicily back in 1943. While liberating that island was a necessary prelude to liberating Europe more generally, the German occupation of Sicily did not pose a direct threat to the Allied cause. So with far weightier matters to attend to—handling Soviet dictator Joseph Stalin and British Prime Minister Winston Churchill, for example—President Franklin Roosevelt wisely left the problem of Sicily to subordinates. FDR thereby demonstrated an aptitude for distinguishing between the genuinely essential and the merely important.

By comparison, today's crop of presidential candidates either are unable to grasp, cannot articulate, or choose to ignore those matters that should rightfully fall under a commander in chief's purview. Instead, they compete with one another in vowing to liberate the twenty-first-century equivalent of Sicily, as if doing so demonstrates their qualifications for the office.

What sort of national security concerns should be front and center in the current election cycle? While conceding that a reasoned discussion of heavily politicized matters like climate change, immigration, or anything to do with Israel is probably impossible, other issues of demonstrable significance deserve attention. What follows are six of them—by no means an exhaustive list—that I've framed as questions a debate moderator might ask of anyone seeking the presidency, along with brief commentaries explaining why neither the posing nor the answering of such questions is likely to happen anytime soon.

1. The War on Terror: Nearly fifteen years after this "war" was launched by George W. Bush, why hasn't "the most powerful military in the world," "the finest fighting force in the history of the world" won it? Why isn't victory anywhere in sight?

As if by informal agreement, the candidates and the journalists covering the race have chosen to ignore the military enterprise inaugurated in 2001, initially called the Global War on Terrorism and continuing today without an agreed-upon name. Since 9/11, the United States has invaded, occupied, bombed, raided, or otherwise established a military presence in numerous countries across much of the Islamic world. How are we doing?

Given the resources expended and the lives lost or ruined, not particularly well it would seem. Intending to promote stability, reduce the incidence of jihadism, and reverse the tide of anti-Americanism among many Muslims, that "war" has done just the opposite. Advance the cause of democracy and human rights? Make that zero for four.

Amazingly, this disappointing record has been almost entirely overlooked in the campaign. The reasons why are not difficult to discern. First and foremost, both parties share in the serial failures of US policy in Afghanistan, Iraq, Syria, Libya, and elsewhere in the region. Pinning the entire mess on George W. Bush is no more persuasive than pinning it all on Obama. An intellectually honest accounting would require explanations that look beyond reflexive partisanship. Among the matters deserving critical scrutiny is Washington's persistent bipartisan belief in military might as an all-purpose problem solver. Not far behind should come questions about simple military competence that no American political figure of note or mainstream media outlet has the gumption to address.

The politically expedient position indulged by the media is to sidestep such concerns in favor of offering endless testimonials to the bravery and virtue of the troops, while calling for yet more of the same or even further escalation. Making a show of supporting the troops takes precedence over serious consideration of what they are continually being asked to do.

2. Nuclear weapons: Today, more than seventy years after Hiroshima and Nagasaki, what purpose do nukes serve? How many nuclear weapons and delivery systems does the United States actually need?

In an initiative that has attracted remarkably little public attention, the Obama administration has announced plans to modernize and upgrade the US nuclear arsenal. Estimated costs of this program reach as high as $1 trillion over the next three decades. Once finished—probably just in time for the one-hundredth anniversary of Hiroshima—the United States will possess more flexible, precise, survivable, and therefore usable nuclear capabilities than anything hitherto imagined.

In effect, the country will have acquired a first-strike capability—even as US officials continue to affirm their earnest hope of removing the scourge of nuclear weapons from the face of the Earth (other powers being the first to disarm, of course).

Whether, in the process, the United States will become more secure or whether there might be far wiser ways to spend that kind of money—shoring up cyber defenses, for example—would seem like questions those who could soon have their finger on the nuclear button might want to consider.

Yet we all know that isn't going to happen. Having departed from the sphere of politics or strategy, nuclear policy has long since moved into the realm of theology. Much as the Christian faith derives from a belief in a Trinity consisting of the Father, the Son, and the Holy Ghost, so nuclear theology has its own triad, comprised of manned bombers, intercontinental ballistic missiles, and submarine-launched missiles. To question the existence of such a holy threesome constitutes rank heresy. It's just not done—especially when there's all that money about to be dropped into the collection plate.

3. Energy security: Given the availability of abundant oil and natural gas reserves in the Western Hemisphere and the potential future abundance of alternative energy systems, why should the Persian Gulf continue to qualify as a vital US national security interest?

Back in 1980, two factors prompted President Jimmy Carter to announce that the United States viewed the Persian Gulf as worth fighting for. The first was a growing US dependence on foreign oil and a belief that American consumers were guzzling gas at a rate that would rapidly deplete domestic reserves. The second was a concern that, having just invaded Afghanistan, the Soviet Union might next have an appetite for going after those giant gas stations in the Gulf, Iran, or even Saudi Arabia.

Today we know that the Western Hemisphere contains more than ample supplies of oil and natural gas to sustain the American way of life (while also heating up the planet). As for the Soviet Union, it no longer exists—a decade spent chewing on Afghanistan having produced a fatal case of indigestion.

No doubt ensuring US energy security should remain a major priority. Yet in that regard, protecting Canada, Mexico, and Venezuela is far more relevant to the nation's well-being than protecting Saudi Arabia, Kuwait, and Iraq, while being far easier and cheaper to accomplish. So who will be the first presidential candidate to call for abrogating the Carter Doctrine? Show of hands, please?

4. Assassination: Now that the United States has normalized assassination as an instrument of policy, how well is it working? What are its benefits and costs?

George W. Bush's administration pioneered the practice of using missile-armed drones as a method of extrajudicial killing. Obama's administration greatly expanded and routinized the practice. The technique is clearly "effective" in the narrow sense of liquidating leaders and "lieutenants" of terror groups that policymakers want done away with. What's less clear is whether the benefits of state-sponsored assassination outweigh the costs, which are considerable. The incidental killing of noncombatants provokes ire directed against the United States and provides terror groups with an excellent recruiting tool. The removal of Mr. Bad Actor from the field adversely affects the organization he leads for no longer than it takes for a successor to emerge. As often as not, the successor turns out to be nastier than Mr. Bad Actor himself.

It would be naïve to expect presidential candidates to interest themselves in the moral implications of assassination as now practiced on a regular basis from the White House. Still, shouldn't they at least wonder whether it actually works as advertised? And as drone technology proliferates, shouldn't they also contemplate the prospect of others—say, Russians, Chinese, and Iranians—following America's lead and turning assassination into a global practice?

5. Europe: Seventy years after World War II and a quarter-century after the Cold War ended, why does European security remain an American

responsibility? Given that Europeans are rich enough to defend themselves, why shouldn't they?

Americans love Europe: old castles, excellent cuisine, and cultural
attractions galore. Once upon a time, the parts of Europe that Americans love best needed protection. Devastated by World War II, Western
Europe faced in the Soviet Union a threat that it could not handle alone.
In a singular act of generosity laced with self-interest, Washington came
to the rescue. By forming NATO, the United States committed itself to
defend its impoverished and vulnerable European allies. Over time this
commitment enabled France, Great Britain, West Germany, and other
nearby countries to recover from the global war and become strong,
prosperous, and democratic countries.

Today Europe is "whole and free," incorporating not only most of
the former Soviet empire, but even parts of the old Soviet Union itself.
In place of the former Soviet threat, there is Vladimir Putin, a bully governing a rickety energy state that, media hype notwithstanding, poses
no more than a modest danger to Europe itself. Collectively, the European Union's economy, at $18 trillion, equals that of the United States
and exceeds Russia's, even in sunnier times, by a factor of nine. Its total
population, easily outnumbering our own, is more than triple Russia's.
What these numbers tell us is that Europe is entirely capable of funding
and organizing its own defense if it chooses to do so.

It chooses otherwise, in effect opting for something approximating
disarmament. As a percentage of the gross domestic product, European
nations spend a fraction of what the United States does on defense.
When it comes to armaments, they prefer to be free riders and Washington indulges that choice. So even today, seven decades after World
War II ended, US forces continue to garrison Europe, and America's
obligation to defend twenty-six countries on the far side of the Atlantic
remains intact.

The persistence of this anomalous situation deserves election-year
attention for one very important reason. It gets to the question of whether
the United States can ever declare mission accomplished. Since the end
of World War II, Washington has extended its security umbrella to

cover not only Europe, but also virtually all of Latin America and large parts of East Asia. More recently, the Middle East, Central Asia, and now Africa have come in for increased attention. As of this writing, US forces alone maintain an active presence in 147 countries.

Do our troops ever really get to "come home"? The question is more than theoretical in nature. To answer it is to expose the implicitly imperial purpose of American globalism, which means, of course, that none of the candidates will touch it with a ten-foot pole.

6. Debt: Does the national debt constitute a threat to national security? If so, what are some politically plausible ways of reining it in?

Together, the administrations of George W. Bush and Barack Obama can take credit for tripling the national debt since 2000. Well before Election Day this coming November, the total debt, now exceeding the entire gross domestic product, will breach the $19 trillion mark.

In 2010, Admiral Mike Mullen, then chairman of the Joint Chiefs of Staff, described that debt as "the most significant threat to our national security." Although in doing so he wandered a bit out of his lane, he performed a rare and useful service by drawing a link between long-term security and fiscal responsibility. Ever so briefly, a senior military officer allowed consideration of the national interest to take precedence over the care and feeding of the military-industrial complex. It didn't last long.

Mullen's comment garnered a bit of attention, but failed to spur any serious congressional action. Again, we can see why, since Congress functions as an unindicted coconspirator in the workings of that lucrative collaboration. Returning to anything like a balanced budget would require legislators to make precisely the sorts of choices that they are especially loath to make—cutting military programs that line the pockets of donors and provide jobs for constituents. (Although the F-35 fighter may be one of the most bloated and expensive weapons programs in history, even Democratic Socialist Senator Bernie Sanders has left no stone unturned in lobbying to get those planes stationed in his hometown of Burlington.)

Recently, the role of Congress in authorizing an increase in the debt ceiling has provided Republicans with an excuse for political posturing, laying responsibility for all that red ink entirely at the feet of President Obama—this despite the fact that he has reduced the annual deficit by two-thirds, from $1.3 trillion the year he took office to $439 billion last year.

Regardless of who takes the prize in November, the United States will continue to accumulate debt at a non-trivial rate. If a Democrat occupies the White House, Republicans will pretend to care. If our next president is a Republican, they will keep mum. In either case, the approach to national security that does so much to keep the books out of balance will remain intact.

Come to think of it, averting real change might just be the one point on which the candidates generally agree.

17

The Decay of
American Politics

An Ode to Ike and Adlai

August 4, 2016

y earliest recollection of national politics dates back exactly sixty
years to the moment, in the summer of 1956, when I watched the
political conventions in the company of that wondrous new addition to our family, television. My parents were supporting President
Dwight D. Eisenhower for a second term and that was good enough for
me. Even as a youngster, I sensed that Ike, the former supreme commander of allied forces in Europe in World War II, was someone of real
stature. In a troubled time, he exuded authority and self-confidence.
By comparison, Democratic candidate Adlai Stevenson came across as
vaguely suspect. Next to the five-star incumbent, he seemed soft, even
foppish, and therefore not up to the job. So at least it appeared to a nine-
year-old living in Chicagoland.

Of the seamy underside of politics I knew nothing, of course. On
the surface, all seemed reassuring. As if by divine mandate, two parties
vied for power. The views they represented defined the allowable range
of opinion. The outcome of any election expressed the collective will of
the people and was to be accepted as such. That I was growing up in the
best democracy the world had ever known—its very existence a daily
rebuke to the enemies of freedom—was beyond question.

Naive? Embarrassingly so. Yet how I wish that Election Day in
November 2016 might present Americans with something even loosely

approximating the alternatives available to them in November 1956. Oh, to choose once more between an Ike and an Adlai.

Don't for a second think that this is about nostalgia. Today, Stevenson doesn't qualify for anyone's list of great Americans. If remembered at all, it's for his sterling performance as President Kennedy's UN ambassador during the Cuban Missile Crisis. Interrogating his Soviet counterpart with cameras rolling, Stevenson barked that he was prepared to wait "until hell freezes over" to get his questions answered about Soviet military activities in Cuba. When the chips were down, Adlai proved anything but soft. Yet in aspiring to the highest office in the land, he had come up well short. In 1952, he came nowhere close to winning, and in 1956 he proved no more successful. Stevenson was to the Democratic Party what Thomas Dewey had been to the Republicans: a luckless two-time loser.

As for Eisenhower, although there is much in his presidency to admire, his errors of omission and commission were legion. During his two terms, from Guatemala to Iran, the CIA overthrew governments, plotted assassinations, and embraced unsavory right-wing dictators—in effect, planting a series of IEDs destined eventually to blow up in the face of Ike's various successors. Meanwhile, binging on nuclear weapons, the Pentagon accumulated an arsenal far beyond what even Eisenhower as commander in chief considered prudent or necessary.

In addition, during his tenure in office, the military-industrial complex became a rapacious juggernaut, an entity unto itself as Ike himself belatedly acknowledged. By no means least of all, Eisenhower fecklessly committed the United States to an ill-fated project of nation-building in a country that just about no American had heard of at the time: South Vietnam. Ike did give the nation eight years of relative peace and prosperity, but at a high price—most of the bills coming due long after he left office.

The Pathology of American Politics

And yet, and yet . . .

To contrast the virtues and shortcomings of Stevenson and Eisenhower with those of Hillary Rodham Clinton and Donald Trump is both instructive and profoundly depressing. Comparing the adversaries of 1956 with their 2016 counterparts reveals with startling clarity what the decades-long decay of American politics has wrought.

In 1956, each of the major political parties nominated a grown-up for the highest office in the land. In 2016, only one has.

In 1956, both parties nominated likeable individuals who conveyed a basic sense of trustworthiness. In 2016, neither party has done so.

In 1956, Americans could count on the election to render a definitive verdict, the vote count affirming the legitimacy of the system itself and allowing the business of governance to resume. In 2016, that is unlikely to be the case. Whether Trump or Clinton ultimately prevails, large numbers of Americans will view the result as further proof of "rigged" and irredeemably corrupt political arrangements. Rather than inducing some semblance of reconciliation, the outcome is likely to deepen divisions.

How in the name of all that is holy did we get into such a mess?

How did the party of Eisenhower, an architect of victory in World War II, choose as its nominee a narcissistic TV celebrity who, with each successive tweet and verbal outburst, offers further evidence that he is totally unequipped for high office? Yes, the establishment media are ganging up on Trump, blatantly displaying the sort of bias normally kept at least nominally under wraps. Yet never have such expressions of journalistic hostility toward a particular candidate been more justified. Trump is a bozo of such monumental proportions as to tax the abilities of our most talented satirists. Were he alive today, Mark Twain at his most scathing would be hard-pressed to do justice to The Donald's blowhard pomposity.

Similarly, how did the party of Adlai Stevenson, but also of Stevenson's hero Franklin Roosevelt, select as its candidate someone so widely disliked and mistrusted even by many of her fellow Democrats? True, antipathy directed toward Hillary Clinton draws some of its energy from incorrigible sexists along with the "vast right-wing conspiracy" whose members thoroughly loath both Clintons. Yet the antipathy is not without basis in fact.

Even by Washington standards, Secretary Clinton exudes a striking sense of entitlement combined with a nearly complete absence of accountability. She shrugs off her misguided vote in support of invading Iraq back in 2003, while serving as senator from New York. She neither explains nor apologizes for pressing to depose Libya's Muammar Gaddafi in 2011, her most notable "accomplishment" as secretary of state. "We came, we saw, he died," she bragged back then, somewhat prematurely given that Libya has since fallen into anarchy and become a haven for ISIS.

She clings to the demonstrably false claim that her use of a private server for State Department business compromised no classified information. Now opposed to the Trans-Pacific Partnership (TPP) that she once described as the "gold standard in trade agreements," Clinton rejects charges of political opportunism. That her change of heart occurred when attacking the TPP was helping Bernie Sanders win one Democratic primary after another is hardly coincidental. Oh, and the big money accepted from banks and Wall Street as well as the tech sector for minimal work and the bigger money still from leading figures in the Israel lobby? Rest assured that her acceptance of such largesse won't reduce by one iota her support for "working-class families" or her commitment to a just peace settlement in the Middle East.

Let me be clear: none of these offer the slightest reason to vote for Donald Trump. Yet together they make the point that Hillary Clinton is a deeply flawed candidate, notably so in matters related to national security. Clinton is surely correct that allowing Trump to make decisions related to war and peace would be the height of folly. Yet her record in that regard does not exactly inspire confidence.

When it comes to foreign policy, Trump's preference for off-the-cuff utterances finds him committing astonishing gaffes with metronomic regularity. Spontaneity serves chiefly to expose his staggering ignorance.

By comparison, the carefully scripted Clinton commits few missteps, as she recites with practiced ease the pabulum that passes for right thinking in establishment circles. But fluency does not necessarily connote soundness. Clinton, after all, adheres resolutely to the highly militarized "Washington playbook" that President Obama himself has disparaged—a faith-based belief in American global primacy to be pursued regardless of how the world may be changing and heedless of costs.

On the latter point, note that Clinton's acceptance speech in Philadelphia included not a single mention of Afghanistan. By Election Day, the war there will have passed its fifteenth anniversary. One might think that a prospective commander in chief would have something to say about the longest conflict in American history, one that continues with no end in sight. Yet, with the Washington playbook offering few answers, Mrs. Clinton chooses to remain silent on the subject.

So while a Trump presidency holds the prospect of the United States driving off a cliff, a Clinton presidency promises to be the equivalent of banging one's head against a brick wall without evident effect, wondering all the while why it hurts so much.

Pseudo-Politics for an Ersatz Era

But let's not just blame the candidates. Trump and Clinton are also the products of circumstances that neither created. As candidates, they are merely exploiting a situation—one relying on intuition and vast stores of brashness, the other putting to work skills gained during a life spent studying how to acquire and employ power. The success both have achieved in securing the nominations of their parties is evidence of far more fundamental forces at work.

In the pairing of Trump and Clinton, we confront symptoms of something pathological. Unless Americans identify the sources of this disease, it will inevitably worsen, with dire consequences in the realm of national security. After all, back in Eisenhower's day, the IEDs planted thanks to reckless presidential decisions tended to blow up only years— or even decades—later. For example, between the 1953 US-engineered coup that restored the Shah to his throne and the 1979 revolution that converted Iran overnight from ally to adversary, more than a quarter of a century elapsed. In our own day, however, detonation occurs so much more quickly—witness the almost instantaneous and explosively unhappy consequences of Washington's post-9/11 military interventions in the Greater Middle East.

So here's a matter worth pondering: How is it that all the months of intensive fundraising, the debates and speeches, the caucuses and primaries, the avalanche of TV ads and annoying robocalls have produced two presidential candidates who tend to elicit from a surprisingly large number of rank-and-file citizens disdain, indifference, or at best hold-your-nose-and-pull-the-lever acquiescence?

Here, then, is a preliminary diagnosis of three of the factors contributing to the erosion of American politics, offered from the conviction that, for Americans to have better choices next time around, fundamental change must occur—and soon.

First, and most important, the evil effects of money: Need chapter and verse? For a tutorial, see this essential 2015 book by Professor Lawrence Lessig of Harvard: *Republic, Lost: Version 2.0.* Those with no time for books might spare eighteen minutes for Lessig's brilliant and deeply disturbing TED talk. Professor Lessig argues persuasively that unless the United States radically changes the way it finances political campaigns, we're pretty much doomed to see our democracy wither and die.

Needless to say, moneyed interests and incumbents who benefit from existing arrangements take a different view and collaborate to maintain the status quo. As a result, political life has increasingly become a pursuit reserved for those like Trump who possess vast personal wealth or for those like Clinton who display an aptitude for persuading the well-to-do to open their purses, with all that implies by way of compromise, accommodation, and the subsequent repayment of favors.

Second, the perverse impact of identity politics on policy: Observers make much of the fact that, in capturing the presidential nomination of a major party, Hillary Clinton has shattered yet another glass ceiling. They are right to do so. Yet the novelty of her candidacy starts and ends with gender. When it comes to fresh thinking, Donald Trump has far more to offer than Clinton—even if his version of "fresh" tends to be synonymous with wacky, off-the-wall, ridiculous, or altogether hair-raising.

The essential point here is that, in the realm of national security, Hillary Clinton is utterly conventional. She subscribes to a worldview (and view of America's role in the world) that originated during the

Cold War, reached its zenith in the 1990s when the United States proclaimed itself the planet's "sole superpower," and persists today remarkably unaffected by actual events. On the campaign trail, Clinton attests to her bona fides by routinely reaffirming her belief in American exceptionalism, paying fervent tribute to "the world's greatest military," swearing that she'll be "listening to our generals and admirals," and vowing to get tough on America's adversaries. These are, of course, the mandatory rituals of the contemporary Washington stump speech, amplified if anything by the perceived need for the first female candidate for president to emphasize her pugnacity.

A Clinton presidency, therefore, offers the prospect of more of the same—muscle-flexing and armed intervention to demonstrate American global leadership—albeit marketed with a garnish of diversity. Instead of different policies, Clinton will offer an administration that has a different look, touting this as evidence of positive change.

Yet while diversity may be a good thing, we should not confuse it with effectiveness. A national security team that "looks like America" (to use the phrase originally coined by Bill Clinton) does not necessarily govern more effectively than one that looks like President Eisenhower's. What matters is getting the job done.

Since the 1990s women have found plentiful opportunities to fill positions in the upper echelons of the national security apparatus. Although we have not yet had a female commander in chief, three women have served as secretary of state and two as national security adviser. Several have filled Adlai Stevenson's old post at the United Nations. Undersecretaries, deputy undersecretaries, and assistant secretaries of like gender abound, along with a passel of female admirals and generals.

So the question needs be asked, Has the quality of national security policy improved compared to the bad old days when men exclusively called the shots? Using as criteria the promotion of stability and the avoidance of armed conflict (along with the successful prosecution of wars deemed unavoidable), the answer would, of course, have to be no. Although Madeleine Albright, Condoleezza Rice, Susan Rice, Samantha Power, and Clinton herself might entertain a different view, actually existing conditions in Afghanistan, Iraq, Libya, Syria, Somalia, Sudan, Yemen, and other countries across the Greater Middle East and significant parts of Africa tell a different story.

The abysmal record of American statecraft in recent years is not remotely the fault of women; yet neither have women made a perceptibly positive difference. It turns out that identity does not necessarily signify wisdom or assure insight. Allocating positions of influence in the State Department or the Pentagon based on gender, race, ethnicity, or sexual orientation—as Clinton will assuredly do—may well gratify previously disenfranchised groups. Little evidence exists to suggest that doing so will produce more enlightened approaches to statecraft, at least not so long as adherence to the Washington playbook figures as a precondition to employment. (Should Clinton win in November, don't expect the redoubtable ladies of CODEPINK to be tapped for jobs at the Pentagon and State Department.)

In the end, it's not identity that matters but ideas and their implementation. To contemplate the ideas that might guide a President Trump along with those he will recruit to act on them—Ivanka as national security adviser?—is enough to elicit shudders from any sane person. Yet the prospect of Madam President surrounding herself with an impeccably diverse team of advisers who share her own outmoded views is hardly cause for celebration.

Putting a woman in charge of national security policy will not in itself amend the defects exhibited in recent years. For that, the obsolete principles with which Clinton along with the rest of Washington remains enamored will have to be jettisoned. In his own bizarre way (albeit without a clue as to a plausible alternative), Donald Trump seems to get that; Hillary Clinton does not.

Third, the substitution of "reality" for reality: Back in 1962, a young historian by the name of Daniel Boorstin published *The Image: A Guide to Pseudo-Events in America.* In an age in which Trump and Clinton vie to determine the nation's destiny, it should be mandatory reading. *The Image* remains, as when it first appeared, a fire bell ringing in the night.

According to Boorstin, more than five decades ago the American people were already living in a "thicket of unreality." By relentlessly indulging in ever more "extravagant expectations," they were forfeiting their capacity to distinguish between what was real and what was illusory. Indeed, Boorstin wrote, "we have become so accustomed to our illusions that we mistake them for reality."

While ad agencies and PR firms had indeed vigorously promoted a world of illusions, Americans themselves had become willing accomplices in the process:

> The American citizen lives in a world where fantasy is more real than reality, where the image has more dignity than its original. We hardly dare to face our bewilderment, because our ambiguous experience is so pleasantly iridescent, and the solace of belief in contrived reality is so thoroughly real. We have become eager accessories to the great hoaxes of the age. These are the hoaxes we play on ourselves.

This, of course, was decades before the nation succumbed to the iridescent allure of Facebook, Google, fantasy football, *Real Housewives of* _____, selfies, smartphone apps, *Game of Thrones*, Pokémon GO— and, yes, the vehicle that vaulted Trump to stardom, *The Apprentice*.

"The making of the illusions which flood our experience has become the business of America," wrote Boorstin. It's also become the essence of American politics, long since transformed into theater, or rather into some sort of (un)reality show.

Presidential campaigns today are themselves, to use Boorstin's famous term, "pseudo-events" that stretch from months into years. By now, most Americans know better than to take at face value anything candidates say or promise along the way. We're in on the joke—or at least we think we are. Reinforcing that perception on a daily basis are media outlets that have abandoned mere reporting in favor of enhancing the spectacle of the moment. This is especially true of the cable news networks, where talking heads serve up a snide and cynical complement to the smarmy fakery that is the office seeker's stock in trade. And we lap it up. It matters little that we know it's all staged and contrived, as long as—a preening Megyn Kelly getting under Trump's skin, Trump himself denouncing "lyin' Ted" Cruz, etc., etc.—it's entertaining.

This emphasis on spectacle has drained national politics of whatever substance it still had back when Ike and Adlai commanded the scene. It hardly need be said that Trump has demonstrated an extraordinary knack—a sort of postmodern genius—for turning this phenomenon to his advantage. Yet in her own way Clinton plays the same game. How else to explain a national convention organized around the idea of "re-introducing to the American people" someone who served eight years as First Lady, was elected to the Senate, failed in a previous high-profile run for the presidency, and completed a term as secretary of state? The just-ended conclave in Philadelphia was, like the Republican one that preceded it, a pseudo-event par excellence, the object of the exercise being to fashion a new "image" for the Democratic candidate.

The thicket of unreality that is American politics has now become all-enveloping. The problem is not Trump and Clinton, per se. It's an identifiable set of arrangements—laws, habits, cultural predisposi-tions—that have evolved over time and promoted the rot that now per-vades American politics. As a direct consequence, the very concept of self-government is increasingly a fantasy, even if surprisingly few Amer-icans seem to mind.

At an earlier juncture back in 1956, out of a population of 168 mil-lion, we got Ike and Adlai. Today, with almost double the population, we get—well, we get what we've got. This does not represent progress. And don't kid yourself that things really can't get much worse. Unless Americans rouse themselves to act, count on it, they will.

18

What We Talk about When We Don't Want to Talk about Nuclear War

Donald and Hillary Take a No-First-Use Pledge on Relevant Information

October 4, 2016

You may have missed it. Perhaps you dozed off. Or wandered into the kitchen to grab a snack. Or by that point in the proceedings were checking out *Seinfeld* reruns. During the latter part of the much hyped but excruciating-to-watch first presidential debate, *NBC Nightly News* anchor Lester Holt posed a seemingly straightforward but cunningly devised question. His purpose was to test whether the candidates understood the essentials of nuclear strategy.

A moderator given to plain speaking might have said this: "Explain why the United States keeps such a large arsenal of nuclear weapons and when you might consider using those weapons."

What Holt actually said was: "On nuclear weapons, President Obama reportedly considered changing the nation's longstanding policy on first use. Do you support the current policy?"

The framing of the question posited no small amount of knowledge on the part of the two candidates. Specifically, it assumed that Trump and Clinton each possess some familiarity with the longstanding policy to which Holt referred and with the modifications that Obama had contemplated making to it.

If you will permit the equivalent of a commercial break as this piece begins, let me explain why I'm about to parse in detail each candidate's actual answer to Holt's question. Amid deep dives into, and expansive punditry regarding, issues like how "fat" a former Miss Universe may have been and how high an imagined future wall on our southern border might prove to be, national security issues likely to test the judgment of a commander in chief have received remarkably little attention. So indulge me. This largely ignored moment in last week's presidential debate is worth examining.

With regard to the issue of "first use," every president since Harry Truman has subscribed to the same posture: the United States retains the prerogative of employing nuclear weapons to defend itself and its allies against even nonnuclear threats. In other words, as a matter of policy, the United States rejects the concept of "no first use," which would prohibit any employment of nuclear weapons except in retaliation for a nuclear attack. According to press reports, President Obama had toyed with but then rejected the idea of committing the United States to a "no first use" posture. Holt wanted to know where the two candidates aspiring to succeed Obama stood on the matter.

Cruelly, the moderator invited Trump to respond first. The look in the Republican nominee's eyes made it instantly clear that Holt could have been speaking Farsi for all he understood. A lesser candidate might then have begun with the nuclear equivalent of "What is Aleppo?"

Yet Trump being Trump, he gamely—or naively—charged headlong into the ambush that Holt had carefully laid, using his allotted two minutes to offer his insights into how as president he would address the nuclear conundrum that previous presidents had done so much to create. The result owed less to early Cold War thinkers-of-the-unthinkable like Herman Kahn or Albert Wohlstetter, who created the field of nuclear strategy, than to Dr. Strangelove. Make that Dr. Strangelove on meth.

Trump turned first to Russia, expressing concern that it might be gaining an edge in doomsday weaponry. "They have a much newer capability than we do," he said. "We have not been updating from the new standpoint." The American bomber fleet in particular, he added, needs modernization. Presumably referring to the recent employment of Vietnam-era bombers in the wars in Afghanistan, Iraq, and Syria, he continued somewhat opaquely, "I looked the other night. I was seeing B-52s, they're old enough that your father, your grandfather, could be flying them. We are not—we are not keeping up with other countries."

Trump then professed an appreciation for the awfulness of nuclear weaponry. "I would like everybody to end it, just get rid of it. But I would certainly not do first strike. I think that once the nuclear alternative happens, it's over."

Give Trump this much: even in a field that tends to favor abstraction and obfuscating euphemisms like "fallout" or "dirty bomb," classifying Armageddon as the "nuclear alternative" represents something of a contribution.

Still, it's worth noting that, in the arcane theology of nuclear strategy, "first strike" and "first use" are anything but synonymous. "First strike" implies a one-sided, preventive war of annihilation. The logic of a first strike, such as it is, is based on the calculation that a surprise nuclear attack could inflict the "nuclear alternative" on your adversary, while sparing your own side from suffering a comparable fate. A successful first strike would be a one-punch knockout, delivered while your opponent still sits in his corner of the ring.

Yet whatever reassurance was to be found in Trump's vow never to order a first strike—not the question Lester Holt was asking—was immediately squandered. The Republican nominee promptly revoked his "no first strike" pledge by insisting, in a cliché much favored in Washington, that "I can't take anything off the table."

Piling non sequitur upon non sequitur, he next turned to the threat posed by a nuclear-armed North Korea, where "we're doing nothing." Yet, worrisome as this threat might be, keeping Pyongyang in check, he added, ought to be Beijing's job. "China should solve that problem for us," he insisted. "China should go into North Korea. China is totally powerful as it relates to North Korea."

If China wouldn't help with North Korea, however, what could be more obvious than that Iran, many thousands of miles away, should do so—and might have, if only President Obama had incorporated the necessary proviso into the Iran nuclear deal. "Iran is one of their biggest trading partners. Iran has power over North Korea." When the Obama administration "made that horrible deal with Iran, they should have included the fact that they do something with respect to North Korea." But why stop with North Korea? Iran "should have done something with respect to Yemen and all these other places," he continued, wandering into the nonnuclear world. US negotiators suitably skilled in the Trumpian art of the deal, he implied, could easily have maneuvered Iran into solving such problems on Washington's behalf.

Veering further off course, Trump then took a passing swipe at Secretary of State John Kerry: "Why didn't you add other things into the deal?" Why, in "one of the great giveaways of all time," did the Obama administration fork over $400 million in cash? At which point, he promptly threw in another figure without the slightest explanation—"It was actually $1.7 billion in cash"—in "one of the worst deals ever made by any country in history."

Trump then wrapped up his meandering tour d'horizon by decrying the one action of the Obama administration that arguably has reduced the prospect of nuclear war, at least in the near future. "The deal with Iran will lead to nuclear problems," he stated with conviction. "All they have to do is sit back ten years, and they don't have to do much. And they're going to end up getting nuclear." For proof, he concluded, talk to the Israelis. "I met with Bibi Netanyahu the other day," he added for no reason in particular. "Believe me, he's not a happy camper."

On this indecipherable note, his allotted time exhausted, Trump's recitation ended. In its way, it had been a Joycean performance.

Bridge Over Troubled Waters?

It was now Clinton's turn to show her stuff. If Trump had responded to Holt like a voluble golf caddy being asked to discuss the finer points of ice hockey, Hillary Clinton chose a different course: she changed the subject. She would moderate her own debate. Perhaps Trump thought Holt was in charge of the proceedings; Clinton knew better.

What followed was vintage Clinton: vapid sentiments, smoothly delivered in the knowing tone of a seasoned Washington operative. During her two minutes, she never came within a country mile of discussing the question Holt had asked or the thoughts she may well entertain about nuclear issues.

"[L]et me start by saying, words matter," she began. "Words matter when you run for president. And they really matter when you are president. And I want to reassure our allies in Japan and South Korea and elsewhere that we have mutual defense treaties and we will honor them."

It was as if Clinton were already speaking from the Oval Office. Trump had addressed his remarks to Lester Holt. Clinton directed hers to the nation at large, to people the world over, indeed to history itself. Warming to her task, she was soon rolling out the sort of profundities that play well at the Brookings Institution, the Carnegie Endowment, or the Council on Foreign Relations, causing audiences to nod—or nod off.

"It is essential that America's word be good," Clinton continued. "And so I know that this campaign has caused some questioning and worries on the part of many leaders across the globe. I've talked with a number of them. But I want to—on behalf of myself, and I think on behalf of a majority of the American people—say that, you know, our word is good."

Then, after inserting a tepid, better-than-nothing endorsement of the Iran nuclear deal, she hammered Trump for not offering an alternative. "Would he have started a war? Would he have bombed Iran?" If you're going to criticize, she pointed out, you need to offer something better. Trump never does, she charged. "It's like his plan to defeat ISIS. He says it's a secret plan, but the only secret is that he has no plan."

With that, she reverted to platitudes. "So we need to be more precise in how we talk about these issues. People around the word follow our presidential campaigns so closely, trying to get hints about what we will do. Can they rely on us? Are we going to lead the world with strength and in accordance with our values? That's what I intend to do. I intend to be a leader of our country that people can count on, both here at home and around the world, to make decisions that will further peace and prosperity, but also stand up to bullies, whether they're abroad or at home."

Like Trump, she offered no specifics. Which bullies? Where? How? In what order? Would she start with Russia's Putin? North Korea's Kim Jong-un? Perhaps Rodrigo Duterte of the Philippines? How about Turkey's Recep Tayyip Erdoğan? Or Bibi?

In contrast to Trump, however, Clinton did speak in complete sentences, which followed one another in an orderly fashion. She thereby came across as at least nominally qualified to govern the country, much like, say, Warren G. Harding nearly a century ago. And what worked for Harding in 1920 may well work for Clinton in 2016.

Of Harding's speechifying, H. L. Mencken wrote at the time, "It reminds me of a string of wet sponges." Mencken characterized Harding's rhetoric as "so bad that a sort of grandeur creeps into it. It drags itself out of the dark abysm of pish, and crawls insanely up the topmost pinnacle of posh. It is rumble and bumble. It is flap and doodle. It is balder and dash." So, too, with Hillary Clinton. She is our Warren G. Harding. In her oratory, flapdoodle and balderdash live on.

The National Security Void

If I've taxed your patience by recounting this non-debate and non-discussion of nuclear first use, it's to make a larger point. The absence of relevant information elicited by Lester Holt's excellent question speaks directly to what has become a central flaw in this entire presidential campaign: the dearth of attention given to matters basic to US national security policy.

In the nuclear arena, the issue of first use is only one of several on which anyone aspiring to become the next commander in chief should be able to offer an informed judgment. Others include questions such as these:

- What is the present-day justification for maintaining the US nuclear "triad," a strike force consisting of manned bombers *and* land-based ballistic missiles *and* submarine-launched ballistic missiles?

- Why is the Pentagon embarking upon a decades-long, trillion-dollar program to modernize that triad, fielding a new generation of bombers, missiles, and submarines along with an arsenal of new warheads? Is that program necessary?
- How do advances in non-nuclear weaponry—for example, in the realm of cyberwarfare—affect theories of nuclear deterrence devised by the likes of Kahn and Wohlstetter during the 1950s and 1960s? Does the logic of those theories still pertain?

Beyond the realm of nuclear strategy, there are any number of other security-related questions about which the American people deserve to hear directly from both Trump and Clinton, testing their knowledge of the subject matter and the quality of their judgments. Among such matters, one in particular screams out for attention. Consider it the question that Washington has declared off-limits: What lessons should be drawn from America's costly and disappointing post-9/11 wars and how should those lessons apply to future policy?

With Election Day now merely a month away, there is no more reason to believe that such questions will receive serious consideration than to expect Trump to come clean on his personal finances or Clinton to release the transcripts of her handsomely compensated Goldman Sachs speeches.

When outcomes don't accord with his wishes, Trump reflexively blames a "rigged" system. But a system that makes someone like Trump a finalist for the presidency isn't rigged. It is manifestly absurd, a fact that has left most of the national media grasping wildly for explanations (albeit none that tag them with having facilitated the transformation of politics into theater).

I'll take a backseat to no one in finding Trump unfit to serve as president. Yet beyond the outsized presence of one particular personality, the real travesty of our predicament lies elsewhere—in the utter shallowness of our political discourse, no more vividly on display than in the realm of national security.

What do our presidential candidates talk about when they don't want to talk about nuclear war? The one, in a vain effort to conceal his own ignorance, offers rambling nonsense. The other, accustomed to making her own rules, simply changes the subject.

The American people thereby remain in darkness. On that score, Trump, Clinton, and the parties they represent are not adversaries. They are collaborators.

19
Prepare, Pursue, Prevail!

Onward and Upward with US Central Command

March 21, 2017

By way of explaining his eight failed marriages, the American bandleader Artie Shaw once remarked, "I am an incurable optimist." In reality, Artie was an incurable narcissist. Utterly devoid of self-awareness, he never looked back, only forward.

So, too, with the incurable optimists who manage present-day American wars. What matters is not past mistakes but future opportunities. This describes the view of General Joseph Votel, current head of US Central Command (CENTCOM). Since its creation in 1983, CENTCOM has emerged as the ne plus ultra of the Pentagon's several regional commands, the place where the action is always hot and heavy. Votel is the latest in a long train of four-star generals to preside over that action.

The title of this essay (exclamation point included) captures in a single phrase the "strategic approach" that Votel has devised for CENTCOM. That approach, according to the command's website, is "proactive in nature and endeavors to set in motion tangible actions in a purposeful, consistent, and continuous manner."

This strategic approach forms but one element in General Votel's multifaceted (if murky) "command narrative," which he promulgated last year upon taking the helm at CENTCOM headquarters in Tampa, Florida. Other components include a "culture," a "vision," a "mission," and "priorities." CENTCOM's *culture* emphasizes "persistent excellence," as the command "strives to understand and help others to comprehend, with granularity and clarity, the complexities of our region."

145

The *vision*, indistinguishable from the *mission* except perhaps for those possessing advanced degrees in hermeneutics, seeks to provide "a more stable and prosperous region with increasingly effective governance, improved security, and trans-regional cooperation." Toward that estimable end, CENTCOM's *priorities* include forging partnerships with other nations "based upon shared values," "actively counter[ing] the malign influence" of hostile regimes, and "degrading and defeating violent extremist organizations and their networks."

At present, CENTCOM is busily implementing the several components of Votel's command narrative across an "area of responsibility" (AOR) consisting of twenty nations, among them Iran, Iraq, Syria, Afghanistan, and Pakistan. As the CENTCOM website puts it, without batting a digital eyelash, that AOR "spans more than 4 million square miles and is populated by more than 550 million people from 22 ethnic groups, speaking 18 languages with hundreds of dialects and confessing multiple religions which transect national borders."

According to the *Department of Defense Dictionary of Military and Associated Terms*, an AOR is the "geographical area associated with a combatant command within which a geographic combatant commander has authority to plan and conduct operations." Yet this anodyne definition fails to capture the spirit of the enterprise in which General Votel is engaged.

One imagines that there must be another *Department of Defense Dictionary*, kept under lock and key in the Pentagon, that dispenses with the bland language and penchant for deceptive euphemisms. That dictionary would define an AOR as "a vast expanse within which the United States seeks to impose order without exercising sovereignty." An AOR combines aspects of colony, protectorate, and contested imperial frontier. In that sense, the term represents the latest incarnation of the informal empire that American elites have pursued in various forms ever since US forces "liberated" Cuba in 1898.

To say that a military officer presiding over an AOR plans and conducts operations is a bit like saying that Jeff Bezos sells books. It's a small truth that evades a larger one. To command CENTCOM is to function as a proconsul, to inhabit as a coequal the rarified realm of kings, presidents, and prime ministers. CENTCOM commanders shape the future of their AOR—or at least fancy that they do.

Sustaining expectations of shaping the future requires a suitably accommodating version of the past. For CENTCOM, history is a record of events selected and arranged to demonstrate progress. By testifying to the achievements of previous CENTCOM commanders, history thereby validates Votel's own efforts to carry on their work. Not for nothing, therefore, does the command's website include this highly sanitized account of its recent past:

> In the wake of 9-11, the international community found Saddam Hussein's continued lack of cooperation with United Nations Security Council (UNSC) Resolutions regarding weapons of mass destruction unacceptable. Hussein's continued recalcitrance led the UNSC to authorize the use of force by a U.S.-led coalition. Operation Iraqi Freedom began 19 March 2003. Following the defeat of both the Taliban regime in Afghanistan (9 November 2001) and Saddam Hussein's government in Iraq (8 April 2003), CENTCOM has continued to provide security to the new freely-elected governments in those countries, conducting counterinsurgency operations and assisting host nation security forces to provide for their own defense.

Setbacks, disappointments, miscalculations, humiliations: you won't hear about them from CENTCOM. Give the Vietnam War the CENTCOM treatment and you would end up with something like this: "Responding to unprovoked North Vietnamese attacks and acting at the behest of the international community, a US-led coalition arrived to provide security to the freely elected South Vietnamese government, conducting counterinsurgency operations and assisting host nation security forces to provide for their own defense." Like Broadway's *Annie*, down at headquarters in Tampa they're "just thinkin' about tomorrow," which "clears away the cobwebs, and the sorrow, till there's none."

In fact, the UN Security Council did not authorize the 2003 invasion of Iraq. Indeed, efforts by George W. Bush's administration to secure such an authorization failed abysmally, collapsing in a welter of half-truths and outright falsehoods. What much of the international community found unacceptable, more so even than Saddam's obstreperousness, was Bush's insistence that he was going to have his war regardless of what others might think. As for celebrating the "defeat" of the Taliban and of Saddam, that's the equivalent of declaring "game over" when the whistle sounds ending the first quarter of a football game.

More to the point, to claim that, in the years since, CENTCOM "has continued to provide security to the new freely-elected governments" of Afghanistan and Iraq whitewashes history in ways that would cause the most shameless purveyor of alt-facts on Fox News to blush. The incontestable truth is that Afghans and Iraqis have not known security since US forces, under the direction of General Votel's various predecessors, arrived on the scene. Rather than providing security, CENTCOM has undermined it.

CENTCOM Headquarters (Where It's Always Groundhog Day)

Even so, as the current steward of CENTCOM's culture, vision, mission, strategic approach, and priorities, General Votel remains undaunted. In his view, everything that happened prior to his assuming ownership of the CENTCOM AOR is irrelevant. What matters is what will happen from now on—in Washington-speak, "going forward." As with Artie Shaw, serial disappointments leave intact the conviction that persistence will ultimately produce a happy ending.

Earlier this month, Votel provided a progress report to the Senate Armed Services Committee and outlined his expectations for future success. In a city that now competes for the title of Comedy Central, few paid serious attention to what the CENTCOM commander had to say. Yet his presentation was, in its own way, emblematic of how, in the Age of Trump, US national security policy has become fully divorced from reality.

General Votel began by inventorying the various "drivers of instability" afflicting his AOR. That list, unsurprisingly enough, turned out to be a long one, including ethnic and sectarian divisions, economic underdevelopment, an absence of opportunity for young people "susceptible to unrest [and] radical ideologies," civil wars, humanitarian crises, large refugee populations, and "competition among outside actors, including Russia and China, seeking to promote their interests and supplant US influence in the region." Not qualifying for mention as destabilizing factors, however, were the presence and activities of US military forces, their footprint dwarfing that of Russia and China.

Indeed, the balance of Votel's sixty-four-page written statement argued, in effect, that US military activities are the key to fixing all that ails the CENTCOM AOR. After making a brief but obligatory bow to the fact that "a solely military response is not sufficient" to address the region's problems, he proceeded to describe at length the military response (and only the military response) that will do just that.

Unfortunately for General Votel, length does not necessarily correlate with substance. Once upon a time, American military professionals prized brevity and directness in their writing. Not so the present generation of generals who are given to logorrhea. Consider just this bit of cliché-ridden drivel—I could quote vast passages of it—that Votel inflicted on members of the United States Senate. "In a region beset by myriad challenges," he reported, "we must always be on the look-out for opportunities to *seize the initiative* to support our objectives and goals." He continued:

Pursuing opportunities means that we are proactive—we don't wait for problems to be presented; we look for ways to get ahead of them. It also means that we have to become comfortable with transparency and flat communications—our ability to understand our AOR better than anyone else gives us the advantage of knowing where opportunities exist. Pursuing opportunities also means we have to take risk—by delegating authority and responsibility to the right level, by trusting our partners, and being willing to trust our best instincts in order to move faster than our adversaries.

In third-tier business schools, bromides of this sort might pass for "best practices." But my guess is that George C. Marshall or Eisenhower would award the author of that paragraph an F and return him to staff college for further instruction.

Frothy verbiage aside, what exactly does General Votel propose? The answer—for those with sufficient patience to wade through the entire sixty-four pages—reduces to this: persist. In concrete terms, that means keeping on killing and enabling our "allies" to do the same until the other side is finally exhausted and gives up. In other words, it's the movie *Groundhog Day* transposed from Punxsutawney, Pennsylvania, to Tampa and then to Afghanistan, Iraq, and other countries where the bodies continue to pile up.

True, the document Votel presented to Congress is superficially comprehensive, with sections touting everything from "Building Partner Capacity" ("we must be forward-leaning and empower our partners to meet internal security challenges") to creating a "Global Engagement Center" ("The best way to defeat an idea is to present a better, more appealing idea"). Strip away the fluff, however, and what's left is nothing more than a call to keep doing what CENTCOM has been doing for years now.

To see what all this really means, practically speaking, just check out CENTCOM press releases for the week of March 5 through 10. The titles alone suffice to describe a situation where every day is like the one that preceded it:

March 5: "Military airstrikes continue against ISIS terrorists in Syria and Iraq"
March 6: "Military airstrikes continue against ISIS terrorists in Syria and Iraq"
March 7: "Military airstrikes continue against ISIS terrorists in Syria and Iraq"

March 8: "Military airstrikes continue against ISIS terrorists in
Syria and Iraq"
March 9: "Military airstrikes continue against ISIS terrorists in
Syria and Iraq"
March 10: "Military airstrikes continue against ISIS terrorists
in Syria and Iraq"

As the good nuns used to tell me back in parochial school, actions
speak louder than words. What the CENTCOM commander says matters less than what CENTCOM forces do. What they are doing is waging an endless war of attrition.

Ludendorff Would Have Approved

"Punch a hole and let the rest follow." During the First World War, that
aphorism, attributed to General Erich Ludendorff, captured the essence
of the German army's understanding of strategy, rooted in the conviction that violence perpetrated on a sufficient scale over a sufficient period
of time will ultimately render a politically purposeless war purposeful.
The formula didn't work for Germany in Ludendorff's day and yielded
even more disastrous results when Hitler revived it two decades later.

Of course, US military commanders today don't make crude references to punching holes. They employ language that suggests discrimination, deliberation, precision, and control as the qualities that define
the American way of war. They steer clear of using terms like attrition.
Yet differences in vocabulary notwithstanding, the US military's present-day MO bears a considerable resemblance to the approach that Ludendorff took fully a century ago. And for the last decade and a half,
US forces operating in the CENTCOM AOR have been no more successful than were German forces on the Western Front in achieving the
purposes that ostensibly made war necessary.

To divert attention from this disturbing fact, General Votel offers
Congress and by extension the American people a sixty-four-page piece
of propaganda. Whether he himself is deluded or dishonest is difficult to say, just as it remains difficult to say whether General William

Westmoreland was deluded or dishonest when he assured Congress in November 1967 that victory in Vietnam was in sight. "With 1968," Westmoreland promised, "a new phase is now starting. We have reached an important point when the end begins now to come into view."

Westmoreland was dead wrong, as the enemy's 1968 Tet Offensive soon demonstrated. That a comparable disaster, no doubt different in form, will expose Votel's own light-at-the-end-of-the-tunnel assessment as equally fraudulent is a possibility, even if one to which American political and military leaders appear to be oblivious. This much is certain: in the CENTCOM AOR the end is not even remotely in view.

What are we to make of this charade of proconsuls parading through Washington to render false or misleading reports on the status of the American empire's outer precincts?

Perhaps the time has come to look elsewhere for advice and counsel. Whether generals like Votel are deluded or dishonest is ultimately beside the point. More relevant is the fact that the views they express—and that inexplicably continue to carry weight in Washington—are essentially of no value. So many years later, no reason exists to believe that they know what they are doing.

To reground US national security policy in something that approximates reality would require listening to new voices, offering views long deemed heretical.

Let me nonetheless offer you an example: "Fifteen years after launching a worldwide effort to defeat and destroy terrorist organizations, the United States finds itself locked in a pathologically recursive loop; we fight to prevent attacks and defend our values, only to incite further violence against ourselves and allies while destabilizing already chaotic regions . . ."

That is not the judgment of some lefty from Cambridge or San Francisco, but of Major John Q. Bolton, a veteran of both the Iraq and Afghan Wars. Within that brief passage is more wisdom than in all of General Votel's sixty-four pages of blather.

I submit that Bolton's grasp of our predicament is infinitely superior to Votel's. The contrast between the two is striking. The officer who wears no stars dares to say what is true; the officer wearing four stars obfuscates. If the four-stars abandon obfuscation for truth, then and only then will they deserve our respectful attention. In the meantime, it's like looking to Artie Shaw for marriage counseling.

20
Unsolicited Advice for an Undeclared Presidential Candidate

A Letter to Elizabeth Warren

(October 16, 2018)

Senator Elizabeth Warren
309 Hart Senate Office Building
Washington, DC

Dear Senator Warren:

As a constituent, I have noted with interest your suggestion that you will "take a hard look" at running for president in 2020, even as you campaign for reelection to the Senate next month. Forgive me for saying that I interpret that comment to mean "I'm in." Forgive me, as well, for my presumption in offering this unsolicited—and perhaps unwanted—advice on how to frame your candidacy.

You are an exceedingly smart and gifted politician, so I'm confident that you have accurately gauged the obstacles ahead. Preeminent among them is the challenge of persuading citizens beyond the confines of New England, where you are known and respected, to cast their ballot for a Massachusetts liberal who possesses neither executive nor military experience and is a woman to boot.

Voters will undoubtedly need reassurance that you have what it takes to keep the nation safe and protect its vital interests. And yes, there is a distinct double standard at work here. Without possessing the most minimal of qualifications to serve as commander in chief, Donald Trump won the presidency in 2016. Who can doubt that gender and race played a role?

So the challenge you face is an enormous one. To meet it, in my estimation, you should begin by exposing the tangle of obsolete assumptions and hitherto unresolvable contradictions embedded in present-day US national security policy. You'll have to demonstrate a superior understanding of how events are actually trending. And you'll have to articulate a plausible way of coping with the problems that lie ahead. To become a viable candidate in 2020, to win the election, and then to govern effectively, you'll need to formulate policies that not only sound better, but *are* better than what we've got today or have had in the recent past. So there's no time to waste in beginning to formulate a Warren Doctrine.

Of course, the city in which you spend your workweek is awash with endless blather about a changing world, emerging challenges, and the need for fresh thinking. Yet, curiously enough, what passes for national security policy has remained largely immune to change, fixed in place by two specific episodes that retain a chokehold on that city's policy elite: the Cold War and the events of 9/11.

The Cold War ended three decades ago in what was ostensibly a decisive victory for the United States. History itself had seemingly anointed us as the "indispensable nation."

Yet here we are, all these years later, gearing up again to duel our old Cold War adversaries, the Ruskies and ChiComs. How, in the intervening decades, did the United States manage to squander the benefits of coming out on top in that "long twilight struggle"? Few members of the foreign policy establishment venture to explain how or why things so quickly went awry. Fewer still are willing to consider the possibility that our own folly offers the principal explanation.

By the time you are elected, the twentieth anniversary of 9/11 will be just around the corner, and with it the twentieth anniversary of the Global War on Terrorism. Who can doubt that when you are inaugurated on January 20, 2021, US forces will still be engaged in combat operations in Afghanistan, Syria, Libya, and various other places across the Greater Middle East and Africa? Yet in present-day Washington, the purpose and prospects of those campaigns elude serious discussion. Does global leadership necessarily entail being permanently at war? In Washington, the question goes not only unanswered, but essentially unasked.

Note that President Trump has repeatedly made plain his desire to extricate the United States from our wars without end, only to be told by his subordinates that he can't. Trump then bows to the insistence of the hawks because, for all his bluster, he's weak and easily rolled. Yet there's a crucial additional factor in play as well: Trump is himself bereft of strategic principles that might provide the basis for a military posture that is not some version of more of the same. When he's told "we have to stay," he simply can't refute the argument. So we stay.

You, too, will meet pressure to perpetuate the status quo. You, too, will be told that no real alternatives exist. Hence, the importance of bringing into office a distinctive strategic vision that offers the possibility of real change.

You will want to tailor that vision so that it finds favor with three disparate audiences. First, to win the nomination, you'll need to persuade members of your own party to prefer your views to those of your potential competitors, including Democrats with far more impressive national security credentials than your own. Among those already hinting at a possible run for the presidency are a well-regarded former vice president and possibly even a former secretary of state who is a decorated combat veteran and chaired the Senate Foreign Relations Committee. Although long in the tooth, they are not to be dismissed.

Second, having won the nomination, you'll have to convince voters who are not Democrats that your vision will, in the words of the preamble to the Constitution, "secure the Blessings of Liberty to ourselves and our Posterity." In this context, convincing should start with education, with, that is, disabusing citizens of the conviction—now prevalent in Washington—that "global leadership" is synonymous with a willingness to use force.

Finally, once you enter the Oval Office, you'll need to get buy-ins from Congress, the national security apparatus, and US allies. That means convincing them that your approach can work, won't entail unacceptable risks, and won't do undue damage to their own parochial interests.

To recap, a Warren Doctrine will need to appeal to progressives likely to have an aversion to the very phrase "national security," even as it inspires middle-of-the-roaders to give you their vote and persuades elites that you can be trusted to exercise power responsibly. All in all, that is a tall order.

Yet I think it can be done. Indeed, it needs to be done if the United States is ever to find a way out of the strategic wilderness in which it is presently wandering, with the likes of Donald Trump, John Bolton, Mike Pompeo, and James Mattis taking turns holding the compass while trying to figure out which way is north.

1 + 3 = You Win

A strategic paradigm worthy of the name begins with a tough-minded appraisal of the existing situation. There is, to put it mildly, a lot going on in our world today, much of it not good: terrorism, whether Islamist or otherwise; unchecked refugee flows; cross-border trafficking in drugs, weapons, and human beings; escalating Saudi-Iranian competition to dominate the Persian Gulf; pent-up resentment among Palestinians, Kurds, and other communities denied their right to self-determination; the provocations of "rogue states" like Russia, Pakistan, and North Korea; and, not to be forgotten, the ever-present danger of unintended nuclear war. As a candidate, you will need to have informed views on each of these.

Yet let me suggest that these are legacy issues, most of them detritus traceable to the twentieth century. None of them are without importance. None can be ignored. If mishandled, two or three of them have the potential to produce apocalyptic catastrophes. Even so, the place to begin formulating a distinctive Warren Doctrine that will resonate with each of those three constituencies—Democrats, the general public, and the establishment—is to posit that these have become secondary concerns.

Eclipsing such legacy issues in immediate significance are three developments that Washington currently neglects or treats as afterthoughts, along with one contradiction that simultaneously permeates and warps any discussion of national security. If properly understood, the items in this quartet would rightly cause Americans to wonder if the blessings of liberty will remain available to their posterity. It's incumbent upon you to provide that understanding. In short, a Warren Doctrine should tackle all four head-on.

Addressing that contradiction should come first. Its essence is that we Americans believe that we are a peaceful people. Our elected and appointed leaders routinely affirm this as true. Yet our nation is permanently at war. We Americans also believe that we have a pronounced aversion to empire. Indeed, our very founding as a republic testifies to our anti-imperial credentials. Yet in Washington, DC—an imperial city if there ever was one—references to the United States of America as the rightful successor to Rome in the era of the Caesars and the British Empire in its heyday abound. And there is more here than mere rhetoric: the military presence of US forces around the planet testifies in concrete terms to our imperial ambitions. We may be what various writers have referred to as an "empire in denial," but we are an empire.

The point of departure for the Warren Doctrine should be to subject this imperial project to an honest cost-benefit appraisal, demonstrating that it leads inexorably to bankruptcy, both fiscal and moral. Allow militarized imperialism to stand as the central theme of US policy and the national security status quo will remain sacrosanct. Expose its defects and the reordering of national security and other priorities becomes eminently possible.

That reordering ought to begin with three neglected developments that should be at the forefront of a Warren Doctrine. The first is a warming planet. The second is an ongoing redistribution of global power, signified by (but not limited to) the rise of China. The third is a growing cyber-threat to our ever more network-dependent way of life. A Warren Doctrine centered on this trio of challenges will both set you apart from your competitors and enable you to take office with clearly defined priorities—at least until some unexpected event, comparable to the fall of the Berlin Wall or the attack on the Twin Towers, obliges you to extemporize, as will inevitably happen.

Here, then, is a CliffsNotes take on each of the Big Three. (You can hire some smart young folk to fill in the details.)

Climate change poses a looming national security threat with existential implications. With this summer's heat waves and recent staggering storms, evidence of this threat has become incontrovertible. Its adverse consequences have already ruined thousands of American lives as evidenced by Hurricanes Katrina (2005), Irma (2017), Harvey (2017), Maria (2017), and Michael (2018), along with Superstorm Sandy (2012), not to mention pervasive drought and increasingly destructive wildfires in a fire season that seems hardly to end. It no longer suffices to categorize these as Acts of God.

The government response to such events has, to say the least, been grossly inadequate. So, too, has government action to cushion Americans from the future impact of far more of the same. A Warren administration needs to make climate change a priority, improving both warning and response to the most immediate dangers and, more importantly, implementing a coherent long-term strategy aimed at addressing (and staunching) the causes of climate change. For those keen for the United States to shoulder the responsibilities of global leadership, here's an opportunity for us to show our stuff.

Second, say goodbye to the conceit of America as the "last" or "sole" superpower. The power shift now well underway, especially in East Asia, but also in other parts of the world, is creating a multipolar global order in which—no matter what American elites might fancy—the United States will no longer qualify as the one and only "indispensable nation." Peace and stability will depend on incorporating into that order other nations with their own claims to indispensability, preeminently China.

And no, China is not our friend and won't be. It's our foremost competitor. Yet China is also an essential partner, especially when it comes to trade, investment, and climate change—that country and the US being the two biggest emitters of greenhouse gases. So classifying China as an enemy, an idea now gaining traction in policy circles, is the height of folly. Similarly, playing games of chicken over artificial islands in the South China Sea, citing as an imperative "freedom of navigation," exemplifies the national security establishment's devotion to dangerously obsolete routines.

Beyond China are other powers, some of them not so new, with interests that the United States will have to take into account. Included in their ranks are India, Russia, Turkey, Japan, a potentially united Korea, Iran (not going away any time soon), and even, if only as a matter of courtesy, Europe. Recognizing the imperative of avoiding a recurrence of the great power rivalries that made the twentieth century a bath of blood, a Warren administration should initiate and sustain an intensive diplomatic dialogue directed at negotiating lasting terms of mutual coexistence—not peace perhaps but at least a reasonable facsimile thereof.

Then there's that cyber-threat, which has multiple facets. First, it places at risk networks on which Americans, even tech-challenged contributors to *TomDispatch* like me, have become dependent. Yet deflecting these threats may invite "solutions" likely to demolish the last remnants of our personal privacy while exposing Americans to comprehensive surveillance by both domestic and foreign intelligence services. A Warren Doctrine would have to ensure that Americans enjoy full access to the "network of things," but on their own terms, not those dictated by corporate entities or governments.

Second, the same technologies that allow the Pentagon to equip US forces with an ever-expanding and ever-more expensive arsenal of "smart" weapons are also creating vulnerabilities that may well render those weapons useless. It's a replication of the Enigma phenomenon: to assume that your secrets are yours alone is to invite disaster, as the Nazis learned in World War II when their unbreakable codes turned out to be breakable. A Warren Doctrine would challenge the assumption, omnipresent in military circles, that equates advances in technology with greater effectiveness. If technology held the key to winning wars, we'd have declared victory in Afghanistan many moons ago.

Finally, there is the dangerous new concept of offensive cyber-warfare, introduced by the United States when it unleashed the Stuxnet virus on Iran's nuclear program back in 2011. Now, as the Trump administration prepares to make American offensive cyber-operations far more likely, it appears to be the coming thing—like strategic bombing in the run-up to World War II or nukes in its aftermath. Yet before charging further down that cyber-path, we would do well to reflect on the consequences of the twentieth century's arms races. They invariably turned out to be far more expensive than anticipated, often with horrific results. A Warren Doctrine should seek to avert the normalization of offensive cyber-warfare.

Let me mention a potential bonus here. Even modest success in addressing the Big Three may create openings to deal with some of those nagging legacy issues as well. Cooperation among great powers on climate change, for example, could create an environment more favorable to resolving regional disputes.

Of course, none of this promises to be easy. Naysayers will describe a Warren Doctrine of this sort as excessively ambitious and insufficiently bellicose. Yet as President Kennedy declared in 1962, when announcing that the United States would go to the moon within the decade, some goals are worthy precisely "because they are hard." Back then, Americans thrilled to Kennedy's promises.

My bet is this may well be another moment when Americans will respond positively to goals that are hard but also daring and of pressing importance. Make yourself the champion of those goals and you just might win yourself a promotion to the White House.

The road between now and November 2020 is a long one. I wish you well as you embark upon the journey.

Respectfully,
Andrew Bacevich

21
Can We Stop
Pretending Now?

The Trump Era as an Occasion for Truth Telling

April 7, 2019

Irony, paradox, contradiction, consternation—these define the times in which we live. On the one hand, the forty-fifth president of the United States is a shameless liar. On the other hand, his presidency offers an open invitation to Americans to confront myths about the way their country actually works. Donald Trump is a bullshit artist of the first order. Yet all art reflects the time in which it's produced, and Trump's art is no exception. Within all the excrement lie nuggets of truth.

Well before Trump rode the down escalator to the center of American politics, there were indicators aplenty that things had gone fundamentally awry. Yet only with the presidential election of 2016 did the chickens come home to roost. And with their arrival, it became apparent that more than a few propositions hitherto accepted as true are anything but.

Let me offer seven illustrative examples of myths that the Trump presidency has once and for all demolished.

Myth #1: The purpose of government is to advance the common good. In modern American politics, the concept of the common good no longer has any practical meaning. It hasn't for decades. The phrase might work for ceremonial occasions—inaugural addresses, prayer breakfasts, that sort of thing—but finds little application in the actual business of governing.

When did politics at the national level become a zero-sum game? Was it during Richard Nixon's presidency? Bill Clinton's? While the question may be of academic interest, more pertinent is the fact that, with Trump in the White House, there is no need to pretend otherwise. Indeed, Trump's popularity with his "base" stems in part from his candid depiction of his political adversaries not as a loyal opposition but an enemy force. Trump's critics return the favor: their loathing for the president and—now that Trump's generals are gone—anyone in his employ knows no bounds.

It's the Mitch McConnell Rule elevated to the status of dogma: If your side wins, mine loses. Therefore, nothing is more important than my side winning. Compromise is for wusses.

Myth #2: Good governance entails fiscal responsibility. This is one of the hoariest shibboleths of modern American politics: feckless Democrats tax and spend; sober Republicans stand for balanced budgets. So President Reagan claimed, en route to racking up the massive deficits that transformed the United States from the world's number one creditor into its biggest debtor. George W. Bush doubled down on Reagan's promise. Yet during his presidency, deficits skyrocketed, eventually exceeding a trillion dollars per annum. No apologies were forthcoming. "Deficits don't matter," his vice president announced.

Then along came Trump. Reciting the standard Republican catechism, he vowed not only to balance the budget but to pay off the entire national debt within eight years. It was going to be a cinch. Instead, the projected deficit in the current fiscal year will once again top a cool trillion dollars while heading skywards. The media took brief note—and moved on.

The naked truth that Trump invites us to contemplate is that both parties are more than comfortable with red ink. As charged, the Democrats are indeed the party of tax and spend. Yet the GOP is the party of spend-at-least-as-much (especially on the Pentagon) while offering massive tax cuts to the rich.

Myth #3: Justice is blind. The nomination of Brett Kavanaugh to the Supreme Court and the controversies surrounding his confirmation af-

firmed in unmistakable terms what had been hidden in plain sight since
at least 1987 when Robert Bork was denied a seat on the court. The
Supreme Court has become a venue for advancing a partisan agenda. It
serves, in effect, as a third legislative body, consisting of unelected members with lifelong tenure, answerable only to itself. So politically active
Americans of whatever stripe believe. Justice impartially administered
is for people who still believe in the Easter Bunny.

As a result, the Supremes now wear invisible labels on their black
robes, identifying members as either liberal or conservative, aligned, in
effect, with Democratic or Republican positions. On hot-button issues—
gun rights and abortion rights are two examples—their job is to act accordingly. Hence, the consternation caused when a member violates those
expectations, as was the case when Chief Justice John Roberts voted to
preserve the Affordable Care Act.

So both parties engage in unapologetic court packing. In recent
years, Mitch McConnell and the Senate Republicans, who blocked dozens of Obama appointees to the federal bench and prevented Merrick
Garland's nomination to the Supreme Court from even being considered, have done so with considerable skill. But Democrats are merely
biding their time. Hence, the imperative of ensuring that Justice Ruth
Bader Ginsburg, now eighty-six and ailing, won't retire until a Democrat once again sits in the Oval Office.

Crucially, neither the left nor the right acknowledges the possibility that a politicized judiciary, however useful in advancing a partisan
agenda, might not serve the nation's long-term interests.

Myth #4: The "wise men" are truly wise. To keep America safe, protect
core US interests, and promote peace, presidents since World War II
have sought advice and counsel from a small self-perpetuating group of
foreign policy insiders claiming specialized knowledge about how the
world works and America's proper role atop that world. In the 1960s,
thanks to the disastrous war in Vietnam, the reputation of this cadre
of "wise men" cratered. Yet they weren't finished, not by a long shot.
Their ranks now including women, they staged a remarkable comeback

in the wake of 9/11. Among the ensuing catastrophes were the wars in Afghanistan, Iraq, Libya, and Syria.

As a candidate, Trump made his contempt for this elite clear. Yet fool that he is, the president now employs a bargain-basement version of the "best and brightest": a national security advisor who believes that "To Stop Iran's Bomb, Bomb Iran"; a secretary of state whose conception of history derives from the Bible; an acting defense secretary on loan from Boeing who reportedly spends time trashing his former employer's competitors; and a CIA director who earned her stripes supervising secret torture chambers.

Members of this posse may carry all the requisite security clearances, but sound thinking or foresight? One might do at least as well and perhaps better consulting a class full of college sophomores. Thanks to Trump, only the truly gullible will persist in thinking that the foreign policy establishment has a lock on wisdom.

Myth #5: The Persian Gulf is a vital US national security interest. For decades now, Americans have been fed this line with unhappy results. Dominating the Persian Gulf, we've been told, is essential to preserving our way of life. Stripped to its essentials, here's the gist of the argument: They have the oil and we need it.

In fact, we don't need their oil. There's plenty right here in our own hemisphere—that is, in what writer Bethany McLean has termed "Saudi America." Moreover, burning all that oil accelerates climate change, which poses a greater proximate threat to the well-being of the American people than anything likely to happen in the Gulf. Meanwhile, several decades of US meddling in that region have produced the inverse of what policymakers promised. Instead of order, there is instability; instead of democracy, illiberalism; instead of peace, death and destruction. In terms of lives lost and damaged and treasure wasted, the cost to the United States has been immense.

To his credit, Trump has now explained the actual basis for the continuing US interest in this part of the world: the Saudis, as well as other Gulf states, have an insatiable appetite for made-in-the-USA armaments. It's all about the Benjamins, baby, and we can't allow Russia or China to horn in on our market. Only to the military-industrial complex and its coconspirators is the Persian Gulf a vital interest. Trump relieves us of the burden of having to pretend otherwise. Thank you, Mr. President.

Myth #6: Prospects for an Israeli-Palestinian peace depend on Washington playing the role of honest broker. Here, too, let's give President Trump his due. He has definitively exposed the entire peace process as a fiction and a fraud. In fulfilling the promise made by previous presidents to move the US embassy to Jerusalem and by endorsing the Israeli claim to the Golan Heights, Trump has stripped away the last vestiges of pretense: Washington favors just one side in this festering dispute, as it has since at least the 1960s.

Why this should even qualify as news is a bit of a mystery. After all, for decades, the United States has been providing Israel with diplomatic cover at the UN Security Council and elsewhere, along with an annual gift of billions of dollars in weaponry—other customers pay cash—even as droves of non-Jewish politicians compete with one another to profess their undying love for and devotion to a country other than their own. Talk about dual loyalty!

Yes, of course, son-in-law Jared is busily hammering out what Trump himself has called "the toughest of all deals." Perhaps there is genius in turning to an amateur when the professionals have failed. If Kushner pulls this off, we'll wonder why Nixon didn't send daughter Tricia to Paris to negotiate an end to the Vietnam War and why Carter didn't dispatch wife Rosalynn to Tehran to sort out the hostage crisis. Yet whether Jared succeeds or not, thanks to Trump, we can now say definitively that when it comes to Israel, the United States is all in, now and forever.

Myth #7: War is the continuation of policy by other means. So, in a riff on Prussian military theorist Carl von Clausewitz's famous maxim, generations of American statesmen and military officers have professed to believe. Yet, in the present century, the challenge of making armed force politically purposeful has turned out to be daunting. Nothing illustrates the point more clearly than America's never-ending war in Afghanistan.

Like the clutter of online ads that our eyes automatically ignore, Americans have learned to tune out this longest war in our history. Originally styled Operation Enduring Freedom, the war itself has certainly endured. It began when this year's crop of high school graduates were just leaving the womb. In terms of total length, it's on track to outlast the Civil War (1861–1865), US participation in the two world wars (1917–1918, 1941–1945), the Korean War (1950–1953), and the Vietnam War (1965–1973) combined.

The Pentagon has never demonstrated more than minimal interest in calculating the war's cumulative costs. While researchers do their best to keep up with the mounting tally, their numbers possess almost no political salience. Congressional Democrats get exercised about the handful of billions of dollars that Trump wants to waste on building his wall, but few members of either party attend to the hundreds of billions wasted in Afghanistan. So like the Energizer Bunny, the war there just keeps on going, while going nowhere in particular.

In his State of the Union Address earlier this year, the president opined that "Great nations do not fight endless wars." It was a commendable declaration. Indeed, Trump has made it unmistakably clear that he wants out of Afghanistan as well as Syria, and the sooner the better. The boss has spoken: We're leaving, pronto, sayonara, gone for good.

Yet as is so often the case with this president, words have not translated into action. So, contrary to Trump's clearly expressed intentions, the Pentagon is planning on keeping seven thousand US troops in Afghanistan for another three to five years while also sustaining an active presence in Syria. In other words, the endless wars won't be ending any time soon.

There's a lesson to be learned here and the lesson is this: while senior military officers will never overtly disobey their president—heaven forbid!—they have evolved a repertoire of tricks over the decades to frustrate any president's intentions. On the eve of his retirement from office in 1961, President Eisenhower went on national television to tell the American people how it's done.

Credit the present generation of generals with having gone one further. Remarkably enough, they have inverted von Clausewitz. No longer does discernible political purpose serve as a necessary precondition for perpetuating a war. If generals (and militarized civilians) don't want a war to end, that suffices as a rationale for its continuation. The boss will comply.

We can therefore thank Trump for inadvertently laying bare the reality of civil-military relations in twenty-first-century Washington: the commander in chief isn't really in command.

Historians are never going to rate Trump as a great or even mediocre president. Even so, they may one day come to appreciate the Trump era as the moment when things long hidden became plain to see, when hitherto widely accepted falsehoods, fabrications, and obsolete assumptions about American democracy finally became untenable. For that, if for nothing else, we may yet have reason to thank our forty-fifth president for services rendered.

22
The Great Reckoning

A Look Back from Mid-Century

July 23, 2019

[Editorial note: This remnant of a manuscript, discovered in a vault near the coastal town of Walpole, Massachusetts, appears to have been part of a larger project, probably envisioned as an interpretive history of the United States since the year 2000. Only a single chapter, probably written near the midpoint of the twenty-first century, has survived. Whether the remainder of the manuscript has been lost or the author abandoned it before its completion is unknown.]

Chapter 1: The Launch

From our present vantage point, it seems clear that, by 2019, the United States had passed a point of no return. In retrospect, this was the moment when indications of things gone fundamentally awry should have become unmistakable. Although at the time much remained hidden in shadows, the historic pivot now commonly referred to as the Great Reckoning had commenced.

Even today, it remains difficult to understand why, given mounting evidence of a grave crisis, passivity persisted for so long across most sectors of society. An epidemic of anomie affected a large swath of the population. Faced with a blizzard of troubling developments, large and small, Americans found it difficult to put things into anything approximating useful perspective. Few even bothered to try. Fewer succeeded. As with predictions of cataclysmic earthquakes or volcanic eruptions, a not-in-my-lifetime mood generally prevailed.

During what was then misleadingly known as the Age of Trump, the political classes dithered. While the antics of President Trump provoked intense interest—the word "intense" hardly covers the attention paid to him—they also provided a convenient excuse for letting partisan bickering take precedence over actual governance or problem solving of any sort. Meanwhile, "thought leaders" (a term then commonly used to describe pontificating windbags) indulged themselves with various pet projects.

In the midst of what commentators were pleased to call the Information Age, most ordinary Americans showed a pronounced affinity for trivia over matters of substance. A staggering number of citizens willingly traded freedom and privacy for convenience, bowing to the dictates of an ever-expanding array of personalized gadgetry. What was then called a "smartphone" functioned as a talisman of sorts, the electronic equivalent of a rosary or prayer beads.

Especially among the young, separation from one's "phone" for more than a few minutes could cause acute anxiety and distress. The novelty of "social media" had not yet worn off, with its most insidious implications just being discovered.

Divided, distracted, and desperately trying to keep up: these emerged then as the abiding traits of life in contemporary America. Craft beer, small-batch bourbon, and dining at the latest farm-to-table restaurant often seemed to matter more than the fate of the nation or, for that matter, the planet as a whole. But all that was about to change.

Scholars will undoubtedly locate the origins of the Great Reckoning well before 2019. Perhaps they will trace its source to the aftermath of the Cold War when American elites succumbed to a remarkable bout of imperial hubris, while ignoring (thanks in part to the efforts of Big Energy companies) the already growing body of information on the human-induced alteration of the planet, which came to be called "climate change" or "global warming." While, generally speaking, the collective story of humankind unfolds along a continuum, by 2019 conditions conducive to disruptive change were forming. History was about to zig sharply off its expected course.

This disruption occurred, of course, within a specific context. During the first two decades of the twenty-first century, American society absorbed a series of punishing blows. First came the contested election of 2000, the president of the United States installed in office by a 5–4 vote of a politicized Supreme Court, which thereby effectively usurped the role of the electorate. And that was just for starters. Following in short order came the terrorist attacks of September 11, 2001, which the world's (self-proclaimed) premier intelligence services failed to anticipate and the world's preeminent military establishment failed to avert.

Less than two years later, the administration of George W. Bush, operating under the delusion that the ongoing war in Afghanistan was essentially won, ordered US forces to invade Iraq, a nation that had played no part in the events of 9/11. The result of this patently illegal war of aggression would not be victory, despite the president's almost instant "mission accomplished" declaration, but a painful replay of the quagmire that US troops had experienced decades before in Vietnam. Expectations of Iraq's "liberation" paving the way for a broader Freedom Agenda that would democratize the Islamic world came to naught. The Iraq War and other armed interventions initiated during the first two decades of the century ended up costing trillions of taxpayer dollars, while sowing the seeds of instability across much of the Greater Middle East and later Africa.

Then, in August 2005, Hurricane Katrina smashed into the Gulf Coast, killing nearly two thousand Americans. US government agencies responded with breathtaking ineptitude, a sign of things to come, as nature itself was turning increasingly unruly. Other natural disasters of unnatural magnitude followed. In 2007, to cite but one example, more than nine thousand wildfires in California swept through more than a million acres. Like swarms of locusts, fires now became an annual (and worsening) plague ravaging the Golden State and the rest of the West Coast. If this weren't enough of a harbinger of approaching environmental catastrophe, the populations of honeybees, vital to American agriculture, began to collapse in these very same years.

Americans were, as it turned out, largely indifferent to the fate of honeybees. They paid far greater attention to the economy, however, which experienced its own form of collapse in 2007–2008. The ensuing Great Recession saw millions thrown out of work and millions more lose their homes as a result of fraudulent mortgage practices. None of the perpetrators were punished. The administration of President Obama chose instead to bail out offending banks and large corporations. Record federal deficits resulted, as the government abandoned once and for all even the pretense of trying to balance the budget. And, of course, the nation's multiple wars dragged on and on and on.

Through all these trials, the American people more or less persevered. If not altogether stoic, they remained largely compliant. As a result, few members of the nation's political, economic, intellectual, or cultural elites showed any awareness that something fundamental might be amiss. The two established parties retained their monopoly on national politics. As late as 2016, the status quo appeared firmly intact. Only with that year's presidential election did large numbers of citizens signal that they had had enough: wearing red MAGA caps rather than wielding pitchforks, they joined Trump's assault on that elite and, thumbing their noses at Washington, installed a reality TV star in the White House.

To the legions who had found the previous status quo agreeable, Trump's ascent to the apex of American politics amounted to an un-bearable affront. They might tolerate purposeless, endless wars, raise more or less any set of funds for the military that was so unsuccessfully fighting them, and turn a blind eye to economic arrangements that fostered inequality on a staggering scale. They might respond to the accelerating threat posed by climate change with lip service and, at best, quarter-measures. But Donald Trump in the Oval Office? That they could not abide.

As a result, from the moment of his election, Trump dominated the American scene. Yet the outrage that he provoked, day in and day out, had the unfortunate side effect that it obscured developments that would in time prove to be of far more importance than the forty-fifth American president himself. Like the "noise" masking signals that, if detected and correctly interpreted, might have averted Pearl Harbor in December 1941 or, for that matter, 9/11, obsessing about Trump caused observers to regularly overlook or discount matters far transcending in significance the daily ration of presidential shenanigans.

Here, then, is a very partial listing of some of the most important of those signals then readily available to anyone bothering to pay attention. On the eve of the Great Reckoning, however, they were generally treated as mere curiosities or matters of limited urgency—problems to be deferred to a later, more congenial moment.

Item: The reality of climate change was now indisputable. All that remained in question was how rapidly it would occur and the extent (and again rapidity) of the devastation that it would ultimately inflict.

Item: Despite everything that was then known about the dangers of further carbon emissions, the major atmospheric contributor to global warming, they only continued to increase, despite the myriad conferences and agreements intended to curb them. (US carbon emissions, in particular, were still rising then, and global emissions were expected to rise by record or near-record amounts as 2019 began.)

Item: The polar icecap was disappearing, with scientists reporting that it had melted more in just twenty years than in the previous ten thousand. This, in turn, meant that sea levels would continue to rise at record rates, posing an increasing threat to coastal cities.

Item: Deforestation and desertification were occurring at an alarming rate.

Item: Approximately eight million metric tons of plastic were seeping into the world's oceans each year, from the ingestion of which vast numbers of seabirds, fish, and marine mammals were dying annually. Payback would come in the form of microplastics contained in seafood consumed by humans.

Item: With China and other Asian countries increasingly refusing to accept American recyclables, municipalities in the United States found themselves overwhelmed by accumulations of discarded glass, plastic, metal, cardboard, and paper. That year, the complete breakdown of the global recycling system already loomed as a possibility.

Item: Worldwide bird and insect populations were plummeting. In other words, the Sixth Mass Extinction had begun.

All of these fall into the category of what we recognize today as planetary issues of existential importance. But even in 2019 there were other matters of less than planetary significance that ought to have functioned as a wake-up call. Among them were:

Item: With the federal government demonstrably unable to secure US borders, immigration authorities were seizing hundreds of thousands of migrants annually. By 2019, the Trump administration was confining significant numbers of those migrants, including small children, in what were, in effect, concentration camps.

Item: Cybercrime had become a major growth industry, on track to rake in $6 trillion annually by 2021. Hackers were already demonstrating the ability to hold large American cities hostage and the authorities proved incapable of catching up.

Item: With the three richest Americans—Jeff Bezos, Bill Gates, and Warren Buffett—controlling more wealth than the bottom fifty percent of the entire population, the United States had become a full-fledged oligarchy. While politicians occasionally expressed their dismay about this reality, prior to 2019 it was widely tolerated.

Item: As measured by roads, bridges, dams, or public transportation systems, the nation's infrastructure was strikingly inferior to what it had been a half-century earlier. (By 2019, China, for instance, had built more than nineteen thousand miles of high-speed rail; the US, not one.) Agreement that this was a problem that needed fixing was universal; corrective action (and government financing), however, was not forthcoming.

Item: Military spending in constant dollars exceeded what it had been at the height of the Cold War when the country's main adversary, the Soviet Union, had a large army with up-to-date equipment and an arsenal of nuclear weapons. In 2019, Iran, the country's most likely adversary, had a modest army and no nuclear weapons.

Item: Incivility, rudeness, bullying, and general nastiness had become rampant, while the White House, once the site of solemn ceremony, deliberation, and decision, played host to politically divisive shouting matches and verbal brawls.

To say that Americans were oblivious to such matters would be inaccurate. Some were, for instance, considering a ban on plastic straws. Yet taken as a whole, the many indications of systemic and even planetary dysfunction received infinitely less popular attention than the pregnancies of British royals, the antics of the justifiably forgotten Kardashian clan, or fantasy football, a briefly popular early twenty-first-century fad.

Of course, decades later, viewed with the benefit of hindsight, the implications of these various trends and data points seem painfully clear: the dominant ideological abstraction of late postmodernity—liberal democratic capitalism—was rapidly failing or had simply become irrelevant to the challenges facing the United States and the human species as a whole. To employ another then-popular phrase, liberal democratic capitalism had become an expression of "fake news," a scam sold to the many for the benefit of the privileged few.

"Toward the end of an age," historian John Lukacs (1924–2019) once observed, "more and more people lose faith in their institutions and finally they abandon their belief that these institutions might still be reformed from within." Lukacs wrote those words in 1970, but they aptly described the situation that had come to exist in that turning-point year of 2019. Basic American institutions—the overworked US military being a singular exception—no longer commanded popular respect.

In essence, the postmodern age was ending, though few seemed to know it—with elites, in particular, largely oblivious to what was occurring. What would replace postmodernity in a planet heading for ruin remained to be seen.

Only when . . .

[Editor's note: Here the account breaks off.]

23
False Security

Donald Trump and the Ten Commandments (Plus One) of the National Security State

October 31, 2019

et us stipulate at the outset that Donald Trump is a vulgar and dishonest fraud without a principled bone in his corpulent frame. Yet history is nothing if not a tale overflowing with irony. Despite his massive shortcomings, President Trump appears intent on recalibrating America's role in the world. Initiating a long-overdue process of aligning US policy with actually existing global conditions just may prove to be his providentially anointed function. Go figure.

The Valhalla of the Indispensable Nation is a capacious place, even if it celebrates mostly white and mostly male diversity. Recall that in the eighteenth century, it was a slaveholding planter from Virginia who secured American independence. In the nineteenth, an ambitious homespun lawyer from Illinois destroyed slavery, thereby clearing the way for his country to become a capitalist behemoth. In the middle third of the twentieth century, a crippled Hudson River grandee delivered the United States to the summit of global power. In that century's difficult later decades, a washed-up movie actor declared that it was "morning in America" and so, however briefly, it seemed to be. Now, in the twenty-first century, to inaugurate the next phase of the American story, history has seemingly designated as its agent a New York real estate developer, casino bankruptee, and reality TV star.

In all likelihood, George Washington, Abraham Lincoln, Franklin Delano Roosevelt, and Ronald Reagan would balk at having Donald

Trump classified as their peer. Yet, however preposterously, in our present moment of considerable crisis, he has succeeded them as the nation's Great Helmsman, albeit one with few ideas about what course to set. Yet somehow Trump has concluded that our existing course has the United States headed toward the rocks. He just might be right.

"Great nations do not fight endless wars." So the president announced in his 2019 State of the Union Address. Implicit in such a seemingly innocuous statement was a genuinely radical proposition, as laden with portent as Lincoln's declaration in 1858 that a house divided cannot stand. Trump appears determined to overturn the prevailing national security paradigm, even if he is largely clueless about what should replace it.

Much as Southerners correctly discerned the import of Lincoln's veiled threat, so, too, have Trump's many critics within the national security apparatus grasped the implications of his insistence that "endless wars" must indeed end. In the unlikely event that he ever delivers on his campaign promise to end the conflicts he inherited, all the claims, assumptions, and practices that together define the US national security praxis will become subject to reexamination. Tug hard enough on this one dangling thread—the wars that drag on and on—and the entire fabric may well unravel.

The Decalogue Plus One

In other words, to acknowledge the folly of this country's endless wars will necessarily call into question the habits that people in and around Washington see as the essence of "American global leadership." Prominent among these are: (1) positioning US forces in hundreds of bases abroad; (2) partitioning the whole planet into several contiguous regional military commands; (3) conferring security guarantees on dozens of nations, regardless of their ability to defend themselves or the values to which they subscribe; (4) maintaining the capability to project power to the remotest corners of the earth; (5) keeping in instant readiness a "triad" of nuclear strike forces; (6) endlessly searching for "breakthrough technologies" that will eliminate war's inherent risks and uncertainties; (7) unquestioningly absorbing the costs of maintaining a sprawling national security bureaucracy; (8) turning a blind eye to the corrupting influence of the military-industrial complex; and easily outpacing all other nations, friend and foe alike, in (9) weapons sales and (10) overall military spending.

Complementing this decalogue, inscribed not on two tablets but in thousands of pages of stupefyingly bureaucratic prose, is an unwritten eleventh commandment: Thou shalt not prevent the commander in chief from doing what he deems necessary. Call it all D+1. In theory, the Constitution endows Congress with the authority to prevent any president from initiating, prolonging, or expanding a war. In practice, Congress has habitually deferred to an increasingly imperial presidency and treated the war powers provisions of the Constitution as nonbinding.

This decalogue-plus-one has been with us for decades. It first emerged during the early phases of the Cold War. Its godfathers included such distinguished (if today largely forgotten) figures as Paul Nitze, principal author of a famously unhinged policy paper known as NSC-68, and General Curtis LeMay, who transformed the Strategic Air Command into a "cocked weapon" capable of obliterating humankind.

During the 1960s, "better-dead-than-red" began to fall from favor and a doctrine of "flexible response" became all the rage. In those years, as an approach to waging, and therefore perpetuating, the Cold War, D+1 achieved maturity. At that very juncture, the search for fresh thinking to justify existing policies vaulted the likes of Robert McNamara and Maxwell Taylor into positions of authority as secretary of defense and chairman of the Joint Chiefs of Staff.

The Vietnam War put the American military establishment's capacity for flexibility to the test. That test did not go well, with Secretary McNamara and General Taylor prominent among the officials whose reputations did not survive. Remarkably, however, amid the carnage of that war, D+1 did survive all but unscathed. Vietnam was surely a debacle, but as long as the Cold War persisted, asking first-order questions about the basic organization of "national security" appeared just too risky. So the decalogue emerged with hardly a scratch. Notwithstanding the disappointing presidencies of Johnson and Nixon, so, too, did the Eleventh Commandment.

More striking still, even after the fall of the Berlin Wall, D+1 persisted. Thirty years ago this month when the Cold War ended, everyone agreed that a new era of global affairs was dawning. The Soviet Union, the threat that had prompted the creation of the decalogue, had vanished. Yet without missing a beat, a new generation of Nitzes and LeMays, McNamaras and Taylors devised an altogether different rationale for preserving their predecessors' handiwork.

That new rationale was nothing if not expansive. During the Cold War, the overarching purpose of D+1 had been to avert the ultimate disaster of Armageddon. Its revised purpose was to promote the ultimate goal of remaking the world in America's image. With a "sole superpower" now presiding over the international order, D+1 offered a recipe for simultaneously cementing permanent US primacy and securing the universal triumph of American values. So, at least, members of an intoxicated foreign policy elite persuaded themselves.

Yet in the wake of the Cold War came not peace and harmony but unprecedented US military activism. Here was the common theme of the otherwise disparate presidencies of George H. W. Bush, Bill Clinton, George W. Bush, and Barack Obama. During the quarter-century that elapsed between the fall of the Berlin Wall and the election of Trump, the United States intervened in or attacked Panama, Iraq, Somalia, Haiti, Bosnia, Kosovo, Afghanistan, Sudan, Afghanistan (again), Iraq (again), Libya, Somalia (again), Yemen, Syria, several West African nations, and, briefly, Pakistan. And given a presidential preference for employing Special Operations forces on highly classified missions, that list is almost surely incomplete. Simply put, reticence regarding the use of force vanished.

As for the Eleventh Commandment, it now achieved a status comparable to the doctrine of papal infallibility. After 9/11, Congress quickly passed an open-ended Authorization for Use of Military Force (AUMF), empowering the president "to take action to deter and prevent acts of international terrorism against the United States." Of course, "terrorism," as we are frequently reminded by the likes of Benjamin Netanyahu, Vladimir Putin, and Recep Tayyip Erdogan, is very much in the eyes of the beholder. In effect, Congress had simply handed the commander in chief a blank check.

That AUMF became law on September 18, 2001, following a unanimous vote in the Senate and with only a single member dissenting in the House of Representatives. In the years since, it has shown both remarkable durability and elasticity. Best illustrating its durability have been the wars launched under its auspices. Best illustrating its elasticity was Barack Obama's "disposition matrix," a secret procedure devised by his administration empowering him to order the killing of just about anyone anywhere on the planet deemed to pose a threat to the United States. All of this transpired with the cool deliberation and thorough consultation that was an Obama signature. Acting pursuant to the provisions of that AUMF, in other words, Obama codified assassination as an integral component of US policy. In Washington, war thereby became a permanent undertaking that recognized no boundaries.

In or Out? Old or New?

Read the papers or watch cable news and you might conclude that the pivotal issue of our moment is the fate of Syria's Kurds, with the United States military deemed uniquely responsible for ensuring their well-being. Yet while such a conclusion may play well with our troubled consciences—and troubled they certainly should be—it is radically misleading.

True enough, Trump's abrupt abandonment of the Kurds qualifies as cruel, callous, and immoral. It also ranks as only the latest in a long string of such American betrayals, as various Native American tribes, Chinese Nationalists, Cuban exiles, South Vietnamese, and prior generations of Kurds (among others) can testify. So Trump has not exactly broken with past precedent.

More to the point, the matter at hand relates less to the Kurds than to a far larger question: Should the United States perpetuate the military enterprise commonly but misleadingly referred to as the "Global War on Terrorism?" Or should the United States recognize that this so-called

GWOT has failed and consider a different approach to policy? Given that the GWOT represents D+1 applied to the Greater Middle East, "different" implies a wholesale reexamination of basic national security policy. It's that prospect that worries the foreign policy establishment.

With the GWOT's twentieth anniversary now within hailing distance, we are in a position to evaluate just what that war has actually achieved. Honest differences of opinion may be possible, but in my judgment the results rank somewhere between disappointing and catastrophic. This much is certain: we have not won and victory is nowhere in sight.

Granted, Iraq's Saddam Hussein is gone, as is Libya's Muammar Gaddafi, both of them guilty of terrible crimes (although innocent of any direct involvement in 9/11). For the moment at least, the repressive Taliban do not rule in Kabul. And Osama bin Laden and Abu Bakr al-Baghdadi are dead. Proponents of the GWOT and of D+1 can point to these as positive achievements.

Yet widen the aperture slightly and the outcome appears less impressive. George W. Bush's much ballyhooed Freedom Agenda came to naught. Regime change in Kabul, Baghdad, and Tripoli produced not liberal democracy but chronic instability, pervasive corruption, and endemic violence. In Afghanistan, the Taliban never admitted defeat and today threaten the Western-installed Afghan government. Rather than affirming American military mastery and benign intentions, the reckless and illegal invasion of Iraq, advertised under the banner of Operation Iraqi Freedom, became a gift to our adversaries. If anyone can be said to have won the Iraq War, that honor must surely belong to the Islamic Republic of Iran. Worse still, by upending the existing regional order, US forces created a power vacuum that facilitated the emergence of new terrorist movements like ISIS.

America's ongoing post-9/11 wars deserve to be called "endless" because, despite contributing to hundreds of thousands of deaths and squandering trillions of dollars over the course of many years, the United States has come nowhere close to fulfilling its declared political aims. The plight of the Kurds in Syria offers a small but telling illustration of the magnitude of that failure.

Now the president of the United States, acting pursuant to the authority granted him by the Eleventh Commandment, says he wants to call it quits. It's like Adam in the Garden of Eden: the one thing he's forbidden to do, he does—or in Trump's case makes a show of intending to do at least.

In response, in a show of near-unanimity Democratic and Republican defenders of the decalogue-plus-one insist that President Trump may not do what he declares himself intent on doing. Recall that George W. Bush's doctrine of preventive war—sometimes disguised as "anticipatory self-defense"—elicited only modest opposition at best, largely along partisan lines. Much the same can be said of Obama's self-appointment as assassin in chief. But Trump's declared intention to withdraw US troops from Syria as a preliminary step toward reducing our regional military presence has elicited bipartisan condemnation expressed in the strongest terms.

Senate Majority Leader Mitch McConnell, typically the president's most stalwart defender, took to the pages of the *Washington Post* to denounce Trump's decision in no uncertain terms. Riddled with half-truths and hyperbole, his op-ed qualifies as a model of "fake news." Yet credit McConnell with this much: he understands that, in the dispute between Trump and the foreign policy establishment, the fate of Syria's Kurds rates as no more than incidental.

The real issue, according to McConnell, is preserving "the post–World War II international system" that, he asserts, "has sustained an unprecedented era of peace, prosperity, and technological development." Furthermore, having created that system, the United States remains "its indispensable nation," a phrase introduced by Madeleine Albright and Bill Clinton in the early 1990s. Preserving that system's benefits requires keeping faith with the Kurds, maintaining the US military presence throughout the Middle East, and above all preserving the established framework of national security policy. In short, compliance with the decalogue is mandatory. Even (or especially) presidents must obey.

Now, if you believe that the world we live in today does not differ in any significant way from the one that existed in the wake of World

War II, McConnell's argument might just possess some merit. Yet back then, the American economy led the pack in every conceivable measure. America's European allies had been ravaged by war and desperately needed US assistance. Both they and the defeated Axis powers, Germany and Japan, appeared vulnerable to the siren song of communism.

To some observers, the Soviet Union appeared intent on taking over the world. China was poor, weak, backward, and divided. Imperial powers like Great Britain, France, and the Netherlands still clung to the illusion that they could keep a lid on demands for national self-determination in South and Southeast Asia, the Middle East, and Africa. Nuclear weapons offered a source of reassurance rather than concern— apart from the United States no one had them. Finally, that a climate crisis attributable to human activity might one day cause grievous harm on a planetary scale was literally beyond imagining.

Time has rendered every bit of this inoperative. McConnell's "post–World War II international system" is now a fantasy about as relevant to contemporary reality as belief in the tooth fairy.

In what may be the sole redeeming feature of his otherwise abysmal presidency, Trump appears determined to blow the whistle on this charade. Sadly, his efforts do not extend much beyond making noise. Even the troop withdrawals that he announces with such fanfare tend to result in little more than repositioning within the region rather than redeployment back to the United States. Worse still, the motley band of mediocrities who surround the president consists almost entirely of believers in D+1. In his impulsive and ignorant way, Trump wants change; they oppose it.

As a result, diplomatic initiatives that might actually open a pathway to ending endless wars—negotiating the restoration of normal diplomatic relations with Tehran, for example, or curtailing weapons sales (and giveaways) to nations that use US-manufactured arms to create mayhem, or demonstrating leadership by declaring a no-first-use policy on nuclear weapons—don't even qualify for discussion. So Trump is left to flail about on his own, haplessly posing legitimate questions that he is incapable of answering.

The fears of the decalogue's defenders are not misplaced: Syria is the loose tip of a dangling thread. Give that thread a good yank and the entire moth-eaten fabric of US national security policy just might become undone. Yet it will take someone with greater determination, consistency, and strength of character than Trump to perform this necessary task.

24
Judgment Day for the National Security State

The Coronavirus and the Real Threats to American Safety and Freedom

March 26, 2020

mericans are facing "a spring unlike any before." So warned a front-page article in the March 13 *New York Times*.

That phrasing, however hyperbolic, was all too apt. The coming of spring has always promised relief from the discomforts of winter. Yet, far too often, it also brings its own calamities and afflictions.

According to the poet T. S. Eliot, "April is the cruellest month." Yet while April has certainly delivered its share of cataclysms, March and May haven't lagged far behind. In fact, cruelty has seldom been a respecter of seasons. The infamous influenza epidemic of 1918, frequently cited as a possible analogue to our current crisis, began in the spring of that year, but lasted well into 1919.

That said, something about the coronavirus pandemic does seem to set this particular spring apart. At one level, that something is the collective panic now sweeping virtually the entire country. President Trump's grotesque ineptitude and tone-deafness have only fed that panic. And in their eagerness to hold Trump himself responsible for the pandemic, as if he were the bat that first transmitted the disease to a human being, his critics magnify further a growing sense of events spinning out of control.

Yet to heap the blame for this crisis on Trump alone (though he certainly deserves plenty of blame) is to miss its deeper significance.

Deferred for far too long, Judgment Day may at long last have arrived for the national security state.

Origins of a Colossus

That state within a state's origins date from the early days of the Cold War. Its ostensible purpose has been to keep Americans safe and so, by extension, to guarantee our freedoms. From the 1950s through the 1980s, keeping us safe provided a seemingly adequate justification for maintaining a sprawling military establishment along with a panoply of "intelligence" agencies—the CIA, the DIA, the NRO, the NSA—all engaged in secret activities hidden from public view. From time to time, the scope, prerogatives, and actions of that conglomeration of agencies attracted brief critical attention—the Cuban Bay of Pigs fiasco in 1961, the Vietnam War of the 1960s and early 1970s, and the Iran-Contra Affair during the presidency of Ronald Reagan being prime examples. Yet at no time did such failures come anywhere close to jeopardizing its existence.

Indeed, even when the implosion of the Soviet Union and the end of the Cold War removed the original justification for its creation, the entire apparatus persisted. With the Soviet Empire gone, Russia in a state of disarray, and communism having lost its appeal as an alternative to democratic capitalism, the managers of the national security state wasted no time in identifying new threats and new missions.

The new threats included autocrats like Panama's Manuel Noriega and Iraq's Saddam Hussein, once deemed valuable American assets, but now, their usefulness gone, classified as dangers to be eliminated. Prominent among the new missions was a sudden urge to repair broken places like the Balkans, Haiti, and Somalia, with American power deployed under the aegis of "humanitarian intervention" and pursuant to a "responsibility to protect." In this way, in the first decade of the post–Cold War era, the national security state kept itself busy. While the results achieved, to put it politely, were mixed at best, the costs incurred appeared tolerable. In sum, the entire apparatus remained impervious to serious scrutiny.

During that decade, however, both the organs of national security and the American public began taking increased notice of what was called "anti-American terrorism"—and not without reason. In 1993, Islamic fundamentalists detonated a bomb in a parking garage of New York's World Trade Center. In 1996, terrorists obliterated an apartment building used to house US military personnel in Saudi Arabia. Two years later, the US embassies in Kenya and Tanzania were blown up, and, in 2000, suicide bombers nearly sank the USS *Cole*, a Navy destroyer making a port call in Aden at the tip of the Arabian Peninsula. To each of these increasingly brazen attacks, all occurring during the administration of President Bill Clinton, the national security state responded ineffectually.

Then, of course, came September 11, 2001. Orchestrated by Osama bin Laden and carried out by nineteen suicidal al-Qaeda operatives, this act of mass murder inflicted incalculable harm on the United States. In its wake, it became common to say that "9/11 changed everything."

In fact, however, remarkably little changed. Despite its seventeen intelligence agencies, the national security state failed utterly to anticipate and thwart that devastating attack on the nation's political and financial capitals. Yet apart from minor adjustments—primarily expanding surveillance efforts at home and abroad—those outfits mostly kept doing what they had been doing, even as their leaders evaded accountability. After Pearl Harbor, at least, one admiral and one general were fired. After 9/11, no one lost his or her job. At the upper echelons of the national security state, the wagons were circled and a consensus quickly formed: no one had screwed up.

Once President George W. Bush identified an "Axis of Evil" (Iraq, Iran, and North Korea), three nations that had had nothing whatsoever to do with the 9/11 attacks, as the primary target for his administration's Global War on Terrorism, it became clear that no wholesale reevaluation of national security policy was going to occur. The Pentagon and the Intelligence Community, along with their sprawling support network of profit-minded contractors, could breathe easy. All of them would get ever more money. That went without saying. Meanwhile, the underlying premise of US policy since the immediate aftermath of World War II—that projecting hard power globally would keep Americans safe—remained sacrosanct.

Viewed from this perspective, the sequence of events that followed was probably overdetermined. In late 2001, US forces invaded Afghanistan, overthrew the Taliban regime, and set out to install a political order more agreeable to Washington. In early 2003, with the mission in Afghanistan still anything but complete, US forces set out to do the same in Iraq. Both of those undertakings have dragged on, in one fashion or another, without coming remotely close to success. Today, the military undertaking launched in 2001 continues, even if it no longer has a name or an agreed-upon purpose.

Nonetheless, at the upper echelons of the national security state, the consensus forged after 9/11 remains firmly in place: no one screws up. In Washington, the conviction that projecting hard power keeps Americans safe likewise remains sacrosanct.

In the nearly two decades since 9/11, willingness to challenge this paradigm has rarely extended beyond nonconforming publications like *TomDispatch*. Until Trump came along, rare was the ambitious politician of either political party who dared say aloud what Trump himself has repeatedly said—that, as he calls them, the "ridiculous endless wars" launched in response to 9/11 represent the height of folly.

Astonishingly enough, within the political establishment that point has still not sunk in. So, in 2020, as in 2016, the likely Democratic nominee for president will be someone who vigorously supported the 2003 invasion of Iraq. Imagine, if you will, Democrats in 1880 nominating not a former union general (as they did) but a former confederate who, twenty years before, had advocated secession. Back then, some sins were unforgivable. Today, politicians of both parties practice self-absolution and get away with it.

The Real Threat

Note, however, the parallel narrative that has unfolded alongside those post-9/11 wars. Taken seriously, that narrative exposes the utter irrelevance of the national security state as currently constituted. The coronavirus pandemic will doubtless prove to be a significant learning experience. Here is one lesson that Americans cannot afford to overlook.

Presidents now routinely request and Congress routinely appropri-ates more than a trillion dollars annually to satisfy the national security state's supposed needs. Even so, Americans today do not feel safe and, to a degree without precedent, they are being denied the exercise of basic everyday freedoms. Judged by this standard, the apparatus created to keep them safe and free has failed. In the face of a pandemic, nature's version of an act of true terror, that failure, the consequences of which Americans will suffer through for months to come, should be seen as definitive.

But wait, some will object. Don't we find ourselves in uncharted waters? Is this really the moment to rush to judgment?

In fact, judgment is long overdue.

While the menace posed by the coronavirus may differ in scope, it does not differ substantively from the myriad other perils that Ameri-cans have endured since the national security state wandered off on its quixotic quest to pacify Afghanistan and Iraq and purge the planet of terrorists. Since 9/11, a partial roster of those perils would include Hur-ricane Katrina (2005), Superstorm Sandy (2012), Hurricanes Harvey, Irma, and Maria (2017), and massive wildfires that have devastated vast stretches of the West Coast on virtually an annual basis. The cumulative cost of such events exceeds a half-trillion dollars. Together, they have taken the lives of several thousand more people than were lost in the 2001 attack on the World Trade Center and the Pentagon.

Earlier generations might have written all of these off as acts of God. Today, we know better. As with blaming Trump, blaming God won't do. Human activities, ranging from the hubristic reengineering of rivers like the Mississippi to the effects of climate change stemming from the use of fossil fuels, have substantially exacerbated such "natural" catastrophes.

And unlike faraway autocrats or terrorist organizations, such phe-nomena, from extreme weather events to pandemics, directly and imme-diately threaten the safety and well-being of the American people. Don't tell the Central Intelligence Agency or the Joint Chiefs of Staff but the principal threats to our collective wellbeing are right here where we live.

Apart from modest belated efforts at mitigation, the existing na-tional security state is about as pertinent to addressing such threats as

President Trump's cheery expectations that the coronavirus will simply evaporate once warmer weather appears. Terror has indeed arrived on our shores and it has nothing to do with al-Qaeda or ISIS or Iranian-backed militias. Americans are terrorized because it has now become apparent that our government, whether out of negligence or stupidity, has left them exposed to dangers that truly put life and liberty at risk. As it happens, all these years in which the national security state has been preoccupied with projecting hard power abroad have left us naked and vulnerable right here at home.

Protecting Americans *where they live* ought to be the national security priority of our time. The existing national security state is incapable of fulfilling that imperative, while its leaders, fixated on waging distant wars, have yet to even accept that they have a responsibility to do so.

Worst of all, even in this election year, no one on the national political scene appears to recognize the danger now fully at hand.

III
ON AND ON THEY GO

25
Writing a Blank Check on War for the President

How the United States Became a Prisoner of War and Congress Went MIA

April 5, 2016

et's face it: In times of war, the Constitution tends to take a beating. With the safety or survival of the nation said to be at risk, the basic law of the land—otherwise considered sacrosanct—becomes nonbinding, subject to being waived at the whim of government authorities who are impatient, scared, panicky, or just plain pissed off.

The examples are legion. During the Civil War, Abraham Lincoln arbitrarily suspended the writ of habeas corpus and ignored court orders that took issue with his authority to do so. After US entry into World War I, the administration of Woodrow Wilson mounted a comprehensive effort to crush dissent, shutting down anti-war publications in complete disregard of the First Amendment. Amid the hysteria triggered by Pearl Harbor, Franklin Roosevelt issued an executive order consigning to concentration camps more than 100,000 Japanese Americans, many of them native-born citizens. Asked in 1944 to review this gross violation of due process, the Supreme Court endorsed the government's action by a 6-3 vote.

More often than not, the passing of the emergency induces second thoughts and even remorse. The further into the past a particular war recedes, the more dubious the wartime arguments for violating the Constitution appear. Americans thereby take comfort in the "lessons learned" that will presumably prohibit any future recurrence of such folly.

194

Even so, the onset of the next war finds the Constitution once more being ill-treated. We don't repeat past transgressions, of course. Instead, we devise new ones. So it has been during the ongoing post-9/11 period of protracted war.

During the presidency of George W. Bush, the United States embraced torture as an instrument of policy in clear violation of the Eighth Amendment prohibiting cruel and unusual punishment. Bush's successor, Obama, ordered the extrajudicial killing of an American citizen, a death by drone that was visibly in disregard of the Fifth and Fourteenth Amendments. Both administrations—Bush's with gusto, Obama's with evident regret—imprisoned individuals for years on end without charge and without anything remotely approximating the "speedy and public trial, by an impartial jury" guaranteed by the Sixth Amendment. Should the present state of hostilities ever end, we can no doubt expect Guantánamo to become yet another source of "lessons learned" for future generations of rueful Americans.

Congress on the Sidelines

Yet one particular check-and-balance constitutional proviso now appears exempt from this recurring phenomenon of disregard followed by professions of dismay, embarrassment, and "never again-ism" once the military emergency passes. I mean, of course, Article I, Section 8 of the Constitution, which assigns to Congress the authority "to declare war" and still stands as testimony to the genius of those who drafted it. There can be no question that the responsibility for deciding when and whether the United States should fight resides with the legislative branch, not the executive, and that this was manifestly the intent of the framers.

On parchment at least, the division of labor appears straightforward. The president's designation as commander in chief of the armed forces in no way implies a blanket authorization to employ those forces however he sees fit or anything faintly like it. Quite the contrary: legitimizing presidential command requires explicit congressional sanction.

Actual practice has evolved into something altogether different. The portion of Article I, Section 8 cited above has become a dead letter, about as operative as blue laws still on the books in some American cities and towns that purport to regulate Sabbath day activities. Superseding the written text is an unwritten counterpart that goes something like this: *with legislators largely consigned to the status of observers, presidents pretty much wage war whenever, wherever, and however they see fit.* Whether the result qualifies as usurpation or forfeiture is one of those chicken-and-egg questions that's interesting but practically speaking beside the point.

This is by no means a recent development. It has a history. In the summer of 1950, when President Truman decided that a UN Security Council resolution provided sufficient warrant for him to order US forces to fight in Korea, congressional war powers took a hit from which they would never recover.

Congress soon thereafter bought into the notion, fashionable during the Cold War, that formal declarations of hostilities had become passé. Waging the "long twilight struggle" ostensibly required deference to the commander in chief on all matters related to national security. To sustain the pretense that it still retained some relevance, Congress took to issuing what were essentially permission slips, granting presidents maximum freedom of action to do whatever they might decide needed to be done in response to the latest perceived crisis.

The Tonkin Gulf Resolution of 1964 offers a notable example. With near unanimity, legislators urged President Johnson "to take all necessary measures to repel any armed attack against the forces of the United States and to prevent further aggression" across the length and breadth of Southeast Asia. Through the magic of presidential interpretation, a mandate to prevent aggression provided legal cover for an astonishingly brutal and aggressive war in Vietnam, as well as Cambodia and Laos. Under the guise of repelling attacks on US forces, Johnson and his successor, Nixon, thrust millions of American troops into a war they could not win, even if more than fifty-eight thousand died trying.

To leap almost four decades ahead, think of the Authorization for Use of Military Force (AUMF) that was passed by Congress in the immediate aftermath of 9/11 as the grandchild of the Tonkin Gulf Resolution. This document required (directed, called upon, requested, invited, urged) President George W. Bush "to use all necessary and appropriate force against those nations, organizations, or persons he determines planned, authorized, committed, or aided the terrorist attacks that occurred on September 11, 2001, or harbored such organizations or persons, in order to prevent any future acts of international terrorism against the United States by such nations, organizations, or persons." In plain language: here's a blank check; feel free to fill it in any way you like.

Forever War

As a practical matter, one specific individual—Osama bin Laden—had hatched the 9/11 plot. A single organization—al-Qaeda—had conspired to pull it off. And just one nation—backward, Taliban-controlled Afghanistan—had provided assistance, offering sanctuary to bin Laden and his henchmen. Yet nearly fifteen years later, the AUMF remains operative and has become the basis for military actions against innumerable individuals, organizations, and nations with no involvement whatsoever in the murderous events of September 11, 2001.

Consider the following less than comprehensive list of four developments, all of which occurred just within the last month and a half:

- In Yemen, a US air strike killed at least fifty individuals, said to be members of an Islamist organization that did not exist on 9/11.
- In Somalia, another US air strike killed a reported 150 militants, reputedly members of al-Shabaab, a very nasty outfit, even if one with no real agenda beyond Somalia itself.
- In Syria, pursuant to the campaign of assassination that is the latest spin-off of the Iraq War, US Special Operations forces bumped off the reputed "finance minister" of the Islamic State, another terror group that didn't even exist in September 2001.
- In Libya, according to press reports, the Pentagon is again gearing up for "decisive military action"—that is, a new round of air strikes and special operations attacks to quell the disorder resulting from the US-orchestrated air campaign that in 2011 destabilized that country. An air strike conducted in late February gave a

hint of what is to come: it killed approximately fifty Islamic State militants (and possibly two Serbian diplomatic captives).

Yemen, Somalia, Syria, and Libya share at least this in common: none of them, nor any of the groups targeted, had a hand in the 9/11 attacks.

Imagine if, within a matter of weeks, China were to launch raids into Vietnam, Thailand, and Taiwan, with punitive action against the Philippines in the offing. Or if Russia, having given a swift kick to Ukraine, Georgia, and Azerbaijan, leaked its plans to teach Poland a lesson for mismanaging its internal affairs. Were Chinese President Xi Jinping or Russian President Vladimir Putin to order such actions, the halls of Congress would ring with fierce denunciations. Members of both houses would jostle for places in front of the TV cameras to condemn the perpetrators for recklessly violating international law and undermining the prospects for world peace. Having no jurisdiction over the actions of other sovereign states, senators and representatives would break down the doors to seize the opportunity to get in their two cents worth. No one would be able to stop them. Who does Xi think he is?! How dare Putin?!

Yet when an American president undertakes analogous actions over which the legislative branch *does* have jurisdiction, members of Congress either yawn or avert their eyes.

In this regard, Republicans are especially egregious offenders. On matters where President Obama is clearly acting in accordance with the Constitution—for example, in nominating someone to fill a vacancy on the Supreme Court—they spare no effort to thwart him, concocting bizarre arguments nowhere found in the Constitution to justify their obstructionism. Yet when this same president cites the 2001 AUMF as the basis for initiating hostilities hither and yon, something that is on the face of it not legal but ludicrous, they passively assent.

Indeed, when Obama in 2015 went so far as to ask Congress to pass a new AUMF addressing the specific threat posed by the Islamic State— that is, essentially rubber-stamping the war he had already launched on his own in Syria and Iraq—the Republican leadership took no action. Looking forward to the day when Obama departs office, Senator Mitch

McConnell with his trademark hypocrisy worried aloud that a new AUMF might constrain his successor. The next president will "have to clean up this mess, created by all of this passivity over the last eight years," the majority leader remarked. In that regard, "an authorization to use military force that ties the president's hands behind his back is not something I would want to do." The proper role of Congress was to get out of the way and give this commander in chief carte blanche so that the next one would enjoy comparably unlimited prerogatives.

Collaborating with a president they roundly despise—implicitly concurring in Obama's questionable claim that "existing statutes [already] provide me with the authority I need" to make war on ISIS—the GOP-controlled Congress thereby transformed the post-9/11 AUMF into what has now become, in effect, a writ of permanent and limitless armed conflict. In Iraq and Syria, for instance, what began as a limited but open-ended campaign of air strikes authorized by President Obama in August 2014 has expanded to include an ever-larger contingent of US trainers and advisers for the Iraqi military, special operations forces conducting raids in both Iraq and Syria, the first new all-US forward fire base in Iraq, and at least five thousand US military personnel now on the ground, a number that continues to grow incrementally.

Remember Obama campaigning back in 2008 and solemnly pledging to end the Iraq War? What he neglected to mention at the time was that he was retaining the prerogative to plunge the country into another Iraq War on his own ticket. So has he now done, with members of Congress passively assenting and the country essentially a prisoner of war.

By now, through its inaction, the legislative branch has, in fact, surrendered the final remnant of authority it retained on matters relating to whether, when, against whom, and for what purpose the United States should go to war. Nothing now remains but to pay the bills, which Congress routinely does, citing a solemn obligation to "support the troops." In this way does the performance of lesser duties provide an excuse for shirking far greater ones.

In military circles, there is a term to describe this type of behavior. It's called cowardice.

26
Milestones
(or What Passes for
Them in Washington)

A Multitrillion-Dollar Bridge to Nowhere
in the Greater Middle East

May 31, 2016

We have it on highest authority: the recent killing of Taliban leader Mullah Akhtar Muhammad Mansour by a US drone strike in Pakistan marks "an important milestone." So the president of the United States has declared, with that claim duly echoed and implicitly endorsed by media commentary—the *New York Times* reporting, for example, that Mansour's death leaves the Taliban leadership "shocked" and "shaken."

But a question remains: A milestone toward what exactly?

Toward victory? Peace? Reconciliation? At the very least, toward the prospect of the violence abating? Merely posing the question is to imply that US military efforts in Afghanistan and elsewhere in the Islamic world serve some larger purpose.

Yet for years now that has not been the case. The assassination of Mansour instead joins a long list of previous milestones, turning points, and landmarks briefly heralded as significant achievements only to prove much less than advertised.

One imagines that Obama himself understands this perfectly well. Just shy of five years ago, he was urging Americans to "take comfort in knowing that the tide of war is receding." In Iraq and Afghanistan, the president insisted, "the light of a secure peace can be seen in the distance." "These long wars," he promised, were finally coming to a "responsible end." We were, that is, finding a way out of Washington's dead-end conflicts in the Greater Middle East.

Who can doubt Obama's sincerity, or question his oft-expressed wish to turn away from war and focus instead on unattended needs here at home? But wishing is the easy part. Reality has remained defiant. Even today, the wars in Iraq and Afghanistan that George W. Bush bequeathed to Obama show no sign of ending.

Like Bush, Obama will bequeath to *his* successor wars he failed to finish. Less remarked upon, he will also pass along to President Clinton or President Trump new wars that are his own handiwork. In Libya, Somalia, Yemen, and several other violence-wracked African nations, the Obama legacy is one of ever-deepening US military involvement. The almost certain prospect of a further accumulation of briefly celebrated and quickly forgotten "milestones" beckons.

During the Obama era, the tide of war has not receded. Instead, Washington finds itself drawn ever deeper into conflicts that, once begun, become interminable—wars for which the vaunted US military has yet to devise a plausible solution.

The Oldest (Also Latest) Solution: Bombs Away

Once upon a time, during the brief, if heady, interval between the end of the Cold War and 9/11 when the United States ostensibly reigned supreme as the world's "sole superpower," Pentagon field manuals credited US forces with the ability to achieve "quick, decisive victory—on and off the battlefield—anywhere in the world and under virtually any conditions." Bold indeed (if not utterly delusional) would be the staff officer willing to pen such words today.

To be sure, the United States military routinely demonstrates astonishing technical prowess—putting a pair of Hellfire missiles through the roof of the taxi in which Mansour was riding, for example. Yet if winning—that is, ending wars on conditions favorable to our side—offers the measure of merit by which to judge a nation's military forces, then when put to the test ours have been found wanting.

Not for lack of trying, of course. In their quest for a formula that might actually accomplish the mission, those charged with directing US military efforts in the Greater Middle East have demonstrated notable flexibility. They have employed overwhelming force and "shock and awe." They have tried regime change (bumping off Saddam Hussein and Muammar Gaddafi, for example) and "decapitation" (assassinating Mansour and a host of other militant leaders, including Osama bin Laden). They have invaded and occupied countries, even giving military-style nation-building a whirl. They have experimented with counterinsurgency and counterterrorism, peacekeeping and humanitarian intervention, retaliatory strikes and preventive war. They have operated overtly, covertly, and through proxies. They have equipped, trained, and advised—and when the beneficiaries of these exertions have folded in the face of the enemy, they have equipped, trained, and advised some more. They have converted American reservists into quasi-regulars, subject to repeated combat tours. In imitation of the corporate world, they have outsourced as well, handing over to profit-oriented "private security" firms functions traditionally performed by soldiers. In short, they have labored doggedly to translate American military power into desired political outcomes.

In this one respect at least, an endless parade of three- and four-star generals exercising command in various theaters over the past several decades have earned high marks. In terms of effort, they deserve an A.

As measured by outcomes, however, they fall well short of a passing grade. However commendable their willingness to cast about for some method that might actually work, they have ended up waging a war of attrition. Strip away the light-at-the-end-of-the-tunnel reassurances regularly heard at Pentagon press briefings or in testimony presented on Capitol Hill, and America's War for the Greater Middle East proceeds on this unspoken assumption: if we kill enough people for a long enough period of time, the other side will eventually give in.

On that score, the prevailing Washington gripe directed at commander in chief Obama is that he has not been willing to kill enough.

Take, for example, a recent *Wall Street Journal* op-ed penned by that literary odd couple, retired General David Petraeus and Brookings Institution analyst Michael O'Hanlon, that appeared under the pugnacious headline "Take the Gloves Off Against the Taliban." To turn around the longest war in American history, Petraeus and O'Hanlon argue, the United States just needs to drop more bombs.

The rules of engagement currently governing air operations in Afghanistan are, in their view, needlessly restrictive. Air power "represents an asymmetric Western advantage, relatively safe to apply, and very effective." (The piece omits any mention of incidents such as the October 2015 destruction of a Doctors Without Borders hospital in the Afghan provincial capital of Kunduz by a US Air Force gunship.) More ordnance will surely produce "some version of victory." The path ahead is clear. "Simply waging the Afghanistan air-power campaign with the vigor we are employing in Iraq and Syria," the authors write with easy assurance, should do the trick.

When armchair generals cite the ongoing US campaign in Iraq and Syria as a model of effectiveness, you know that things must be getting desperate.

Granted, Petraeus and O'Hanlon are on solid ground in noting that as the number of US and NATO troops in Afghanistan has decreased, so, too, has the number of air strikes targeting the Taliban. Back when more allied boots were on the ground, more allied planes were, of course, overhead. And yet the 100,000 close-air-support sorties flown between 2011 and 2015—that's more than one sortie per Taliban fighter—did not, alas, yield "some version of victory."

In short, we've already tried the Petraeus-O'Hanlon take-the-gloves-off approach to defeating the Taliban. It didn't work. With the Afghanistan War's fifteenth anniversary now just around the corner, to suggest that we can bomb our way to victory there is towering nonsense.

In Washington, Big Thinking and Small

Petraeus and O'Hanlon characterize Afghanistan as "the eastern bulwark in our broader Middle East fight." Eastern sinkhole might be a more apt description. Note, by the way, that they have nothing useful to say about the "broader fight" to which they allude. Yet that broader fight—undertaken out of the conviction, still firmly in place today, that American military assertiveness can somehow repair the Greater Middle East—is far more deserving of attention than how to employ very expensive airplanes against insurgents armed with inexpensive Kalashnikovs.

To be fair, in silently passing over the broader fight, Petraeus and O'Hanlon are hardly alone. On this subject no one has much to say—not other stalwarts of the onward-to-victory school, nor officials presently charged with formulating US national security policy, nor members of the Washington commentariat eager to pontificate about almost anything. Worst of all, the subject is one on which each of the prospective candidates for the presidency is mum.

From Secretary of Defense Ashton Carter and Chairman of the Joint Chiefs of Staff General Joseph Dunford on down to the lowliest blogger, opinions about how best to wage a particular campaign in that broader fight are readily available. Need a plan for rolling back the Islamic State? Glad you asked. Concerned about that new ISIS franchise in Libya? Got you covered. Boko Haram? Here's what you need to know. Losing sleep over al-Shabaab? Take heart—big thinkers are on the case.

As to the broader fight itself, however, no one has a clue. Indeed, it seems fair to say that merely defining our aims in that broader fight, much less specifying the means to achieve them, heads the list of issues that people in Washington studiously avoid. Instead, they prattle endlessly about the Taliban and ISIS and Boko Haram and al-Shabaab.

Here's the one thing you need to know about the broader fight: *there is no strategy*. None. Zilch. We're on a multi-trillion-dollar bridge to nowhere, with members of the national security establishment more or less content to see where it leads.

May I suggest that we find ourselves today in what might be called a Khe Sanh moment? Older readers will recall that back in late 1967 and early 1968, in the midst of the Vietnam War, one particular question gripped the national security establishment and those paid to attend to its doings: Can Khe Sanh hold?

Now almost totally forgotten, Khe Sanh was then a battlefield as well known to Americans as Fallujah was to become in our own day. Located in the northern part of South Vietnam, it was the site of a besieged and outnumbered Marine garrison, surrounded by two full enemy divisions. In the eyes of some observers, the outcome of the Vietnam War appeared to hinge on the ability of the Marines there to hold out—to avoid the fate that had befallen the French garrison at Dien Bien Phu slightly more than a decade earlier. For France, the fall of Dien Bien Phu had indeed spelled final defeat in Indochina.

Was history about to repeat itself at Khe Sanh? As it turned out, no . . . and yes.

The Marines did hold—a milestone!—and the United States lost the war anyway.

In retrospect, it seems pretty clear that those responsible for formulating US policy back then fundamentally misconstrued the problem at hand. Rather than worrying about the fate of Khe Sanh, they ought to have been asking questions like these: Is the Vietnam War winnable? Does it even make sense? If not, why are we there? And above all, does no alternative exist to simply pressing on with a policy that shows no signs of success?

Today the United States finds itself in a comparable situation. What to do about the Taliban or ISIS is not a trivial question. Much the same can be said regarding the various other militant organizations with which US forces are engaged in a variety of countries—many now failing states—across the Greater Middle East.

But the question of how to take out organization X or put country Y back together pales in comparison with the other questions that should by now have come to the fore but haven't. Among the most salient are these: Does waging war across a large swath of the Islamic world make sense? When will this broader fight end? What will it cost? Short of reducing large parts of the Middle East to rubble, is that fight winnable in any meaningful sense? Above all, does the world's most powerful nation have no other choice but to persist in pursuing a manifestly futile endeavor?

Try this thought experiment: Imagine the opposing candidates in a presidential campaign each refusing to accept war as the new normal. Imagine them actually taking stock of the broader fight that's been ongoing for decades now. Imagine them offering alternatives to armed conflicts that just drag on and on. Now *that* would be a milestone.

27
Winning

Trump Loves to Do It, but American Generals Have Forgotten How

November 29, 2016

resident-elect Donald Trump's message for the nation's senior military leadership is ambiguously unambiguous. Here is he on *60 Minutes* just days after winning the election.

Trump: "We have some great generals. We have great generals."

Lesley Stahl: "You said you knew more than the generals about ISIS."

Trump: "Well, I'll be honest with you, I probably do because look at the job they've done. OK, look at the job they've done. They haven't done the job."

In reality, Trump, the former reality show host, knows next to nothing about ISIS, one of many gaps in his education that his impending encounter with actual reality is likely to fill. Yet when it comes to America's generals, our president-to-be is onto something. No doubt our three- and four-star officers qualify as "great" in the sense that they mean well, work hard, and are altogether fine men and women. That they have not "done the job," however, is indisputable—at least if their job is to bring America's wars to a timely and successful conclusion.

Trump's unhappy verdict—that the senior US military leadership doesn't know how to win—applies in spades to the two principal conflicts of the post-9/11 era: the Afghanistan War, now in its sixteenth year, and the Iraq War, launched in 2003 and (after a brief hiatus) once more grinding on. Yet the verdict applies equally to lesser theaters of conflict, largely overlooked by the American public, that in recent years have engaged the attention of US forces, a list that would include conflicts in Libya, Somalia, Syria, and Yemen.

Granted, our generals have demonstrated an impressive aptitude for moving pieces around on a dauntingly complex military chessboard. Brigades, battle groups, and squadrons shuttle in and out of various war zones, responding to the needs of the moment. The sheer immensity of the enterprise across the Greater Middle East and Northern Africa—the sorties flown, munitions expended, the seamless deployment and redeployment of thousands of troops over thousands of miles, the vast stockpiles of material positioned, expended, and continuously resupplied—represents a staggering achievement. Measured by these or similar quantifiable outputs, America's military has excelled. No other military establishment in history could have come close to duplicating the logistical feats being performed year in, year out by the armed forces of the United States.

Nor should we overlook the resulting body count. Since the autumn of 2001, something like 370,000 combatants and noncombatants have been killed in the various theaters of operations where US forces have been active. Although modest by twentieth-century standards, this post-9/11 harvest of death is hardly trivial.

Yet in evaluating military operations, it's a mistake to confuse *how much* with *how well*. Only rarely do the outcomes of armed conflicts turn on comparative statistics. Ultimately, the one measure of success that really matters involves achieving war's political purposes. By that standard, victory requires not simply the defeat of the enemy, but accomplishing the nation's stated war aims, and not just in part or temporarily but definitively. Anything less constitutes failure, not to mention utter waste for taxpayers, and for those called upon to fight, it constitutes cause for mourning.

By that standard, having been "at war" for virtually the entire twenty-first century, the United States military is still looking for its first win. And however strong the disinclination to concede that Donald Trump could be right about anything, his verdict on American generalship qualifies as apt.

A Never-Ending Parade of Commanders
for Wars That Never End

That verdict brings to mind three questions. First, with Trump a rare exception, why have the recurring shortcomings of America's military leadership largely escaped notice? Second, to what degree does faulty generalship suffice to explain why actual victory has proven so elusive? Third, to the extent that deficiencies at the top of the military hierarchy bear directly on the outcome of our wars, how might the generals improve their game?

As to the first question, the explanation is quite simple. During protracted wars, traditional standards for measuring generalship lose their salience. Without pertinent standards, there can be no accountability. Absent accountability, failings and weaknesses escape notice. Eventually, what you've become accustomed to seems tolerable. Twenty-first century Americans inured to wars that never end have long since forgotten that bringing such conflicts to a prompt and successful conclusion once defined the very essence of what generals were expected to do.

Senior military officers were presumed to possess unique expertise in designing campaigns and directing engagements. Not found among mere civilians or even among soldiers of lesser rank, this expertise provided the rationale for conferring status and authority on generals.

In earlier eras, the very structure of wars provided a relatively straightforward mechanism for testing such claims to expertise. Events on the battlefield rendered harsh judgments, creating or destroying reputations with brutal efficiency.

Back then, standards employed in evaluating generalship were clear-cut and uncompromising. Those who won battles earned fame, glory, and the gratitude of their countrymen. Those who lost battles got fired or were put out to pasture.

During the Civil War, for example, Lincoln did not need an advanced degree in strategic studies to conclude that Union generals like John Pope, Ambrose Burnside, and Joseph Hooker didn't have what it took to defeat the Army of Northern Virginia. Humiliating defeats sustained by the Army of the Potomac at the Second Battle of Bull Run,

Fredericksburg, and Chancellorsville made that obvious enough. Similarly, the victories Ulysses S. Grant and William T. Sherman gained at Shiloh, at Vicksburg, and in the Chattanooga campaign strongly suggested that here was the team to which the president could entrust the task of bringing the Confederacy to its knees.

Today, public drunkenness, petty corruption, or sexual shenanigans with a subordinate might land generals in hot water. But as long as they avoid egregious misbehavior, senior officers charged with prosecuting America's wars are largely spared judgments of any sort. Trying hard is enough to get a passing grade.

With the country's political leaders and public conditioned to conflicts seemingly destined to drag on for years, if not decades, no one expects the current general in chief in Iraq or Afghanistan to bring things to a successful conclusion. His job is merely to manage the situation until he passes it along to a successor, while duly adding to his collection of personal decorations and perhaps advancing his career.

Today, for example, Army General John Nicholson commands US and allied forces in Afghanistan. He's only the latest in a long line of senior officers to preside over that war, beginning with General Tommy Franks in 2001 and continuing with Generals Mikolashek, Barno, Eikenberry, McNeill, McKiernan, McChrystal, Petraeus, Allen, Dunford, and Campbell. The title carried by these officers changed over time. So, too, did the specifics of their "mission" as Operation Enduring Freedom evolved into Operation Freedom's Sentinel. Yet even as expectations slipped lower and lower, none of the commanders rotating through Kabul delivered. Not a single one has, in our president-elect's concise formulation, "done the job." Indeed, it's increasingly difficult to know what that job is, apart from preventing the Taliban from quite literally toppling the government.

In Iraq, meanwhile, Army Lieutenant General Stephen Townsend currently serves as the—count 'em—ninth American to command US and coalition forces in that country since the George W. Bush administration ordered the invasion in 2003. The first in that line (once again), General Tommy Franks, overthrew the Saddam Hussein regime and thereby broke Iraq. The next five, Generals Sanchez, Casey, Petraeus, Odierno, and Austin, labored for eight years to put it back together again.

At the end of 2011, President Obama declared that they had done just that and terminated the US military occupation. The Islamic State soon exposed Obama's claim as specious when its militants put a US-trained Iraqi army to flight and annexed large swathes of that country's territory. Following in the footsteps of his immediate predecessors Generals James Terry and Sean MacFarland, General Townsend now shoulders the task of trying to restore Iraq's status as a more or less genuinely sovereign state. He directs what the Pentagon calls Operation Inherent Resolve, dating from June 2014, the follow-on to Operation New Dawn (September 2010–December 2011), which was itself the successor to Operation Iraqi Freedom (March 2003–August 2010).

When and how Inherent Resolve will conclude is difficult to forecast. We can, however, say with some confidence that with the end nowhere in sight, General Townsend won't be its last commander. Other generals are waiting in the wings with their own careers to polish. As in Kabul, the parade of US military commanders through Baghdad will continue.

For some readers, this listing of mostly forgotten names and dates may have a soporific effect. Yet it should also drive home Trump's point. The United States may today have the world's most powerful and capable military—so at least we are constantly told. Yet the record shows that it does not have a corps of senior officers who know how to translate capability into successful outcomes.

Draining Which Swamp?

That brings us to the second question: Even if commander in chief Trump were somehow able to identify modern-day equivalents of Grant and Sherman to implement his war plans, secret or otherwise, would they deliver victory?

On that score, we would do well to entertain doubts. Although senior officers charged with running recent American wars have not exactly covered themselves in glory, it doesn't follow that their shortcomings offer the sole or even a principal explanation for why those wars have yielded such disappointing results. The truth is that some wars aren't winnable and shouldn't be fought.

So, yes, Trump's critique of American generalship possesses merit, but whether he knows it or not, the question truly demanding his attention as the incoming commander in chief isn't, Who should I hire (or fire) to fight my wars? Instead, far more urgent is, Does further war promise to solve any of my problems?

One mark of a successful business executive is knowing when to cut your losses. It's also the mark of a successful statesman. Trump claims to be the former. Whether his putative business savvy will translate into the world of statecraft remains to be seen. Early signs are not promising.

As a candidate, Trump vowed to "defeat radical Islamic terrorism," destroy ISIS, "decimate al-Qaeda," and "starve funding for Iran-backed Hamas and Hezbollah." Those promises imply a significant escalation of what Americans used to call the Global War on Terrorism.

Toward that end, the incoming administration may well revive some aspects of the George W. Bush playbook, including repopulating the military prison at Guantanamo Bay, Cuba, and, "if it's so important to the American people," reinstituting torture. The Trump administration will at least consider reimposing sanctions on countries like Iran. It may aggressively exploit the offensive potential of cyber-weapons, betting that America's cyber-defenses will hold.

Yet President Trump is also likely to double down on the use of conventional military force. In that regard, his promise to "quickly and decisively bomb the hell out of ISIS" offers a hint of what is to come. His appointment of the uber-hawkish Lieutenant General Michael Flynn as his national security adviser and his rumored selection of retired Marine Corps General James ("Mad Dog") Mattis as defense secretary suggest that he means what he says. In sum, a Trump administration seems unlikely to reexamine the conviction that the problems roiling the Greater Middle East will someday, somehow yield to a US-imposed military solution. Indeed, in the face of massive evidence to the contrary, that conviction will deepen, with genuinely ironic implications for the Trump presidency.

In the immediate wake of 9/11, George W. Bush concocted a fantasy of American soldiers liberating oppressed Afghans and Iraqis and thereby "draining the swamp" that served to incubate anti-Western terrorism. The results achieved proved beyond disappointing, while the costs exacted in terms of lives and dollars squandered were painful indeed. Incrementally, with the passage of time, many Americans concluded that perhaps the swamp most in need of attention was not on the far side of the planet but much closer at hand—right in the imperial city nestled alongside the Potomac River.

To a very considerable extent, Trump defeated Hillary Clinton, preferred candidate of the establishment, because he advertised himself as just the guy disgruntled Americans could count on to drain that swamp.

Yet what too few of those Americans appreciate, even today is that war created that swamp in the first place. War empowers Washington. It centralizes. It provides a rationale for federal authorities to accumulate and exercise new powers. It makes government bigger and more intrusive. It lubricates the machinery of waste, fraud, and abuse that causes tens of billions of taxpayer dollars to vanish every year. When it comes to sustaining the swamp, nothing works better than war.

Were Trump really intent on draining that swamp—if he genuinely seeks to "Make America Great Again"—then he would extricate the United States from war. His liquidation of Trump University, which was to higher education what Freedom's Sentinel and Inherent Resolve are to modern warfare, provides a potentially instructive precedent for how to proceed.

But don't hold your breath on that one. All signs indicate that, in one fashion or another, our combative next president will perpetuate the wars he's inheriting. Trump may fancy that, as a veteran of *Celebrity Apprentice* (but not of military service), he possesses a special knack for spotting the next Grant or Sherman. But acting on that impulse will merely replenish the swamp in the Greater Middle East along with the one in Washington. And soon enough, those who elected him with expectations of seeing the much-despised establishment dismantled will realize that they've been had.

Which brings us, finally, to that third question: To the extent that deficiencies at the top of the military hierarchy do affect the outcome of wars, what can be done to fix the problem?

The most expeditious approach? Purge all currently serving three- and four-star officers; then, make a precondition for promotion to those ranks confinement in a reeducation camp run by Iraq and Afghanistan war amputees, with a curriculum designed by Veterans for Peace. Graduation should require each student to submit an essay reflecting on these words of wisdom from U. S. Grant himself: "There never was a time when, in my opinion, some way could not be found to prevent the drawing of the sword."

True, such an approach may seem a bit draconian. But this is no time for half measures—as even Trump may eventually recognize.

28
Forbidden Questions?

Twenty-Four Key Issues That Neither the Washington Elite nor the Media Consider Worth Their Bother

May 7, 2017

onald Trump's election has elicited impassioned affirmations of a renewed commitment to unvarnished truth-telling from the prestige media. The common theme: you know you can't trust *him*, but trust *us* to keep dogging him on your behalf. The *New York Times* has even unveiled a portentous new promotional slogan: "The truth is now more important than ever."

For its part, the *Washington Post* grimly warns that "democracy dies in darkness," and is offering itself as a source of illumination now that the rotund figure of the forty-fifth president has produced the political equivalent of a total eclipse of the sun. Meanwhile, National Public Radio fundraising campaigns are sounding an increasingly panicky note: give, listener, lest you be personally responsible for the demise of the republic that we are bravely fighting to save from extinction.

If only it were so. How wonderful it would be if President Trump's ascendancy had coincided with a revival of hard-hitting, deep-dive, no-holds-barred American journalism. Alas, that's hardly the case. True, the big media outlets are demonstrating both energy and enterprise in exposing the ineptitude, inconsistency, and dubious ethical standards, as well as outright lies and fake news, that are already emerging as Trump era signatures. That said, pointing out that the president has (again) uttered a falsehood, claimed credit for a nonexistent achievement, or abandoned some position to which he had previously sworn fealty requires something less than the sleuthing talents of a Sherlock Holmes. As for beating up on poor Sean Spicer for his latest sequence of gaffes—well, that's more akin to sadism than reporting.

Apart from a commendable determination to discomfit Trump and members of his inner circle (select military figures excepted, at least for now), journalism remains pretty much what it was prior to November 8 of last year: personalities built up only to be torn down; fads and novelties discovered, celebrated, then mocked; "extraordinary" stories of ordinary people granted fifteen seconds of fame only to once again be consigned to oblivion—all served with a side dish of that day's quota of suffering, devastation, and carnage. These remain journalism's stock-in-trade. As practiced in the United States, with certain honorable (and hence unprofitable) exceptions, journalism remains superficial, voyeuristic, and governed by the attention span of a two-year-old.

As a result, all those editors, reporters, columnists, and talking heads who characterize their labors as "now more important than ever" ill serve the public they profess to inform and enlighten. Rather than clearing the air, they befog it further. If anything, the media's current obsession with Trump—his every utterance or tweet treated as "breaking news!"—just provides one additional excuse for highlighting trivia, while slighting issues that deserve far more attention than they currently receive.

To illustrate the point, let me cite some examples of national security issues that presently receive short shrift or are ignored altogether by those parts of the fourth estate said to help set the nation's political agenda. To put it another way: Hey, Big Media, here are two dozen matters to which you're not giving faintly adequate thought and attention:

1. *Accomplishing the "mission"*: Since the immediate aftermath of World War II, the United States has been committed to defending key allies in Europe and East Asia. Not long thereafter, US security guarantees were extended to the Middle East as well. Under what circumstances can Americans expect nations in these regions to assume responsibility for managing their own affairs? To put it another way, when (if ever) might US forces actually come home? And if it is incumbent

upon the United States to police vast swaths of the planet in perpetuity,
how should momentous changes in the international order—the rise of
China, for example, or accelerating climate change—affect the US approach to doing so?

2. *American military supremacy*: The United States military is undoubtedly the world's finest. It's also far and away the most generously
funded, with policymakers offering US troops no shortage of opportunities to practice their craft. So why doesn't this great military ever win
anything? Or put another way, why in recent decades have those forces
been unable to accomplish Washington's stated wartime objectives?
Why has the now fifteen-year-old War on Terrorism failed to result in
even a single real success anywhere in the Greater Middle East? Could
it be that we've taken the wrong approach? What should we be doing
differently?

3. *America's empire of bases*: The US military today garrisons the
planet in a fashion without historical precedent. Successive administrations, regardless of party, justify and perpetuate this policy by insisting that positioning US forces in distant lands fosters peace, stability,
and security. In the present century, however, perpetuating this practice
has visibly had the opposite effect. In the eyes of many of those called
upon to "host" American bases, the permanent presence of such forces
smacks of occupation. They resist. Why should US policymakers expect
otherwise?

4. *Supporting the troops*: In present-day America, expressing reverence for those who serve in uniform is something akin to a religious
obligation. Everyone professes to cherish America's "warriors." Yet such
bountiful, if superficial, expressions of regard camouflage a growing gap
between those who serve and those who applaud from the sidelines.
Our present-day military system, based on the misnamed all-volunteer
force, is neither democratic nor effective. Why has discussion and debate about its deficiencies not found a place among the nation's political
priorities?

5. *Prerogatives of the commander in chief*: Are there any military actions that the president of the United States may not order on his own

authority? If so, what are they? Bit by bit, decade by decade, Congress has abdicated its assigned role in authorizing war. Today, it merely rubber-stamps what presidents decide to do (or simply stays mum). Who does this deference to an imperial presidency benefit? Have US policies thereby become more prudent, enlightened, and successful?

6. *Assassin in chief:* A policy of assassination, secretly implemented under the aegis of the CIA during the early Cold War, yielded few substantive successes. When the secrets were revealed, however, the US government suffered considerable embarrassment, so much so that presidents foreswore politically motivated murder. After 9/11, however, Washington returned to the assassination business in a big way and on a global scale, using drones. Today, the only secret is the sequence of names on the current presidential hit list, euphemistically known as the White House "disposition matrix." But does assassination actually advance US interests (or does it merely recruit replacements for the terrorists it liquidates)? How can we measure its costs, whether direct or indirect? What dangers and vulnerabilities does this practice invite?

7. *The war formerly known as the "Global War on Terrorism":* What precisely is Washington's present strategy for defeating violent jihadism? What sequence of planned actions or steps is expected to yield success? If no such strategy exists, why is that the case? How is it that the absence of strategy—not to mention an agreed upon definition of "success"—doesn't even qualify for discussion here?

8. *The campaign formerly known as Operation Enduring Freedom:* The conflict commonly referred to as the Afghanistan War is now the longest in US history, having lasted longer than the Civil War, World War I, and World War II combined. What is the Pentagon's plan for concluding that conflict? When might Americans expect it to end? On what terms?

9. *The Gulf:* Americans once believed that their prosperity and way of life depended on having assured access to Persian Gulf oil. Today, that is no longer the case. The United States is once more an oil exporter. Available and accessible reserves of oil and natural gas in North America are far greater than was once believed. Yet the assumption that

the Persian Gulf still qualifies as crucial to American national security persists in Washington. Why?

10. *Hyping terrorism*: Each year terrorist attacks kill far fewer Americans than do auto accidents, drug overdoses, or even lightning strikes. Yet in the allocation of government resources, preventing terrorist attacks takes precedence over preventing all three of the others combined. Why is that?

11. *Deaths that matter and deaths that don't*: Why do terrorist attacks that kill a handful of Europeans command infinitely more American attention than do terrorist attacks that kill far larger numbers of Arabs? A terrorist attack that kills citizens of France or Belgium elicits from the United States heartfelt expressions of sympathy and solidarity. A terrorist attack that kills Egyptians or Iraqis elicits shrugs. Why the difference? To what extent does race provide the answer to that question?

12. *Israeli nukes*: What purpose is served by indulging the pretense that Israel does not have nuclear weapons?

13. *Peace in the Holy Land*: What purpose is served by indulging illusions that a "two-state solution" offers a plausible resolution to the Israeli-Palestinian conflict? As remorselessly as white settlers once encroached upon territory inhabited by Native American tribes, Israeli settlers expand their presence in the occupied territories year by year. As they do, the likelihood of creating a viable Palestinian state becomes ever more improbable. To pretend otherwise is the equivalent of thinking that one day President Trump might prefer the rusticity of Camp David to the glitz of Mar-a-Lago.

14. *Merchandizing death*: When it comes to arms sales, there is no need to "Make America Great Again." The US ranks number one by a comfortable margin, with longtime allies Saudi Arabia and Israel leading recipients of those arms. Each year, the Saudis (per capita gross domestic product $20,000) purchase hundreds of millions of dollars of US weapons. Israel (per capita gross domestic product $38,000) gets several billion dollars worth of such weaponry annually courtesy of the American taxpayer. If the Saudis pay for US arms, why shouldn't the Israelis? They can certainly afford to do so.

15. *Our friends the Saudis (I)*: Fifteen of the nineteen hijackers on September 11, 2001, were Saudis. What does that fact signify?

16. *Our friends the Saudis (II)*: If indeed Saudi Arabia and Iran are competing to determine which nation will enjoy the upper hand in the Persian Gulf, why should the United States favor Saudi Arabia? In what sense do Saudi values align more closely with American values than do Iranian ones?

17. *Our friends the Pakistanis*: Pakistan behaves like a rogue state. It is a nuclear weapons proliferator. It supports the Taliban. For years, it provided sanctuary to Osama bin Laden. Yet US policymakers treat Pakistan as if it were an ally. Why? In what ways do US and Pakistani interests or values coincide? If there are none, why not say so?

18. *Free-loading Europeans*: Why can't Europe, "whole and free," its population and economy considerably larger than Russia's, defend itself? It's altogether commendable that US policymakers should express support for Polish independence and root for the Baltic republics. But how does it make sense for the United States to care more about the well-being of people living in Eastern Europe than do people living in Western Europe?

19. *The mother of all "special relationships"*: The United States and the United Kingdom have a "special relationship" dating from the days of Franklin Roosevelt and Winston Churchill. Apart from keeping the Public Broadcasting Service supplied with costume dramas and stories featuring eccentric detectives, what is the rationale for that partnership today? Why should US relations with Great Britain, a fading power, be any more "special" than its relations with a rising power like India? Why should the bonds connecting Americans and Britons be any more intimate than those connecting Americans and Mexicans? Why does a republic now approaching the 241st anniversary of its independence still need a "mother country"?

20. *The old nuclear disarmament razzmatazz*: American presidents routinely cite their hope for the worldwide elimination of nuclear weapons. Yet the US maintains nuclear strike forces on full alert, has embarked on a costly and comprehensive trillion-dollar modernization of

its nuclear arsenal, and even refuses to adopt a no-first-use posture when it comes to nuclear war. The truth is that the United States will consider surrendering its nukes only after every other nation on the planet has done so first. How does American nuclear hypocrisy affect the prospects for global nuclear disarmament or even simply for the nonproliferation of such weaponry?

21. *Double standards (I)*: American policymakers take it for granted that their country's sphere of influence is global, which, in turn, provides the rationale for the deployment of US military forces to scores of countries. Yet when it comes to nations like China, Russia, or Iran, Washington takes the position that spheres of influence are obsolete and a concept that should no longer be applicable to the practice of statecraft. So Chinese, Russian, and Iranian forces should remain where they belong—in China, Russia, and Iran. To stray beyond that constitutes a provocation, as well as a threat to global peace and order. Why should these other nations play by American rules? Why shouldn't similar rules apply to the United States?

22. *Double standards (II)*: Washington claims that it supports and upholds international law. Yet when international law gets in the way of what American policymakers want to do, they disregard it. They start wars, violate the sovereignty of other nations, and authorize agents of the United States to kidnap, imprison, torture, and kill. They do these things with impunity, only forced to reverse their actions on the rare occasions when US courts find them illegal. Why should other powers treat international norms as sacrosanct since the United States does so only when convenient?

23. *Double standards (III)*: The United States condemns the indiscriminate killing of civilians in wartime. Yet over the last three-quarters of a century, it killed civilians regularly and often on a massive scale. By what logic, since the 1940s, has the killing of Germans, Japanese, Koreans, Vietnamese, Laotians, Cambodians, Afghans, and others by US air power been any less reprehensible than the Syrian government's use of "barrel bombs" to kill Syrians today? On what basis should Americans accept Pentagon claims that, when civilians are killed these days by

US forces, the acts are invariably accidental, whereas Syrian forces kill civilians intentionally and out of malice? Why exclude incompetence or the fog of war as explanations? And why, for instance, does the United States regularly gloss over or ignore altogether the noncombatants that Saudi forces (with US assistance) are routinely killing in Yemen?

24. *Moral obligations*: When confronted with some egregious violation of human rights, members of the chattering classes frequently express an urge for the United States to "do something." Holocaust analogies sprout like dandelions. Newspaper columnists recycle copy first used when Cambodians were slaughtering other Cambodians en masse or whenever Hutus and Tutsis went at it. Proponents of action— typically advocating military intervention—argue that the United States has a moral obligation to aid those victimized by injustice or cruelty anywhere on earth. But what determines the pecking order of such moral obligations? Which comes first, a responsibility to redress the crimes of others or a responsibility to redress crimes committed by Americans? Who has a greater claim to US assistance, Syrians suffering today under the boot of Bashar al-Assad, or Iraqis, their country shattered by the US invasion of 2003? Where do the Vietnamese fit into the queue? How about the Filipinos, brutally denied independence and forcibly incorporated into an American empire as the nineteenth century ended? Or African Americans, whose ancestors were enslaved? Or, for that matter, dispossessed and disinherited Native Americans? Is there a statute of limitations that applies to moral obligations? And if not, shouldn't those who have waited longest for justice or reparations receive priority attention?

Let me suggest that any one of these two dozen issues—none seriously covered, discussed, or debated in the American media or in the political mainstream—bears more directly on the well-being of the United States and our prospects for avoiding global conflict than anything Trump may have said or done during his first one hundred days as president. Collectively, they define the core of the national security challenges that presently confront this country, even as they languish on the periphery of American politics.

How much damage Trump's presidency wreaks before it ends remains to be seen. Yet he himself is a transient phenomenon. To allow his pratfalls and shenanigans to divert attention from matters sure to persist when he finally departs the stage is to make a grievous error. It may well be that, as the *Times* insists, the truth is now more important than ever. If so, finding the truth requires looking in the right places and asking the right questions.

29
Autopilot Wars

Sixteen Years, but Who's Counting?

October 8, 2017

onsider, if you will, these two indisputable facts. First, the United States is today more or less permanently engaged in hostilities in not one faraway place, but at least seven. Count 'em: Afghanistan, Iraq, Syria, Pakistan, Somalia, Yemen, and Libya. Second, the vast majority of the American people could not care less.

Nor can it be said that we don't care because we don't know. True, government authorities withhold certain aspects of ongoing military operations or release only details that they find convenient. Yet information describing what US forces are doing (and where) is readily available, even if buried in recent months by barrages of presidential tweets. Here, for anyone interested, are press releases issued by United States Central Command for just one recent week:

September 19: "Military airstrikes continue against ISIS terrorists in Syria and Iraq"

September 20: "Military airstrikes continue against ISIS terrorists in Syria and Iraq";

"Iraqi Security Forces begin Hawijah offensive"

September 21: "Military airstrikes continue against ISIS terrorists in Syria and Iraq"

September 22: "Military airstrikes continue against ISIS terrorists in Syria and Iraq"

September 23: "Military airstrikes continue against ISIS terrorists in Syria and Iraq";

224

"Operation Inherent Resolve Casualty"

September 25: "Military airstrikes continue against ISIS terrorists in Syria and Iraq"

September 26: "Military airstrikes continue against ISIS terrorists in Syria and Iraq"

Ever since the United States launched its War on Terrorism, oceans of military press releases have poured forth. And those are just for starters. To provide updates on the US military's various ongoing campaigns, generals, admirals, and high-ranking defense officials regularly testify before congressional committees or brief members of the press. From the field, journalists offer updates that fill in at least some of the details—on civilian casualties, for example—that government authorities prefer not to disclose. Contributors to newspaper op-ed pages and "experts" booked by network and cable TV news shows, including passels of retired military officers, provide analysis. Trailing behind come books and documentaries that put things in a broader perspective.

But here's the truth of it: none of it matters.

Like traffic jams or robocalls, war has fallen into the category of things that Americans may not welcome, but have learned to live with. In twenty-first-century America, war is not that big a deal.

While serving as defense secretary in the 1960s, Robert McNamara once mused that the "greatest contribution" of the Vietnam War might have been to make it possible for the United States "to go to war without the necessity of arousing the public ire." With regard to the conflict once widely referred to as McNamara's War, his claim proved grotesquely premature. Yet a half-century later, his wish has become reality.

Why do Americans today show so little interest in the wars waged in their name and at least nominally on their behalf? Why, as our wars drag on and on, doesn't the disparity between effort expended and benefits accrued arouse more than passing curiosity or mild expressions of dismay? Why, in short, don't we give a [*expletive deleted*]?

Perhaps just posing such a question propels us instantly into the realm of the unanswerable, like trying to figure out why people idolize Justin Bieber, shoot birds, or watch golf on television.

Without any expectation of actually piercing our collective ennui, let me take a stab at explaining why we don't give a @#$%&! Here are eight distinctive but mutually reinforcing explanations, offered in a sequence that begins with the blindingly obvious and ends with the more speculative.

Americans don't attend all that much to ongoing American wars because:

1. *US casualty rates are low.* By using proxies and contractors, and relying heavily on airpower, America's war managers have been able to keep a tight lid on the number of US troops being killed and wounded. Thus far in 2017, for example, a grand total of eleven American soldiers have been lost in Afghanistan—about equal to the number of shooting deaths in Chicago over the course of a typical week. True, in Afghanistan, Iraq, and other countries where the US is engaged in hostilities, whether directly or indirectly, plenty of people who are not Americans are being killed and maimed. (The estimated number of Iraqi civilians killed this year alone exceeds twelve thousand.) But those casualties have next to no political salience as far as the United States is concerned. As long as they don't impede US military operations, they literally don't count (and generally aren't counted).

2. *The true costs of Washington's wars go untabulated.* In a famous speech, dating from early in his presidency, Eisenhower said that "Every gun that is made, every warship launched, every rocket fired signifies, in the final sense, a theft from those who hunger and are not fed, those who are cold and are not clothed." Dollars spent on weaponry, Ike insisted, translated directly into schools, hospitals, homes, highways, and power plants that would go unbuilt. "This is not a way of life at all, in any true sense," he continued. "[I]t is humanity hanging from a cross of iron." More than six decades later, Americans have long since accommodated themselves to that cross of iron. Many actually see it as a boon, a source of corporate profits, jobs, and, of course, campaign contributions. As such, they avert their eyes from the opportunity costs of our never-ending wars. The dollars expended pursuant to our post-9/11 conflicts will ultimately number in the multi-trillions. Imagine the

benefits of investing such sums in upgrading the nation's aging infrastructure. Yet don't count on congressional leaders, other politicians, or
just about anyone else to pursue that connection.

3. *On matters related to war, American citizens have opted out.* Others have made the point so frequently that it's the equivalent of hearing
"Rudolph the Red-Nosed Reindeer" at Christmastime. Even so, it bears
repeating: the American people have defined their obligation to "support the troops" in the narrowest imaginable terms, ensuring above all
that such support requires absolutely no sacrifice on their part. Members of Congress abet this civic apathy, while also taking steps to insulate themselves from responsibility. In effect, citizens and their elected
representatives in Washington agree that supporting the troops means
deferring to the commander in chief, without inquiring about whether
what he has the troops doing makes the slightest sense. Yes, we set down
our beers long enough to applaud those in uniform and boo those who
decline to participate in mandatory rituals of patriotism. What we don't
do is demand anything remotely approximating actual accountability.

4. *Terrorism gets hyped and hyped and hyped some more.* While international terrorism isn't a trivial problem (and wasn't for decades before
9/11), it comes nowhere close to posing an existential threat to the United
States. Indeed, other threats, notably the impact of climate change, constitute a far greater danger to the well-being of Americans. Worried about
the safety of your children or grandchildren? The opioid epidemic constitutes an infinitely greater danger than "Islamic radicalism." Yet having been sold a bill of goods about a "war on terror" that is essential for
"keeping America safe," mere citizens are easily persuaded that scattering
US troops throughout the Islamic world while dropping bombs on designated evildoers is helping win the former while guaranteeing the latter.
To question that proposition becomes tantamount to suggesting that God
might not have given Moses two stone tablets after all.

5. *Blather crowds out substance.* When it comes to foreign policy,
American public discourse is—not to put too fine a point on it—vacu-
ous, insipid, and mindlessly repetitive. William Safire of the *New York
Times* once characterized American political rhetoric as BOMFOG,

with those running for high office relentlessly touting the Brotherhood of Man and the Fatherhood of God. Ask a politician, Republican or Democrat, to expound on this country's role in the world, and then brace yourself for some variant of WOSFAD, as the speaker insists that it is incumbent upon the World's Only Superpower to spread Freedom and Democracy. Terms like *leadership* and *indispensable* are introduced, along with warnings about the dangers of *isolationism* and *appeasement*, embellished with ominous references to *Munich*. Such grandiose posturing makes it unnecessary to probe too deeply into the actual origins and purposes of American wars, past or present, or assess the likelihood of ongoing wars ending in some approximation of actual success. Cheerleading displaces serious thought.

6. *Besides, we're too busy.* Think of this as a corollary to point five. Even if the present-day American political scene included figures like Senators Robert La Follette or J. William Fulbright, who long ago warned against the dangers of militarizing US policy, Americans may not retain a capacity to attend to such critiques. Responding to the demands of the Information Age is not, it turns out, conducive to deep reflection. We live in an era (so we are told) when frantic multitasking has become a sort of duty and when being overscheduled is almost obligatory. Our attention span shrinks and with it our time horizon. The matters we attend to are those that happened just hours or minutes ago. Yet like the great solar eclipse of 2017—hugely significant and instantly forgotten—those matters will, within another few minutes or hours, be superseded by some other development that briefly captures our attention. As a result, a dwindling number of Americans—those not compulsively checking Facebook pages and Twitter accounts—have the time or inclination to ponder questions like, When will the Afghanistan War end? Why has it lasted almost sixteen years? Why doesn't the finest fighting force in history actually win? Can't package an answer in 140 characters or a thirty-second made-for-TV sound bite? Well, then, slowpoke, don't expect anyone to attend to what you have to say.

7. *Anyway, the next president will save us.* At regular intervals, Americans indulge in the fantasy that, if we just install the right person

in the White House, all will be well. Ambitious politicians are quick to exploit this expectation. Presidential candidates struggle to differentiate themselves from their competitors, but all of them promise in one way or another to wipe the slate clean and "Make America Great Again." Ignoring the historical record of promises broken or unfulfilled, and presidents who turn out not to be deities but flawed human beings, Americans—members of the media above all—pretend to take all this seriously. Campaigns become longer, more expensive, more circus-like, and ever less substantial. One might think that the election of Donald Trump would prompt a downward revision in the exalted expectations of presidents putting things right. Instead, especially in the anti-Trump camp, getting rid of Trump himself (Collusion! Corruption! Obstruction! Impeachment!) has become the overriding imperative, with little attention given to restoring the balance intended by the framers of the Constitution. The irony of Trump perpetuating wars that he once roundly criticized and then handing the conduct of those wars to generals devoid of ideas for ending them almost entirely escapes notice.

8. *Our culturally progressive military has largely immunized itself from criticism.* As recently as the 1990s, the US military establishment aligned itself with the retrograde side of the culture wars. Who can forget the gays-in-the-military controversy that rocked Bill Clinton's administration during his first weeks in office, as senior military leaders publicly denounced their commander in chief? Those days are long gone. Culturally, the armed forces have moved left. Today, the services go out of their way to project an image of tolerance and a commitment to equality on all matters related to race, gender identity, and sexual preference. So when President Trump announced his opposition to transgendered persons serving in the armed forces, tweeting that the military "cannot be burdened with the tremendous medical costs and disruption that transgender in the military would entail," senior officers politely but firmly disagreed and pushed back. Given the ascendency of cultural issues near the top of the US political agenda, the military's embrace of diversity helps to insulate it from criticism and from being called to account for a less than sterling performance in waging wars. Put simply,

critics who in an earlier day might have blasted military leaders for their inability to bring wars to a successful conclusion hold their fire. Having women graduate from Ranger School or command Marines in combat more than compensates for not winning.

A collective indifference to war has become an emblem of contemporary America. But don't expect your neighbors down the street or the editors of the *New York Times* to lose any sleep over that fact. Even to notice it would require them—and us—to care.

30
Still Waiting

A Harvey Weinstein Moment for America's Wars?

December 10, 2017

What makes a Harvey Weinstein moment? The now-disgraced Hollywood mogul is hardly the first powerful man to stand accused of having abused women. The Harveys who preceded Harvey himself are legion, their prominence matching or exceeding his own and the misdeeds with which they were charged at least as reprehensible.

In the relatively recent past, a roster of prominent offenders would include Bill Clinton, Bill Cosby, Roger Ailes, Bill O'Reilly, and, of course, Donald Trump. Throw in various jocks, maestros, senior military officers, members of the professoriate and you end up with quite a list. Yet in virtually all such cases, the alleged transgressions were treated as instances of individual misconduct, egregious perhaps but possessing at best transitory political resonance.

All that, though, was pre-Harvey. As far as male sexual malfeasance is concerned, we might compare Weinstein's epic fall from grace to the stock market crash of 1929: one week it's the anything-goes Roaring Twenties, the next we're smack dab in a Great Depression.

How profound is the change? Up here in Massachusetts where I live, we've spent the past year marking John F. Kennedy's one-hundredth birthday. If Kennedy were still around to join in the festivities, it would be as a Class A sex offender who used his position of power to prey upon young women. Rarely in American history has the cultural landscape shifted so quickly or so radically.

In our post-Harvey world, men charged with sexual misconduct are guilty until proven innocent, all crimes are capital offenses, and there exists no statute of limitations. Once a largely empty corporate slogan, "zero tolerance" has become a battle cry.

All of this serves as a reminder that, on some matters at least, the American people retain an admirable capacity for outrage. We *can* distinguish between the tolerable and the intolerable. And we *can* demand accountability of powerful individuals and institutions.

Everything They Need to Win (Again!)

What's puzzling is why that capacity for outrage and demand for accountability doesn't extend to our now well-established penchant for waging war across much of the planet.

In no way would I wish to minimize the pain, suffering, and humiliation of the women preyed upon by the various reprobates now getting their belated comeuppance. But to judge from published accounts, the women (and in some cases, men) abused by Weinstein, Louis C.K., Mark Halperin, Leon Wieseltier, Kevin Spacey, Al Franken, Charlie Rose, Matt Lauer, Garrison Keillor, my West Point classmate Judge Roy Moore, and their compadres at least managed to survive their encounters. None of the perpetrators are charged with having committed murder. No one died.

Compare their culpability to that of the high-ranking officials who have presided over or promoted this country's various military misadventures of the present century. Those wars have, of course, resulted in hundreds of thousands of deaths and will ultimately cost American taxpayers many trillions of dollars. Nor have those costly military efforts eliminated "terrorism," as President George W. Bush promised back when today's GIs were still in diapers.

Bush told us that, through war, the United States would spread freedom and democracy. Instead, our wars have sown disorder and instability, creating failing or failed states across the Greater Middle East and Africa. In their wake have sprung up ever more, not fewer, jihadist groups, while acts of terror are soaring globally. These are indisputable facts.

It discomfits me to reiterate this mournful litany of truths. I feel a bit like the doctor telling the lifelong smoker with stage-four lung cancer that an addiction to cigarettes is adversely affecting his health. His mute response: I know and I don't care. Nothing the doc says is going to budge the smoker from his habit. You go through the motions, but wonder why.

In a similar fashion, war has become a habit to which the United States is addicted. Except for the terminally distracted, most of us know that. We also know—*we cannot not know*—that, in places like Afghanistan and Iraq, US forces have been unable to accomplish their assigned mission, despite more than sixteen years of fighting in the former and more than a decade in the latter.

It's not exactly a good news story, to put it mildly. So forgive me for saying it, but most of us simply don't care, which means that we continue to allow a free hand to those who preside over those wars, while treating with respect the views of pundits and media personalities who persist in promoting them. What's past doesn't count; we prefer to sustain the pretense that tomorrow is pregnant with possibilities. Victory lies just around the corner.

By way of example, consider a recent article in *U.S. News and World Report*. The headline: "Victory or Failure in Afghanistan: 2018 Will Be the Deciding Year." The title suggests a balance absent from the text that follows, which reads like a Pentagon press release. Here in its entirety is the nut graf (my own emphasis added):

> Armed with a *new strategy* and renewed support from old allies, the Trump administration now believes it has *everything it needs to win* the war in Afghanistan. Top military advisers all the way up to Defense Secretary Jim Mattis say they can accomplish what two previous administrations and multiple troop surges could not: the *defeat of the Taliban* by Western-backed local forces, a negotiated peace and the establishment of a popularly supported government in Kabul capable of keeping the country from once again becoming a haven to any terrorist group.

Now if you buy this, you'll believe that Harvey Weinstein has learned his lesson and can be trusted to interview young actresses while wearing his bathrobe.

For starters, there is no "new strategy." Trump's generals, apparently with a nod from their putative boss, are merely modifying the old "strategy," which was itself an outgrowth of previous strategies tried, found wanting, and eventually discarded before being rebranded and eventually recycled.

Short of using nuclear weapons, US forces fighting in Afghanistan over the past decade and a half have experimented with just about every approach imaginable: invasion, regime change, occupation, nation-building, pacification, decapitation, counterterrorism, and counterinsurgency, not to mention various surges, differing in scope and duration. We have had a big troop presence and a smaller one, more bombing and less, restrictive rules of engagement and permissive ones. In the military equivalent of throwing in the kitchen sink, a US Special Operations Command four-engine prop plane recently deposited the largest nonnuclear weapon in the American arsenal on a cave complex in eastern Afghanistan. Although that MOAB made a big boom, no offer of enemy surrender materialized.

In truth, US commanders have quietly shelved any expectations of achieving an actual victory—traditionally defined as "imposing your will on the enemy"—in favor of a more modest conception of success. In year XVII of America's Afghanistan War, the hope is that training, equipping, advising, and motivating Afghans to assume responsibility for defending their country may someday allow American forces and their coalition partners to depart. By 2015, that project, building up the Afghan security forces, had already absorbed at least $65 billion in US taxpayer dollars. And under the circumstances, consider that a mere down payment.

According to General John Nicholson, our seventeenth commander in Kabul since 2001, the efforts devised and implemented by his many predecessors have resulted in a "stalemate"—a generous interpretation given that the Taliban presently controls more territory than it has held since the US invasion. Officers no less capable than Nicholson himself, David Petraeus and Stanley McChrystal among them, didn't get it done. Nicholson's argument: trust me.

In essence, the "new strategy" devised by Trump's generals, Secretary of Defense Mattis and Nicholson among them, amounts to this: persist a tad longer with a tad more. A modest uptick in the number of US and allied troops on the ground will provide more trainers, advisers, and motivators to work with and accompany their Afghan counterparts in the field. The Mattis/Nicholson plan also envisions an increasing number of air strikes, signaled by the recent use of B-52s to attack illicit Taliban "drug labs," a scenario that Stanley Kubrick himself would have been hard-pressed to imagine.

Notwithstanding the novelty of using strategic bombers to destroy mud huts, there's not a lot new here. Dating back to 2001, coalition forces have already dropped tens of thousands of bombs in Afghanistan. Almost as soon as the Taliban were ousted from Kabul, coalition efforts to create effective Afghan security forces commenced. So, too, did attempts to reduce the production of the opium that has funded the Taliban insurgency, alas with essentially no effect whatsoever. What Trump's generals want a gullible public (and astonishingly gullible and inattentive members of Congress) to believe is that this time they've somehow devised a formula for getting it right.

Turning the Corner

With his trademark capacity to intuit success, President Trump already sees clear evidence of progress. "We're not fighting anymore to just walk around," he remarked in his Thanksgiving message to the troops. "We're fighting to win. And you people [have] turned it around over the last three to four months like nobody has seen." The president, we may note, has yet to visit Afghanistan.

I'm guessing that the commander in chief is oblivious to the fact that, in US military circles, the term *winning* has acquired notable elasticity. Trump may think that it implies vanquishing the enemy—white flags and surrender ceremonies on the USS *Missouri*. General Nicholson knows better. "Winning," the field commander says, "means delivering a negotiated settlement that reduces the level of violence and protecting the homeland." (Take that definition at face value and we can belatedly move Vietnam into the win column!)

Should we be surprised that Trump's generals, unconsciously imitating General William Westmoreland a half-century ago, claim once again to detect light at the end of the tunnel? Not at all. Mattis and Nicholson (along with White House Chief of Staff John Kelly and National Security Adviser H. R. McMaster) are following the Weinstein playbook: keep doing it until they make you stop. Indeed, with what can only be described as chutzpah, Nicholson himself recently announced that we have "turned the corner" in Afghanistan. In doing so, of course, he is counting on Americans not to recall the various war managers, military and civilian alike, who have made identical claims going back years now, among them Secretary of Defense Leon Panetta in 2012.

From on high, assurances of progress; in the field, results that, year after year, come nowhere near what's promised; on the home front, an astonishingly credulous public. The war in Afghanistan has long since settled into a melancholy and seemingly permanent rhythm.

The fact is that the individuals entrusted by President Trump to direct US policy believe with iron certainty that difficult political problems will yield to armed might properly employed. That proposition is one to which generals like Mattis and Nicholson have devoted a considerable part of their lives, not just in Afghanistan but across much of the Islamic world. They are no more likely to question the validity of that proposition than the Pope is to entertain second thoughts about the divinity of Jesus Christ.

In Afghanistan, their entire worldview—not to mention the status and clout of the officer corps they represent—is at stake. No matter how long the war there lasts, no matter how many "generations" it takes, no matter how much blood is shed to no purpose, and no matter how much money is wasted, they will never admit to failure—nor will any of the militarists-in-mufti cheering them on from the sidelines in Washington, Trump not the least among them.

Meanwhile, the great majority of the American people, their attention directed elsewhere, remain studiously indifferent to the charade being played out before their eyes.

It took a succession of high-profile scandals before Americans truly woke up to the plague of sexual harassment and assault. How long will it take before the public concludes that they have had enough of wars that don't work? Here's hoping it's before our president, in a moment of ill temper, unleashes "fire and fury" on the world.

31

What Happens When a Few Volunteer and the Rest Just Watch

The American Military System Dissected

April 10, 2018

"The purpose of all wars, is peace." So observed St. Augustine early in the first millennium A.D. Far be it from me to disagree with the esteemed bishop of Hippo, but his crisply formulated aphorism just might require a bit of updating.

I'm not a saint or even a bishop, merely an interested observer of this nation's ongoing military misadventures early in the third millennium A.D. From my vantage point, I might suggest the following amendment to Augustine's dictum: *Any war failing to yield peace is purposeless and, if purposeless, both wrong and stupid.*

War is evil. Large-scale, state-sanctioned violence is justified only when all other means of achieving genuinely essential objectives have been exhausted or are otherwise unavailable. A nation should go to war only when it has to—and even then, ending the conflict as expeditiously as possible should be an imperative.

Some might take issue with these propositions, President Trump's latest national security adviser doubtless among them. Yet most observers—even, I'm guessing, most high-ranking US military officers—would endorse them. How is it then that *peace* has essentially vanished as a US policy objective? Why has war joined death and taxes in that select category of things that Americans have come to accept as unavoidable?

The United States has taken Thucydides's famed Melian Dialogue and turned it inside out. Centuries before Augustine, the great Athenian historian wrote, "The strong do what they will, while the weak suffer what they must." Strength confers choice; weakness restricts it. That's the way the world works, so at least Thucydides believed. Yet the inverted Melian Dialogue that prevails in present-day Washington seemingly goes like this: *strength imposes obligations and limits choice.* In other words, we gotta keep doing what we've been doing, no matter what.

Making such a situation all the more puzzling is the might and majesty of America's armed forces. By common consent, the United States today has the world's best military. By some estimates, it may be the best in recorded history. It's certainly the most expensive and hardest working on the planet.

Yet in the post–Cold War era, when the relative strength of US forces reached its zenith, our well-endowed, well-trained, well-equipped, and highly disciplined troops have proven unable to accomplish any of the core tasks to which they've been assigned. This has been especially true since 9/11.

We send the troops off to war, but they don't achieve peace. Instead, America's wars and skirmishes simply drag on, seemingly without end. We just keep doing what we've been doing, a circumstance that both Augustine and Thucydides would undoubtedly have found baffling.

Prosecuting War, Averting Peace

How to explain this paradox of a superb military that never gets the job done? Let me suggest that the problem lies with the present-day American military system, the principles to which the nation adheres in raising, organizing, supporting, and employing its armed forces. By its very existence, a military system expresses an implicit contract between the state, the people, and the military itself.

Here, as I see it, are the principles—seven in all—that define the prevailing military system of the United States.

First, we define military service as entirely voluntary. In the US, there is no link between citizenship and military service. It's up to you as an individual to decide if you want to take up arms in the service of your country. If you choose to do so, that's okay. If you choose otherwise, that's okay, too. Either way, your decision is of no more significance than whether you root for the Yankees or the Mets.

Second, while non-serving citizens are encouraged to "support the troops," we avoid stipulating how this civic function is to be performed. In practice, there are many ways of doing so, some substantive, others merely symbolic. Most citizens opt for the latter. This means that they cheer when invited to do so. Cheering is easy and painless. It can even make you feel good about yourself.

Third, when it comes to providing the troops with actual support, we expect Congress to do the heavy lifting. Our elected representatives fulfill that role by routinely ponying up vast sums of money for what is misleadingly called a defense budget. In some instances, Congress appropriates even more money than the Pentagon asks for, as was the case this year.

Meanwhile, under the terms of our military system, attention to how this money actually gets spent by our yet-to-be-audited Pentagon tends to be—to put the matter politely—spotty.

Only rarely does the Congress insert itself forcefully into matters relating to what US forces scattered around the world are actually doing. Yes, there are periodic hearings, with questions posed and testimony offered. But unless there is some partisan advantage to be gained, oversight tends to be, at best, pro forma. As a result, those charged with implementing national security policy—another Orwellian phrase—enjoy very considerable latitude.

Fourth, under the terms of our military system, this latitude applies in spades to the chief executive. The commander in chief occupies the apex of our military system. The president may bring to office very little expertise pertinent to war or the art of statecraft, yet his authority regarding such matters is essentially unlimited.

Consider, if you will, the sobering fact that our military system empowers the president to order a nuclear attack, should he see the need—or feel the impulse—to do so. He need not obtain congressional consent. He certainly doesn't need to check with the American people.

Since Harry Truman ordered the destruction of Hiroshima and Nagasaki in 1945, presidents have not exercised this option, for which we should all be grateful. Yet on more occasions than you can count, they have ordered military actions, large and small, on their own authority or after only the most perfunctory consultation with Congress. When Donald Trump, for instance, threatened North Korea's Kim Jong-un with "fire and fury the likes of which the world has never seen," he gave no hint that he would even consider asking for prior congressional authorization to do so. Trump's words were certainly inflammatory. Yet were he to act on those words, he would merely be exercising a prerogative enjoyed by his predecessors going back to Truman himself.

The Constitution invests in Congress the authority to declare war. The relevant language is unambiguous. In practice, as countless commentators have noted, that provision has long been a dead letter. This, too, forms an essential part of our present military system.

Fifth, under the terms of that system, there's no need to defray the costs of military actions undertaken in our name. Supporting the troops does not require citizens to pay anything extra for what the US military is doing out there, wherever it may be. The troops are asked to sacrifice; for the rest of us, sacrifice is anathema.

Indeed, in recent years, presidents who take the nation to war or perpetuate wars they inherit never even consider pressing Congress to increase our taxes accordingly. On the contrary, they advocate tax cuts, especially for the wealthiest among us, which lead directly to massive deficits.

Sixth, pursuant to the terms of our military system, the armed services have been designed not to defend the country but to project military power on a global basis. For the Department of Defense actually defending the United States qualifies as an afterthought, trailing well behind other priorities such as trying to pacify Afghanistan's Kandahar Province or jousting with militant groups in Somalia. The United States Army, Navy, Air Force, and Marine Corps are all designed to fight elsewhere, relying on a constellation of perhaps eight hundred bases around the world to facilitate the conduct of military campaigns "out there," wherever "there" may happen to be. They are, in other words, expeditionary forces.

Reflect for a moment on the way the Pentagon divvies the world up into gigantic swathes of territory and then assigns a military command to exercise jurisdiction over each of them: European Command, Africa Command, Central Command, Southern Command, Northern Command, and Indo-Pacific Command. With the polar ice cap continuing to melt, a US Arctic Command is almost surely next on the docket. Nor is the Pentagon's mania for creating new headquarters confined to terra firma. We already have US Cyber Command. Now that we have a Space Command, can US Galactic Command be far behind?

No other nation adheres to this practice. Nor would the United States permit any other nation to do so. Imagine the outcry in Washington if President Xi Jinping had the temerity to create a "PRC Latin America Command," headed by a four-star Chinese general charged with maintaining order and stability from Mexico to Argentina.

Seventh (and last), our military system invests great confidence in something called the military profession. The legal profession exists to implement the rule of law. We hope that the result is some approximation of justice. The medical profession exists to repair our bodily ailments. We hope that health and longevity will result. The military profession exists to master war. With military professionals in charge, it's our hope that America's wars will conclude quickly and successfully with peace the result.

To put it another way, we look to the military profession to avert the danger of long, costly, and inconclusive wars. History suggests that these sap the collective strength of a nation and can bring about its premature decline. We count on military professionals to forestall that prospect.

Our military system assigns the immediate direction of war to our most senior professionals, individuals who have ascended step by step to the very top of the military hierarchy. We expect three- and four-star generals and admirals to possess the skills needed to make war politically purposeful. This expectation provides the rationale for the status they enjoy and the many entitlements they are accorded.

America, the (Formerly) Indispensable

Now, the nation that has created this military system is not some "shithole country," to use a phrase made famous by President Trump. We are, or at least claim to be, a democratic republic in which all power ultimately derives from the people. We believe in—indeed, are certain that we exemplify—freedom, even as we continually modify the meaning of that term.

In the aggregate, we are very rich. Since the latter part of the nineteenth century we have taken it for granted that the United States ought to be the richest country on the planet, notwithstanding the fact that large numbers of ordinary Americans are themselves anything but rich. Indeed, as a corollary to our military system, we count on these less affluent Americans to volunteer for military service in disproportionate numbers. Offered sufficient incentives, they do so.

Finally, since 1945 the United States has occupied *the* preeminent place in the global order, a position affirmed with the collapse of the Soviet Union and the end of the Cold War in 1991. Indeed, we have come to believe that American primacy reflects the will of God or of some cosmic authority.

From the early years of the Cold War, we have come to believe that the freedom, material abundance, and primacy we cherish all depend upon the exercise of "global leadership." In practice, that seemingly benign term has been a euphemism for unquestioned military superiority and the self-assigned right to put our military to work as we please wherever we please. Back in the 1990s, Secretary of State Madeleine Albright said it best: "If we have to use force, it is because we are America. We are the indispensable nation. We stand tall. We see further into the future."

Other countries might design their military establishments to protect certain vital interests. As Albright's remark suggests, American designs have been far more ambitious.

Here, then, is a question: How do the principles and attitudes that undergird our military system actually suit twenty-first-century America? And if they don't, what are the implications of clinging to such a system? Finally, what alternative principles might form a more reasonable basis for raising, organizing, supporting, and employing our armed forces?

Spoiler alert: Let me acknowledge right now that I consider our present-day military system irredeemably flawed and deeply harmful. For proof we need look no further than the conduct of our post-9/11 wars, especially in Iraq and Afghanistan, but also in Libya, Pakistan, Somalia, Syria, Yemen, and parts of sub-Saharan Africa.

These myriad undertakings of the last nearly seventeen years have subjected our military system to a comprehensive real-world examination. Collectively, they have rendered a judgment on that system. And the judgment is negative. Put to the test, the American military system has failed.

And the cost so far? Trillions of dollars expended (with trillions more to come), thousands of American lives lost, tens of thousands of Americans grievously damaged, and even greater numbers of non-Americans killed, injured, and displaced.

One thing is certain: our wars have not brought about peace by even the loosest definition of the word.

A Military Report Card

There are many possible explanations for why our recent military record has been so dismal. One crucial explanation—perhaps the most important of all—relates to those seven principles that undergird our military system.

Let me review them in reverse order.

Principle 7, the military profession: Tally up the number of three- and four-star generals who have commanded the Afghan War since 2001. It's roughly a dozen. None of them has succeeded in bringing it to a successful conclusion. Nor does any such happy ending seem likely to be in the offing anytime soon. The senior officers we expect to master war have demonstrated no such mastery.

The generals who followed one another in presiding over that war are undoubtedly estimable, well-intentioned men, but they have not accomplished the job for which they were hired. Imagine if you contracted with a dozen different plumbers—each highly regarded—to fix a leaking sink in your kitchen and you ended up with a flooded basement. You might begin to think that there's something amiss in the way that plumbers are trained and licensed. Similarly, perhaps it's time to reexamine our approach to identifying and developing very senior military officers.

Or alternatively, consider this possibility: Perhaps our theory of war as an enterprise where superior generalship determines the outcome is flawed. Perhaps war cannot be fully mastered, by generals or anyone else.

It might just be that war is inherently unmanageable. Take it from Winston Churchill, America's favorite confronter of evil. "The statesman who yields to war fever," Churchill wrote, "must realize that once the signal is given, he is no longer the master of policy but the slave of unforeseeable and uncontrollable events."

If Churchill is right, perhaps our expectations that senior military professionals will tame war—control the uncontrollable—are misplaced. Perhaps our military system should put greater emphasis on avoiding war altogether or at least classifying it as an option to be exercised with great trepidation, rather than as the political equivalent of a handy-dandy, multifunctional Swiss Army knife.

Principle 6, organizing our forces to emphasize global power projection: Reflect for a moment on the emerging security issues of our time. The rise of China is one example. A petulant and over-armed Russia offers a second. Throw in climate change and mushrooming cyber-threats and you have a daunting set of problems. It's by no means impertinent to wonder about the relevance of the current military establishment to these challenges.

Every year the United States spends hundreds of billions of dollars to maintain and enhance the lethality of a force configured for conventional power projection and to sustain the global network of bases that goes with it. For almost two decades, that force has been engaged in a futile war of attrition with radical Islamists that has now spread across much of the Greater Middle East and parts of Africa.

I don't know about you, but I worry more about the implications of China's rise and Russian misbehavior than I do about Islamic terrorism. And I worry more about changing weather patterns here in New England or somebody shutting down the electrical grid in my hometown than I do about what Beijing and Moscow may be cooking up. Bluntly put, our existing military system finds us focused on the wrong problem set.

We need a military system that accurately prioritizes actual and emerging threats. The existing system does not. This suggests the need for radically reconfigured armed services, with the hallowed traditions of George Patton, John Paul Jones, Billy Mitchell, and Chesty Puller honorably but permanently retired.

Principle 5, paying—or not paying—for America's wars: If you want it, you should be willing to pay for it. That hoary axiom ought to guide our military system as much as it should our personal lives. Saddling millennials or members of Generation Z with the cost of paying for wars mostly conceived and mismanaged by my fellow baby boomers strikes me as downright unseemly.

One might expect the young to raise quite a ruckus over such an obvious injustice. In recent weeks, we've witnessed their righteous anger over the absence of effective gun controls in this country. That they aren't comparably incensed about the misuse of guns by their own contemporaries deployed to distant lands represents a real puzzle, especially since they're the ones who will ultimately be stuck with the bill.

Principles 4 and 3, the role of Congress and the authority of the commander in chief: Whatever rationale may once have existed for allowing the commander in chief to circumvent the Constitution's plainly specified allocation of war powers to Congress should long since have lapsed. Well before Donald Trump became president, a responsible Congress would have reasserted its authority to declare war. That Trump sits in the Oval Office and now takes advice from the likes of John Bolton invests this matter with great urgency.

Surely President Trump's bellicose volatility drives home the point that it's past time for Congress to assert itself in providing responsible oversight regarding all aspects of US military policy. Were it to do so, the chances of fixing the defects permeating our present military system would improve appreciably.

Of course, the likelihood of that happening is nil until the money changers are expelled from the temple. And that won't occur until Americans who are not beholden to the military-industrial complex and its various subsidiaries rise up, purge the Congress of its own set of complexes, and install in office people willing to do their duty. And that brings us back to . . .

Principles 2 and 1, the existing relationship between the American people and their military and our reliance on a so-called all-volunteer force: Here we come to the heart of the matter. I submit that the relationship between the American people and their military is shot through with hypocrisy. It is, in fact, nothing short of fraudulent. Worse still, most of us know it, even if we are loath to fess up. In practice, the informal mandate to "support the troops" has produced an elaborate charade. It's theater, as phony as Trump's professed love for DACA recipients.

If Americans were genuinely committed to supporting the troops, they would pay a great deal more attention to what President Trump and his twenty-first-century predecessors have tasked those troops to accomplish—with what results and at what cost. Of course, that would imply doing more than cheering and waving the flag on cue. Ultimately, the existence of the all-volunteer force obviates any need for such an effort. It provides Americans with an ample excuse for ignoring our endless wars and allowing our flawed military system to escape serious scrutiny.

Having outsourced responsibility for defending the country to people few of us actually know, we've ended up with a military system that is unfair, undemocratic, hugely expensive, and largely ineffective, not to mention increasingly irrelevant to the threats coming our way. The perpetuation of that system finds us mired in precisely the sort of long, costly, inconclusive wars that sap the collective strength of a nation and may bring about its premature decline.

The root cause of our predicament is the all-volunteer force. Only when we ordinary citizens conclude that *we* have an obligation to contribute to the country's defense will it become possible to devise a set of principles for raising, organizing, supporting, and employing US forces that align with our professed values and our actual security requirements.

Stormy Daniels figured out that an existing contract had outlived its purpose. Hopefully, the rest of us can do the same.

32
Our Man in Riyadh

Abizaid of Arabia

November 27, 2018

hat does President Trump's recent nomination of retired Army General John Abizaid to become the next US ambassador to Saudi Arabia signify? Next to nothing—and arguably quite a lot.

Abizaid's proposed appointment is both a nonevent and an opportunity not to be wasted. It means next to nothing in this sense: While once upon a time, American diplomats abroad wielded real clout—Benjamin Franklin and John Quincy Adams offer prominent examples—that time is long past. Should he receive Senate confirmation, Ambassador Abizaid will not actually shape US policy toward Saudi Arabia. At most, he will convey policy, while keeping officials back in Washington apprised regarding conditions in the kingdom. "Conditions" in this context will mean the opinions, attitudes, whims, and mood of one particular individual: Mohammed bin Salman. MBS, as he is known, is the Saudi crown prince and the kingdom's de facto absolute ruler. By no means incidentally, he is also that country's assassin in chief as well as the perpetrator of atrocities in a vicious war that he launched in neighboring Yemen in 2015.

Implicit in Abizaid's job description will be a requirement to cozy up to MBS. "Cozy up" in this context implies finding ways to befriend, influence, and seduce; that is, seeking to replicate in Riyadh the achievements in Washington of Prince Bandar bin Sultan, who from 1983 to 2005 served as Saudi ambassador to the United States.

With plenty of money to spread around, Bandar charmed—which in this context means suborned—the Washington establishment, while ingratiating himself with successive presidents and various other power brokers. With his fondness for nicknames, George W. Bush dubbed him "Bandar Bush," informally designating the Saudi prince a member of his own dynastic clan.

After 9/11, the Saudi envoy made the most of those connections, deflecting attention away from the role Saudis had played in the events of that day while fingering Saddam Hussein's Iraq as the true font of Islamist terrorism. Bush came around to endorsing Bandar's view—although he may not have needed much urging. So while Bandar may not rank alongside the likes of Vice President Dick Cheney, Secretary of Defense Donald Rumsfeld, and Deputy Secretary of Defense Paul Wolfowitz among the architects of the ensuing Iraq War, he certainly deserves honorable mention.

That Abizaid will come anywhere close to replicating Bandar's notable (or nefarious) achievements seems unlikely. For starters, at age sixty-seven, he may not want to spend the next twenty years or so in the Saudi capital, Riyadh, sucking up to the kingdom's royals. At least as significantly, he lacks Bandar's bankroll. However much dough Abizaid may have raked in via his consulting firm since leaving the army a decade ago, it doesn't qualify as real money in Saudi circles, where a billion dollars is a mere rounding error. The mega-rich do not sell themselves cheaply, unless perhaps your surname is Trump.

So the substantive implications of Abizaid's appointment for US-Saudi relations will likely be negligible. Trump's son-in-law Jared Kushner will undoubtedly continue to wield greater influence over MBS than Ambassador Abizaid does—or at least will fancy that he is doing so.

Long (and Wrong) War

In another sense, however, Abizaid's appointment to this post (vacant since Trump became president) could mean quite a lot. It offers an ideal opportunity to take stock of the "Long War."

Now that phrase "Long War" is one that presidents, national security advisors, defense secretaries, and their minions assiduously avoid. Yet, in military circles, it long ago superseded the Global War on Terrorism as an umbrella term describing what US forces have been doing across the Greater Middle East all these many years.

Already by 2005, for example, hawkish analysts employed by a conservative Washington think tank were marketing their recipe for *Winning the Long War*. And that was just for starters. For more than a decade now, the *Long War Journal* has been offering authoritative analysis of US military operations across the Greater Middle East and Africa. In the meantime, West Point's Combating Terrorism Center churns out monographs with titles like "Fighting the Long War." Always quick to recognize another golden goose of government contracts, the RAND Corporation weighed in with *Unfolding the Future of the Long War*. After publishing a lengthy essay in the *New York Times Magazine* called "My Long War," correspondent Dexter Filkins went a step further and titled his book *The Forever War*. (And for creative types, *Voices from the Long War* invites Iraq and Afghan War vets to reflect on their experiences before a theatrical audience.)

But where, you might wonder, did that dour phrase originate? As it happens, General Abizaid himself coined it back in 2004 when he was still an active duty four-star and head of US Central Command, the regional headquarters principally charged with waging that conflict. In other words, just a year after the US invaded Iraq and President George W. Bush posed under a White House–produced "Mission Accomplished" banner, with administration officials and their neoconservative boosters looking forward to many more "Iraqi Freedom"–style victories to come, the senior officer presiding over that war went on record to indicate that victory wasn't going to happen anytime soon. Oops.

And so it has come to pass. The Long War has now lasted twice as long as the average length of marriages in the United States, with no end in sight. Whether intuitively or after careful study, General Abizaid had divined something important indeed.

Crucially, however, his critique went beyond the question of duration. Abizaid also departed from the administration's line in describing the actual nature of the problem at hand. "Terrorists" per se were not the enemy, he insisted at the time. The issue was much bigger than any one organization such as al-Qaeda. The real threat facing the United States came from what he called "Salafist jihadists," radicalized Sunni Muslims committed by whatever means necessary to propagating a strict and puritanical form of Islam around the world. To promote their cause, Salafists eagerly embraced violence.

Back in 2004, when Abizaid was venturing heretical thoughts, the United States had gotten itself all tangled up in a nasty scuffle in Iraq. A year earlier, the US had invaded that country to overthrow Saddam Hussein. Now the Iraqi dictator was indubitably a bad actor. At least some of the charges that George W. Bush and his subordinates, amplified by a neoconservative chorus, lodged against him were true. Yet Saddam was the inverse of a Salafist.

Indeed, even before plunging into Iraq, looking beyond an expected easy win over Saddam, George W. Bush had identified Iran as a key member of an "Axis of Evil" and implicitly next in line for liberation. Sixteen years later, members of the Trump administration still hanker to have it out with the ayatollahs governing Shiite-majority Iran. Yet, as was the case with Saddam, those ayatollahs are anything but Salafists.

Now, it's worth noting that Abizaid was not some dime-a-dozen four-star. He speaks Arabic, won a fellowship to study in Jordan, and earned a graduate degree in Middle East Studies at Harvard. If the post-9/11 American officer corps had in its ranks an equivalent of Lawrence of Arabia, he was it, even if without T. E. Lawrence's (or Peter O'Toole's) charisma and flair for self-promotion. Nonetheless, with Abizaid suggesting, in effect, that the Iraq War was "the wrong war at the wrong place at the wrong time against the wrong enemy," just about no one in Washington was willing to listen.

That once-familiar quotation dates from 1951, when General Omar Bradley warned against extending the then-ongoing Korean War into China. Bradley's counsel carried considerable weight—and limiting the scope of the Korean War made it possible to end that conflict in 1953.

Abizaid's counsel turned out to carry next to no weight at all. So the Long War just keeps getting longer, even as its strategic rationale becomes ever more difficult to discern.

The Real Enemy

Posit, for the sake of discussion, that back in 2004 Abizaid was onto something—as indeed he was. Who then, in this Long War of ours, *is* our adversary? Who is in league with those Salafi jihadists? Who underwrites their cause?

The answer to those questions is not exactly a mystery. It's the Saudi royal family. Were it not for Saudi Arabia's role in promoting militant Salafism over the course of several decades, it would pose no bigger problem than anti-government cattle ranchers taking on the Bureau of Land Management.

To put it another way, while the Long War has found US troops fighting the wrong enemy for years on end in places like Iraq and Afghanistan, the nexus of the problem remains Saudi Arabia. The Saudis have provided billions to fund madrassas and mosques, spreading Salafism to the far reaches of the Islamic world. Next to oil, violent jihadism is Saudi Arabia's principal export. Indeed, the former funds the latter.

Those Saudi efforts have borne fruit of a poisonous character. Recall that Osama bin Laden was a Saudi. So, too, were fifteen of the nineteen hijackers on September 11, 2001. These facts are not incidental, even if—to expand on Donald Rumsfeld's famous typology of known knowns, known unknowns, and unknown unknowns—Washington treats them as knowns we prefer to pretend we don't know.

So from the outset, in the conflict that the United States dates from September 2001, our ostensible ally has been the principal source of the problem. In the Long War, Saudi Arabia represents what military theorists like to call the center of gravity, defined as "the source of power that provides moral or physical strength, freedom of action, or will to act" to the enemy. When it comes to Salafist jihadism, Saudi Arabia fits that definition to a T.

So there is more than a little poetic justice—or is it irony?—in General Abizaid's proposed posting to Riyadh. The one senior military officer who early on demonstrated an inkling of understanding of the Long War's true nature now prepares to take up an assignment in what is, in essence, the very center of the enemy's camp. It's as if President Lincoln had dispatched Ulysses S. Grant to Richmond, Virginia, in 1864 as his liaison to Jefferson Davis.

Which brings us to the opportunity referred to at the outset of this essay. The opportunity is not Abizaid's. He can look forward to a frustrating and probably pointless assignment. Yet Trump's nomination of Abizaid presents an opportunity to the US senators charged with approving his appointment. While we can take it for granted that Abizaid will be confirmed, the process of confirmation offers the Senate, and especially members of the Senate Foreign Relations Committee, a chance to take stock of this Long War of ours and, in particular, to assess how Saudi Arabia fits into the struggle.

Who better to reflect on these matters than John Abizaid? Imagine the questions:

General, can you describe this Long War of ours? What is its nature? What is it all about?

Are we winning? How can we tell?

How much longer should Americans expect it to last?

What are we up against? Give us a sense of the enemy's intentions, capabilities, and prospects.

With MBS in charge, is Saudi Arabia part of the solution or part of the problem?

Take all the time you need, sir. Be candid. We're interested in your opinion.

After the embarrassment of the Kavanaugh confirmation hearings, the Senate is badly in need of refurbishing its reputation. The Abizaid nomination provides a ready-made chance to do just that. Let's see if the "world's greatest deliberative body" rises to the occasion. Just don't hold your breath.

33
Lost in TrumpWorld

War in the Shadows

February 5, 2019

The news, however defined, always contains a fair amount of pap. Since Donald Trump's ascent to the presidency, however, the trivia quotient in the average American's daily newsfeed has grown like so many toadstools in a compost heap, overshadowing or crowding out matters of real substance. We're living in TrumpWorld, folks. Never in the history of journalism have so many reporters, editors, and pundits expended so much energy fixating on one particular target, while other larger prey frolic unmolested within sight.

As diversion or entertainment—or as a way to make a buck or win fifteen seconds of fame—this development is not without value. Yet the overall impact on our democracy is problematic. It's as if all the nation's sportswriters obsessed 24/7 about beating New England Patriots coach Bill Belichick.

In TrumpWorld, journalistic importance now correlates with relevance to the ongoing saga of Donald J. Trump. To members of the mainstream media (Fox News, of course, excepted), that saga centers on efforts to oust the president from office before he destroys the republic or blows up the planet.

Let me stipulate for the record: this cause is not entirely meritless. Yet to willingly embrace such a perspective is to forfeit situational awareness bigly. All that ends up mattering are the latest rumors, hints, signs, or surefire indicators that The Day of Reckoning approaches. Meanwhile, the president's own tweets, ill-tempered remarks, and outlandish decisions each serve as a reminder that the moment when he becomes an ex-president can't arrive too soon.

Hotels in Moscow, MAGA Caps, and a Nixon Tattoo

Ostensibly big stories erupt, command universal attention, and then evaporate like the dewfall on a summer morning, their place taken by the next equally big, no less ephemeral story. Call it the Michael Wolff syndrome. Just a year ago, Wolff's *Fire and Fury: Inside the Trump White House* took the political world by storm, bits and pieces winging across the Internet while the book itself reportedly sold a cool million copies in the first four days of its release. Here was the unvarnished truth of TrumpWorld with a capital T. Yet as quickly as *Fire and Fury* appeared, it disappeared, leaving nary a trace.

Today, ninety-nine cents will get you a copy of that same hardcover book. As a contribution to deciphering our times, the value of Wolff's volume is about a dollar less than its current selling price. A mere year after its appearance, it's hard to recall what all the fuss was about.

Smaller scale versions of the Wolff syndrome play themselves out almost daily. Remember the recent bombshell BuzzFeed report charging that Trump had ordered his lawyer Michael Cohen to lie about a proposed hotel project in Moscow? For a day or so, it was the all-encompassing, stop-the-presses-get-me-rewrite version of reality, the revelation—finally!—that would bring down the president. Then the office of Special Counsel Robert Mueller announced that key aspects of the report were "not accurate" and the 24/7 buzz created by that scoop vanished as quickly as it had appeared.

Immediately thereafter, Rudy Giuliani, once "America's mayor," now Trump's Barney Fife–equivalent of a personal lawyer, announced on national television that he had never said "there was no collusion" between the Trump campaign and Russian authorities in election 2016. Observers on the lookout for the proverbial smoking gun quickly interpreted that odd formulation as an admission that collusion must, in fact, have occurred.

The headlines were thunderous. Yet within hours, the gotcha interpretation fell apart. Alternative explanations appeared, suggesting that

Giuliani was suffering from dementia or that his drinking habit had gotten out of hand. With the ex-mayor wasting little time walking back his own comment, another smoking gun morphed into a cap pistol.

Fortunately for what little survives of his reputation, Giuliani's latest gaffe was promptly eclipsed by video clips that seemed to show white students from an all-boys Catholic high school in Kentucky (strike one!), who had just participated in the annual March for Life in Washington (strike two!), taunting an elderly Native American Vietnam War veteran using tomahawk chops while sporting MAGA hats on the steps of the Lincoln Memorial (strike three!).

The ensuing rush to judgment became a wind sprint. Here was the distilled essence of every terrible thing that Trump had done to America. The pro-Trump baseball caps said it all. As a columnist in my hometown newspaper put it, "Like a white hood, that cap represents a provocation and a threat: 'You know where we stand. You've been warned. And the president of the United States has our back.' And, yes, I do equate MAGA gear with traditional Klan attire. The sartorial choices change, the racism remains the same." For those too obtuse to grasp the underlying point, the title of the essay drove it home: "White America, come get your children."

As luck would have it, however, the events that actually unfolded on the steps of the Lincoln Memorial turned out to be more complicated than was first reported. No matter: in TrumpWorld, all sides treat facts as malleable and striking the right moral posture counts for far more than balance or accuracy.

Anyway, soon after, with news that Trump confidant Roger Stone had been indicted on various charges, the boys from Covington could return to the obscurity from which they briefly emerged. To judge from the instantaneous media reaction, Stone's first name might as well have been Rosetta. Here at last—for sure this time—was the key to getting the real dirt.

Rest assured, though, that by the time this essay appears, Stone and his Nixon tattoo will have been superseded by yet another sensational Trump-related revelation (or two or three).

And so it goes, in an endlessly churning cycle: "breaking news" goes viral; commentators rush in to explain what-it-all-means; the president himself retaliates by lashing out on Twitter ("The Greatest Witch Hunt in the History of our Country!"), much to the delight of his critics. This tit-for-tat exchange continues until the next fresh tidbit of "breaking news" gives the cycle another vigorous turn.

When Does a Hill of Beans Become a Mountain?
Do all of the words spoken or written result in citizens who are better informed and better able to reach sensible conclusions about the global situation in which our country finds itself? Not as far as I can tell. Granted, if I spent more time watching those gabbling heads on CNN, MSNBC, and Fox News, I might feel differently. But I doubt it.

Still, having been involuntarily shanghaied into TrumpWorld, I worry that my fellow citizens are losing their ability to distinguish between what truly matters and what doesn't, between what's vital and what's merely interesting. True, Donald J. Trump has a particular knack for simplifying and thereby distorting almost any subject to which he gives even the slightest attention, ranging from border security to forest management. Yet almost everywhere in TrumpWorld, this very tendency has become endemic, with nuance and perspective sacrificed to the larger cause of cleansing the temple of the president's offending presence. Nothing, it appears, comes close to the importance of this effort.

Not even wars.

I admit to a preoccupation with the nation's seemingly never-ending armed conflicts. These days it's not the conduct of our wars that interests me—they have become all but indecipherable—but their duration, aimlessness, and cumulative costs. Yet even more than all of these, what's fascinating is the way that they continue more or less on autopilot.

I don't wish to imply that political leaders and media outlets ignore our wars altogether. That would be unfair. Yet in TrumpWorld, while the president's performance in office receives intensive and persistent coverage day in, day out, the attention given to America's wars has been sparse and perfunctory, when not positively bizarre.

As a case in point, consider the op-ed that recently appeared in the *New York Times* (just as actual peace talks between the US and the Taliban seemed to be progressing), making the case for prolonging the US war in Afghanistan, while chiding President Trump for considering a reduction in the number of US troops currently stationed there. Any such move, warned Michael O'Hanlon of the Brookings Institution, would be a "mistake" of the first order.

The ongoing Afghan War dates from a time when some of today's recruits were still in diapers. Yet O'Hanlon counsels patience: a bit more time and things just might work out. This is more or less comparable to those who suggested back in the 1950s that African Americans might show a bit more patience in their struggle for equality: Hey, what's the rush?

I don't pretend to know what persuaded the editors of the *Times* that O'Hanlon's call to make America's longest war even longer qualifies as something readers of the nation's most influential newspaper just now need to ponder. Yet I do know this: the dearth of critical attention to the costs and consequences of our various post-9/11 wars is nothing short of shameful, a charge to which politicians and journalists alike should plead equally guilty.

I take it as a given that President Trump is an incompetent nitwit, precisely as his critics charge. Yet his oft-repeated characterization of those wars as profoundly misguided has more than a little merit. Even more striking than Trump's critique is the fact that so few members of the national security establishment are willing to examine it seriously. As a consequence, the wars persist, devoid of purpose.

Still, I find myself wondering: If a proposed troop drawdown in Afghanistan qualifies as a "mistake," as O'Hanlon contends, then what term best describes a war that has cost something like a trillion dollars, killed and maimed tens of thousands, and produced a protracted stalemate?

Disaster? Debacle? Catastrophe? Humiliation?

And, if recent press reports prove true, with US government officials accepting Taliban promises of good behavior as a basis for calling it quits, then this longest war in our history will not have provided much of a return on investment. Given the disparity between the US aims announced back in 2001 and the results actually achieved, defeat might be an apt characterization.

Yet the fault is not Trump's. The fault belongs to those who have allowed their immersion in the dank precincts of TrumpWorld to preclude serious reexamination of misguided and reckless policies that predate the Trump presidency by at least fifteen years.

34
Illusions of Victory

How the United States Did Not Reinvent War but Thought It Did

May 5, 2019

"War is the great auditor of institutions," the historian Correlli Barnett once observed. Since 9/11, the United States has undergone such an audit and been found wanting. That adverse judgment applies in full to America's armed forces.

Valor does not offer the measure of an army's greatness, nor does fortitude, nor durability, nor technological sophistication. A great army is one that accomplishes its assigned mission. Since George W. Bush inaugurated his Global War on Terror, the armed forces of the United States have failed to meet that standard.

In the aftermath of September 11, 2001, Bush conceived of a bold, offensive strategy, vowing to "take the battle to the enemy, disrupt his plans, and confront the worst threats before they emerge." The military offered the principal means for undertaking this offensive, and US forces soon found themselves engaged on several fronts.

Two of those fronts—Afghanistan and Iraq—commanded priority attention. In each case, the assigned task was to deliver a knockout blow, leading to a quick, decisive, economical, politically meaningful victory. In each case, despite impressive displays of valor, fortitude, durability, and technological sophistication, America's military came up short. The problem lay not with the level of exertion but with the results achieved.

In Afghanistan, US forces failed to eliminate the leadership of al-Qaeda. Although they toppled the Taliban regime that had ruled most of that country, they failed to eliminate the Taliban movement, which soon began to claw its way back. Intended as a brief campaign, the Afghan War became a protracted one. Nearly seven years after it began, there is no end in sight. If anything, America's adversaries are gaining strength. The outcome remains much in doubt.

In Iraq, events followed a similar pattern, with the appearance of easy success belied by subsequent developments. The US invasion began on March 19, 2003. Six weeks later, against the backdrop of a White House–produced banner proclaiming "Mission Accomplished," President Bush declared that "major combat operations in Iraq have ended." This claim proved illusory.

Writing shortly after the fall of Baghdad, the influential neoconservatives David Frum and Richard Perle declared Operation Iraqi Freedom "a vivid and compelling demonstration of America's ability to win swift and total victory." General Tommy Franks, commanding the force that invaded Iraq, modestly characterized the results of his handiwork as "unequalled in its excellence by anything in the annals of war." In retrospect, such judgments—and they were legion—can only be considered risible. A war thought to have ended on April 9, 2003, in Baghdad's Firdos Square was only just beginning. Fighting dragged on for years, exacting a cruel toll. Iraq became a reprise of Vietnam, although in some respects at least on a blessedly smaller scale.

A New American Way of War?

It wasn't supposed to be this way. Just a few short years ago, observers were proclaiming that the United States possessed military power such as the world had never seen. Here was the nation's strong suit. "The troops" appeared unbeatable. Writing in 2002, for example, Max Boot, a well-known commentator on military matters, attributed to the United States a level of martial excellence "that far surpasses the capabilities of such previous would-be hegemons as Rome, Britain, and Napoleonic France." With US forces enjoying "unparalleled strength in every facet of warfare," allies, he wrote, had become an encumbrance: "We just don't need anyone else's help very much."

Boot dubbed this the Doctrine of the Big Enchilada. Within a year, after US troops had occupied Baghdad, he went further: America's army even outclassed Germany's *Wehrmacht*. The mastery displayed in knocking off Saddam, Boot gushed, made "fabled generals such as Erwin Rommel and Heinz Guderian seem positively incompetent by comparison."

All of this turned out to be hot air. If the Global War on Terror has produced one undeniable conclusion, it is that estimates of US military capabilities have turned out to be wildly overstated. The Bush administration's misplaced confidence in the efficacy of American arms represents a strategic misjudgment that has cost the country dearly. Even in an age of stealth, precision weapons, and instant communications, armed force is not a panacea. Even in a supposedly unipolar era, American military power turns out to be quite limited.

How did it happen that Americans so utterly over-appraised the utility of military power? The answer to that question lies at the intersection of three great illusions.

According to the first illusion, the United States during the 1980s and 1990s had succeeded in reinventing armed conflict. The result was to make force more precise, more discriminating, and potentially more humane. The Pentagon had devised a new American way of war, investing its forces with capabilities unlike any the world had ever seen. As President Bush exuberantly declared shortly after the fall of Baghdad in April 2003, "We've applied the new powers of technology to strike an enemy force with speed and incredible precision. By a combination of creative strategies and advanced technologies, we are redefining war on our terms. In this new era of warfare, we can target a regime, not a nation."

The distinction between regime and nation was a crucial one. By employing these new military techniques, the United States could eliminate an obstreperous foreign leader and his cronies, while sparing the population over which that leader ruled. Putting a missile through the roof of a presidential palace made it unnecessary to incinerate an entire capital city, endowing force with hitherto undreamed-of political utility and easing ancient moral inhibitions on the use of force. Force had been a club; it now became a scalpel. By the time the president spoke, such sentiments had already become commonplace among many (although by no means all) military officers and national security experts.

Here lay a formula for certain victory. Confidence in military prowess both reflected and reinforced a post–Cold War confidence in the universality of American values. Harnessed together, they made a seemingly unstoppable one-two punch.

With that combination came expanded ambitions. In the 1990s, the very purpose of the Department of Defense changed. Sustaining American global preeminence, rather than mere national security, became its explicit function. In the most comprehensive articulation of this new American way of war, the Joint Chiefs of Staff committed the armed services to achieving what they called "full spectrum dominance"—unambiguous supremacy in all forms of warfare, to be achieved by tapping the potential of two "enablers"—"technological innovation and information superiority."

Full spectrum dominance stood in relation to military affairs as the political scientist Francis Fukuyama's well-known proclamation of "the end of history" stood in relation to ideology: each claimed to have unlocked ultimate truths. According to Fukuyama, democratic capitalism represented the final stage in political economic evolution. According to the proponents of full spectrum dominance, that concept represented the final stage in the evolution of modern warfare. In their first days and weeks, the successive invasions of Afghanistan and Iraq both seemed to affirm such claims.

How Not to "Support the Troops"

According to the second illusion, American civilian and military leaders subscribed to a common set of principles for employing their now-dominant forces. Adherence to these principles promised to prevent any recurrence of the sort of disaster that had befallen the nation in Vietnam. If politicians went off half-cocked, as President Lyndon Johnson and Secretary of Defense Robert McNamara had back in the 1960s, generals who had correctly discerned and assimilated the lessons of modern war could be counted on to rein them in.

These principles found authoritative expression in the Weinberger-Powell Doctrine, which specified criteria for deciding when and how to use force. Caspar Weinberger, secretary of defense during most of the Reagan era, first articulated these principles in 1984. General Colin Powell, chairman of the Joint Chiefs of Staff during the early 1990s, expanded on them. Yet the doctrine's real authors were the members of the post-Vietnam officer corps. The Weinberger-Powell principles expressed the military's own lessons taken from that war. Those principles also expressed the determination of senior officers to prevent any recurrence of Vietnam.

Henceforth, according to Weinberger and Powell, the United States would fight only when genuinely vital interests were at stake. It would do so in pursuit of concrete and attainable objectives. It would mobilize the necessary resources—political and moral as well as material—to win promptly and decisively. It would end conflicts expeditiously and then get out, leaving no loose ends. The spirit of the Weinberger-Powell Doctrine was not permissive; its purpose was to curb the reckless or imprudent inclinations of bellicose civilians.

According to the third illusion, the military and American society had successfully patched up the differences that produced something akin to divorce during the divisive Vietnam years. By the 1990s, a reconciliation of sorts was under way. In the wake of Operation Desert Storm, "the American people fell in love again with their armed forces." So, at least, General Powell, one of that war's great heroes, believed. Out of this love affair a new civil-military compact had evolved, one based on the confidence that, in times of duress, Americans could be counted on to "support the troops." Never again would the nation abandon its soldiers.

The all-volunteer force (AVF)—despite its name, a professional military establishment—represented the chief manifestation of this new compact. By the 1990s, Americans were celebrating the AVF as the one component of the federal government that actually worked as advertised. The AVF embodied the nation's claim to the status of sole superpower; it was "America's Team." In the wake of the Cold War, the AVF sustained the global Pax Americana without interfering with the average American's pursuit of life, liberty, and happiness. What was not to like?

Events since 9/11 have exposed these three illusions for what they were. When tested, the new American way of war yielded more glitter than gold. The generals and admirals who touted the wonders of full spectrum dominance were guilty of flagrant professional malpractice, if not outright fraud. To judge by the record of the past twenty years, US forces win decisively only when the enemy obligingly fights on American terms—and Saddam Hussein's demise has drastically reduced the likelihood of finding such accommodating adversaries in the future. As for loose ends, from Somalia to the Balkans, from Central Asia to the Persian Gulf, they have been endemic.

When it came to the Weinberger-Powell Doctrine, civilian willingness to conform to its provisions proved to be highly contingent. Confronting Powell in 1993, Madeleine Albright famously demanded to know, "What's the point of having this superb military that you're always talking about, if we can't use it?" Mesmerized by the prospects of putting American soldiers to work to alleviate the world's ills, Albright soon enough got her way. An odd alliance that combined left-leaning do-gooders with jingoistic politicians and pundits succeeded in chipping away at constraints on the use of force. "Humanitarian intervention" became all the rage. Whatever restraining influence the generals exercised during the 1990s did not survive that decade. Lessons of Vietnam that had once seemed indelible were forgotten.

Meanwhile, the reconciliation of the people and the army turned out to be a chimera. When the chips were down, "supporting the troops" elicited plenty of posturing but little by way of binding commitments. Far from producing a stampede of eager recruits keen to don a uniform, the events of 9/11 reaffirmed a widespread popular preference for hiring someone else's kid to chase terrorists, spread democracy, and ensure access to the world's energy reserves.

In the midst of a global war of ostensibly earthshaking importance, Americans demonstrated a greater affinity for their hometown sports heroes than for the soldiers defending the distant precincts of the

American imperium. Tom Brady makes millions playing quarterback in the NFL and rakes in millions more from endorsements. Pat Tillman quit professional football to become an army ranger and was killed in Afghanistan. Yet, of the two, Brady more fully embodies the contemporary understanding of the term *patriot*.

Demolishing the Doctrine of the Big Enchilada

While they persisted, however, these three illusions fostered gaudy expectations about the efficacy of American military might. Every president since Reagan has endorsed these expectations. Every president since Reagan has exploited his role as commander in chief to expand on the imperial prerogatives of his office. Each has also relied on military power to conceal or manage problems that stemmed from the nation's habits of profligacy.

In the wake of 9/11, these puerile expectations—that armed force wielded by a strong-willed chief executive could do just about anything—reached an apotheosis of sorts. Having manifestly failed to anticipate or prevent a devastating attack on American soil, President Bush proceeded to use his ensuing Global War on Terrorism as a pretext for advancing grandiose new military ambitions married to claims of unbounded executive authority—all under the guise of keeping Americans "safe."

With the president denying any connection between the events of September 11 and past US policies, his declaration of a global war nipped in the bud whatever inclination the public might have entertained to reconsider those policies. In essence, Bush counted on war both to concentrate greater power in his own hands and to divert attention from the political, economic, and cultural bind in which the United States found itself as a result of its own past behavior.

As long as US forces sustained their reputation for invincibility, it remained possible to pretend that the constitutional order and the American way of life were in good health. The concept of waging an open-ended global campaign to eliminate terrorism retained a modicum of plausibility. After all, how could anyone or anything stop the unstoppable American soldier?

Call that reputation into question, however, and everything else unravels. This is what occurred when the Iraq War went sour. The ills afflicting our political system, including a deeply irresponsible Congress, broken national security institutions, and above all an imperial commander in chief not up to the job, became all but impossible to ignore. So, too, did the self-destructive elements inherent in the American way of life—especially an increasingly costly addiction to foreign oil, universally deplored and almost as universally indulged. More noteworthy still, the prospect of waging war on a global scale for decades, if not generations, became preposterous.

To anyone with eyes to see, the events of the past seven years have demolished the Doctrine of the Big Enchilada. A gung ho journalist like Robert Kaplan might still believe that, with the dawn of the twenty-first century, the Pentagon had "appropriated the entire earth, and was ready to flood the most obscure areas of it with troops at a moment's notice," that planet Earth in its entirety had become "battle space for the American military." Yet any buck sergeant of even middling intelligence knew better than to buy such claptrap.

With the Afghanistan War well into its seventh year and the Iraq War marking its fifth anniversary, a commentator like Michael Barone might express absolute certainty that "just about no mission is impossible for the United States military." But Barone was not facing the prospect of being ordered back to the war zone for his second or third combat tour.

Between what President Bush called upon America's soldiers to do and what they were capable of doing loomed a huge gap that defines the military crisis besetting the United States today. For a nation accustomed to seeing military power as its trump card, the implications of that gap are monumental.

IV
OH, HIM (REMEMBERING TRUMP)

35
Don't Cry for Me, America

What Trumpism Means for Democracy

March 1, 2016

Whether or not Donald Trump ultimately succeeds in winning the White House, historians are likely to rank him as the most consequential presidential candidate of at least the past half-century. He has already transformed the tone and temper of American political life. If he becomes the Republican nominee, he will demolish its structural underpinnings as well. Should he prevail in November, his election will alter its very fabric in ways likely to prove irreversible. Whether Trump ever delivers on his promise to "Make America Great Again," he is already transforming American democratic practice.

Trump takes obvious delight in thumbing his nose at the political establishment and flouting its norms. Yet to classify him as an antiestablishment figure is to miss his true significance. He is to American politics what Martin Shkreli is to Big Pharma. Each represents in exaggerated form the distilled essence of a much larger and more disturbing reality. Each embodies the smirking cynicism that has become one of the defining characteristics of our age. Each in his own way is a sign of the times.

In contrast to the universally reviled Shkreli, however, Trump has cultivated a mass following that appears impervious to his missteps, miscues, and misstatements. What Trump actually believes—whether he believes in anything apart from big, splashy self-display—is largely unknown and probably beside the point. Trumpism is not a program or an ideology. It is an attitude or pose that feeds off of, and then reinforces, widespread anger and alienation.

270

The pose works because the anger—always present in certain quarters of the American electorate but especially acute today—is genuine. By acting the part of impish bad boy and consciously trampling on the canons of political correctness, Trump validates that anger. The more outrageous his behavior, the more secure his position at the very center of the political circus. Wondering what he will do next, we can't take our eyes off him. And to quote Marco Rubio in a different context, Trump "knows exactly what he is doing."

Targeting Obama's Presidency

There is a form of genius at work here. To an extent unmatched by any other figure in American public life, Trump understands that previous distinctions between the ostensibly serious and the self-evidently frivolous have collapsed. Back in 1968, then running for president, Richard Nixon, of all people, got things rolling when he appeared on *Laugh-In* and uttered the immortal words, "Sock it to me?" But no one has come close to Trump in grasping the implications of all this. In contemporary America, celebrity confers authority. Mere credentials or qualifications have become an afterthought. How else to explain the host of a "reality" TV show instantly qualifying as a serious contender for high office?

For further evidence of Trump's genius, consider the skill with which he plays the media, especially celebrity journalists who themselves specialize in smirking cynicism. Rather than pretending to take them seriously, he unmasks their preening narcissism, which mirrors his own. He refuses to acknowledge their self-assigned role as gatekeepers empowered to police the boundaries of permissible discourse. As the embodiment of "breaking news," he continues to stretch those boundaries beyond recognition.

In that regard, the spectacle of televised "debates" has offered Trump an ideal platform for promoting his cult of personality. Once a solemn, almost soporific forum for civic education—remember Kennedy and Nixon in 1960?—presidential debates now provide occasions for trading insults, provoking gaffes, engaging in verbal food fights, and marketing magical solutions to problems ranging from war to border security that are immune to magic. For all of that we have Trump chiefly to thank.

Trump's success as a campaigner schools his opponents, of course. In a shrinking Republican field, survival requires mimicking his antics. In that regard, Ted Cruz rates as Trump's star pupil. Cruz is to Trump what Lady Gaga was to Amy Winehouse—a less freewheeling, more scripted, and arguably more calculating version of the original.

Yet if not a clone, Cruz taps into the same vein of pissed-off, give-me-my-country-back rage that Trump himself has so adeptly exploited. Like the master himself, Cruz has demonstrated a notable aptitude for expressing disagreement through denigration and for extravagant, crackpot promises. For his part, Marco Rubio, the only other Republican still seriously in the running, lags not far behind. When it comes to swagger and grandiosity, nothing beats a vow to create a "New American Century," thereby resurrecting a mythic past when all was ostensibly right with the world.

On two points alone do these several Republicans see eye-to-eye. The first relates to domestic policy, the second to America's role in the world.

On point one: with absolute unanimity, Trump, Cruz, and Rubio ascribe to Obama any and all problems besetting the nation. To take their critique at face value, the country was doing swimmingly well back in 2009 when Obama took office. Today, it's FUBAR, due entirely to Obama's malign actions.

Wielding comparable authority, however, a Republican president can, they claim, dismantle Obama's poisonous legacy and restore all that he has destroyed. From "day one," on issues ranging from health care to immigration to the environment, the Republican candidates vow to do exactly this. With the stroke of a pen and the wave of a hand, it will be a breeze.

On point two: ditto. Aided and abetted by Hillary Clinton, Obama has made a complete hash of things abroad. Here the list of Republican grievances is especially long. Thanks to Obama, Russia threatens Europe; North Korea is misbehaving; China is flexing its military muscles;

ISIS is on the march; Iran has a clear path to acquiring nuclear weapons; and perhaps most distressingly of all, Benjamin Netanyahu, the prime minister of Israel, is unhappy with US policy.

Here, too, the Republican candidates see eye-to-eye and have solutions readily at hand. In one way or another, all of those solutions relate to military power. Trump, Cruz, and Rubio are unabashed militarists. (So, too, is Hillary Clinton, but that's an issue deserving an essay of its own.) Their gripe with Obama is that he never put American military might fully to work, a defect they vow to amend. A Republican commander in chief, be it Trump, Cruz, or Rubio, won't take any guff from Moscow or Pyongyang or Beijing or Tehran. He will eradicate "radical Islamic terrorism," put the mullahs back in their box, torture a bunch of terrorists in the bargain, and give Bibi whatever he wants.

In addition to offering Obama a sort of backhanded tribute—so much damage wrought by just one man in so little time—the Republican critique reinforces reigning theories of presidential omnipotence. Just as an incompetent or ill-motivated chief executive can screw everything up, so, too, can a bold and skillful one set things right.

Juan and Evita in Washington?

The ratio between promises made and promises fulfilled by every president in recent memory—Obama included—should have demolished such theories long ago. But no such luck. Fantasies of a great president saving the day still persist, something that Trump, Cruz, and Rubio have all made the centerpiece of their campaigns. Elect me, each asserts. I alone can save the republic.

Here, however, Trump may enjoy an edge over his competitors, including Hillary Clinton and Bernie Sanders. With Americans assigning to their presidents the attributes of demigods—each and every one memorialized before death with a library-shrine—who better to fill the role than an egomaniacal tycoon who already acts the part? The times call for strong leadership. Who better to provide it than a wheeler-dealer unbothered by the rules that constrain mere mortals?

What then lies ahead?

If Trump secures the Republican nomination, now an increasingly imaginable prospect, the party is likely to implode. Whatever rump organization survives will have forfeited any remaining claim to represent principled conservatism.

None of this will matter to Trump, however. He is no conservative and Trumpism requires no party. Even if some new institutional alternative to conventional liberalism eventually emerges, the two-party system that has long defined the landscape of American politics will be gone for good.

Should Trump or a Trump mini-me ultimately succeed in capturing the presidency, a possibility that can no longer be dismissed out of hand, the effects will be even more profound. In all but name, the United States will cease to be a constitutional republic. Once President Trump inevitably declares that he alone expresses the popular will, Americans will find that they have traded the rule of law for a version of caudillismo. Trump's Washington could come to resemble Buenos Aires in the days of Juan Perón, with Melania a suitably glamorous stand-in for Evita, and plebiscites suitably glamorous stand-ins for elections.

That a considerable number of Americans appear to welcome this prospect may seem inexplicable. Yet reason enough exists for their disenchantment. American democracy has been decaying for decades. The people know that they are no longer truly sovereign. They know that the apparatus of power, both public and private, does not promote the common good, itself a concept that has become obsolete. They have had their fill of irresponsibility, lack of accountability, incompetence, and the bad times that increasingly seem to go with them.

So in disturbingly large numbers they have turned to Trump to strip bare the body politic, willing to take a chance that he will come up with something that, if not better, will at least be more entertaining. As Argentines and others who have trusted their fate to demagogues have discovered, such expectations are doomed to disappointment.

In the meantime, just imagine how the Donald J. Trump Presidential Library, no doubt taller than all the others put together, might one day glitter and glisten—perhaps with casino attached.

36
Slouching Toward Mar-a-Lago

The Post–Cold War Consensus Collapses

August 8, 2017

L ike it or not, the president of the United States embodies America itself. The individual inhabiting the White House has become the preeminent symbol of who we are and what we represent as a nation and a people. In a fundamental sense, he is us.

It was not always so. Millard Fillmore, the thirteenth president (1850–1853), presided over but did not personify the American republic. He was merely the federal chief executive. Contemporary observers did not refer to his term in office as the Age of Fillmore. With occasional exceptions, Abraham Lincoln in particular, much the same could be said of Fillmore's successors. They brought to office low expectations, which they rarely exceeded. So when Chester A. Arthur (1881–1885) or William Howard Taft (1909–1913) left the White House, there was no rush to immortalize them by erecting gaudy shrines—now known as "presidential libraries"—to the glory of their presidencies. In those distant days, ex-presidents went back home or somewhere else where they could find work.

Over the course of the past century, all that has changed. Ours is a republic that has long since taken on the trappings of a monarchy, with the president inhabiting rarified space as our king-emperor. The Brits have their woman in Buckingham Palace. We have our man in the White House.

Nominally, the Constitution assigns responsibilities and allocates prerogatives to three coequal branches of government. In practice, the executive branch enjoys primacy. Prompted by a seemingly endless series of crises since the Great Depression and World War II, presidents have accumulated ever-greater authority, partly through usurpation, but more often than not through forfeiture.

At the same time, they also took on various extra-constitutional responsibilities. By the beginning of the present century, Americans took it for granted that the occupant of the Oval Office should function as prophet, moral philosopher, style-setter, interpreter of the prevailing zeitgeist, and—last but hardly least—celebrity in chief. In short, POTUS was the bright star at the center of the American solar system.

As recently as a year ago, few saw in this cult of the presidency cause for complaint. On odd occasions, some particularly egregious bit of executive tomfoolery might trigger grumbling about an "imperial presidency." Yet rarely did such complaints lead to effective remedial action. The War Powers Resolution of 1973 might be considered the exception that proves the rule. Inspired by the disaster of the Vietnam War and intended to constrain presidents from using force without congressional buy-in and support, that particular piece of legislation ranks alongside the Volstead Act of 1919 (enacted to enforce Prohibition) as among the least effective ever to become law.

In truth, influential American institutions—investment banks and multinational corporations, churches and universities, big city newspapers and TV networks, the bloated national security apparatus and both major political parties—have found reason aplenty to endorse a system that elevates the president to the status of demigod. By and large, it's been good for business, whatever that business happens to be.

Furthermore, it's *our* president—not some foreign dude—who is, by common consent, the most powerful person in the universe. For inhabitants of a nation that considers itself both "exceptional" and "indispensable," this seems only right and proper. So Americans generally like it that *their* president is the acknowledged Leader of the Free World rather than some fresh-faced pretender from France or Canada.

Then came the Great Hysteria. Arriving with a Pearl Harbor–like shock, it erupted on the night of November 8, 2016, just as the news that Hillary Clinton was losing Florida and appeared certain to lose much else besides became apparent.

Suddenly, all the habits and precedents that had contributed to empowering the modern American presidency no longer made sense. That a single deeply flawed individual along with a handful of unelected associates and family members should be entrusted with determining the fate of the planet suddenly seemed the very definition of madness.

Emotion-laden upheavals producing behavior that is not entirely rational are hardly unknown in the American experience. Indeed, they recur with some frequency. The Great Awakenings of the eighteenth and early nineteenth centuries are examples of the phenomenon. So also are the two Red Scares of the twentieth century, the first in the early 1920s and the second, commonly known as "McCarthyism," coinciding with the onset of the Cold War.

Yet the response to Donald Trump's election, combining as it has fear, anger, bewilderment, disgust, and something akin to despair, qualifies as an upheaval without precedent. History itself had seemingly gone off the rails. The crude Andrew Jackson's 1828 ousting of an impeccably pedigreed president, John Quincy Adams, was nothing compared to the vulgar Trump's defeat of an impeccably credentialed graduate of Wellesley and Yale who had served as First Lady, United States senator, and secretary of state. A self-evidently inconceivable outcome—all the smart people agreed on that point—had somehow happened anyway.

A vulgar, bombastic, thrice-married real estate tycoon and reality TV host as prophet, moral philosopher, style-setter, interpreter of the prevailing zeitgeist, and chief celebrity? The very idea seemed both absurd and intolerable.

If we have, as innumerable commentators assert, embarked upon the Age of Trump, the defining feature of that age might well be the single-minded determination of those horrified and intent on ensuring its prompt termination. In 2016, *TIME* magazine chose Trump as its person of the year. In 2017, when it comes to dominating the news, that "person" might turn out to be a group—all those fixated on cleansing the White House of Trump's defiling presence.

Egged on and abetted in every way by Trump himself, the anti-Trump resistance has made itself the Big Story. Lies, hate, collusion, conspiracy, fascism: rarely has the everyday vocabulary of American politics been as ominous and forbidding as over the past six months. Take resistance rhetoric at face value and you might conclude that Trump is indeed the fifth horseman of the apocalypse, his presence in the presidential saddle eclipsing all other concerns. Pestilence, war, famine, and death will just have to wait.

The unspoken assumption of those most determined to banish him from public life appears to be this: once he's gone, history will be returned to its intended path, humankind will breathe a collective sigh of relief, and all will be well again. Yet such an assumption strikes me as remarkably wrongheaded—and not merely because, should Trump prematurely depart from office, Mike Pence will succeed him. Expectations that Trump's ouster will restore normalcy ignore the very factors that first handed him the Republican nomination (with a slew of competitors wondering what hit them) and then put him in the Oval Office (with a vastly more seasoned and disciplined, if uninspiring, opponent left to bemoan the injustice of it all).

Not all, but many of Trump's supporters voted for him for the same reason that people buy lottery tickets: Why not? In their estimation, they had little to lose. Their loathing of the status quo is such that they may well stick with Trump even as it becomes increasingly obvious that his promise of salvation—an America made "great again"—is not going to materialize.

Yet those who imagine that Trump's removal will put things right are likewise deluding themselves. To persist in thinking that he defines the problem is to commit an error of the first order. Trump is not cause, but consequence.

For too long, the cult of the presidency has provided an excuse for treating politics as a melodrama staged at four-year intervals and centering on hopes of another Roosevelt or Kennedy or Reagan appearing as the agent of American deliverance. Trump's ascent to the office once inhabited by those worthies should demolish such fantasies once and for all.

How is it that someone like Trump could become president in the first place? Blame sexism, Fox News, James Comey, Russian meddling, and Hillary's failure to visit Wisconsin all you want, but a more fundamental explanation is this: the election of 2016 constituted a de facto referendum on the course of recent American history. That referendum rendered a definitive judgment: the underlying consensus informing US policy since the end of the Cold War has collapsed. Precepts that members of the policy elite have long treated as self-evident no longer command the backing or assent of the American people. Put simply: it's the ideas, stupid.

Rabbit Poses a Question

"Without the Cold War, what's the point of being an American?" As the long twilight struggle was finally winding down, Harry "Rabbit" Angstrom, novelist John Updike's late-twentieth-century everyman, pondered that question. In short order, Rabbit got his answer. So, too, after only perfunctory consultation, did his fellow citizens.

The passing of the Cold War offered cause for celebration. On that point all agreed. Yet, as it turned out, it did not require reflection from the public at large. Policy elites professed to have matters well in hand. The dawning era, they believed, summoned Americans not to think anew, but to keep doing precisely what they were accustomed to doing, albeit without fretting further about communist takeovers or the risks of nuclear Armageddon. In a world where a "single superpower" was calling the shots, utopia was right around the corner. All that was needed was for the United States to demonstrate the requisite confidence and resolve.

Three specific propositions made up the elite consensus that coalesced during the initial decade of the post–Cold War era. According to the first, the globalization of corporate capitalism held the key to wealth creation on a hitherto unimaginable scale. According to the second, jettisoning norms derived from Judeo-Christian religious traditions held the key to the further expansion of personal freedom. According to the third, muscular global leadership exercised by the United States held the key to promoting a stable and humane international order.

Unfettered neoliberalism plus the unencumbered self plus unabashed American assertiveness: these defined the elements of the post–Cold War consensus that formed during the first half of the 1990s—plus what enthusiasts called the information revolution. The miracle of that "revolution," gathering momentum just as the Soviet Union was going down for the count, provided the secret sauce that infused the emerging consensus with a sense of historical inevitability.

The Cold War itself had fostered notable improvements in computational speed and capacity, new modes of communication, and techniques for storing, accessing, and manipulating information. Yet, however impressive, such developments remained subsidiary to the larger East-West competition. Only as the Cold War receded did they move from background to forefront. For true believers, information technology came to serve a quasi-theological function, promising answers to life's ultimate questions. Although God might be dead, Americans found in Bill Gates and Steve Jobs nerdy but compelling idols.

More immediately, in the eyes of the policy elite, the information revolution meshed with and reinforced the policy consensus. For those focused on the political economy, it greased the wheels of globalized capitalism, creating vast new opportunities for trade and investment. For those looking to shed constraints on personal freedom, information promised empowerment, making identity itself something to choose, discard, or modify. For members of the national security apparatus, the information revolution seemed certain to endow the United States with seemingly unassailable military capabilities. That these various enhancements would combine to improve the human condition was taken for granted; that they would, in due course, align everybody—from Afghans to Zimbabweans—with American values and the American way of life seemed more or less inevitable.

The three presidents of the post–Cold War era—Clinton, Bush, and Obama—put these several propositions to the test. Politics as theater requires us to pretend that our forty-second, forty-third, and forty-fourth presidents differed in fundamental ways. In practice, however, their similarities greatly outweighed any of those differences. Taken together, the administrations over which they presided collaborated in pursuing a common agenda, each intent on proving that the post–Cold War consensus could work in the face of mounting evidence to the contrary.

To be fair, it did work for some. "Globalization" made some people very rich indeed. In doing so, however, it greatly exacerbated inequality, while doing nothing to alleviate the condition of the American working class and underclass.

The emphasis on diversity and multiculturalism improved the status of groups long subjected to discrimination. Yet these advances have done remarkably little to reduce the alienation and despair pervading a society suffering from epidemics of chronic substance abuse, morbid obesity, teen suicide, and similar afflictions. Throw in the world's highest incarceration rate, a seemingly endless appetite for porn, urban school systems mired in permanent crisis, and mass shootings that occur with metronomic regularity, and what you have is something other than the profile of a healthy society.

As for militarized American global leadership, it has indeed resulted in various bad actors meeting richly deserved fates. Goodbye, Saddam. Good riddance, Osama. Yet it has also embroiled the United States in a series of costly, senseless, unsuccessful, and ultimately counterproductive wars. As for the vaunted information revolution, its impact has been ambiguous at best, even if those with eyeballs glued to their personal electronic devices can't tolerate being offline long enough to assess the actual costs of being perpetually connected.

In November 2016, Americans who consider themselves ill served by the post–Cold War consensus signaled that they had had enough. Voters not persuaded that neoliberal economic policies, a culture taking its motto from the Outback Steakhouse chain, and a national security strategy that employs the US military as a global police force were working to their benefit provided a crucial margin in the election of Donald Trump.

The response of the political establishment to this extraordinary repudiation testifies to the extent of its bankruptcy. The Republican Party still clings to the notion that reducing taxes, cutting government red tape, restricting abortion, curbing immigration, prohibiting flag-burning, and increasing military spending will alleviate all that ails the country. Meanwhile, to judge by the promises contained in their recently unveiled (and instantly forgotten) program for a "Better Deal," Democrats believe that raising the minimum wage, capping the cost of prescription drugs, and creating apprenticeship programs for the unemployed will return their party to the good graces of the American electorate.

In both parties embarrassingly small-bore thinking prevails, with Republicans and Democrats equally bereft of fresh ideas. Each party is led by aging hacks. Neither has devised an antidote to the crisis in American politics signified by the nomination and election of Donald Trump.

While our emperor tweets, Rome itself fiddles.

Starting Over

I am by temperament a conservative and a traditionalist, wary of revolutionary movements that more often than not end up being hijacked by nefarious plotters more interested in satisfying their own ambitions than in pursuing high ideals. Yet even I am prepared to admit that the status quo appears increasingly untenable. Incremental change will not suffice. The challenge of the moment is to embrace radicalism without succumbing to irresponsibility.

The one good thing we can say about the election of Trump—to borrow an image from Thomas Jefferson—is that it ought to serve as a fire bell in the night. If Americans have an ounce of sense, the Trump presidency will cure them once and for all of the illusion that from the White House comes redemption. By now we ought to have had enough of de facto monarchy.

By extension, Americans should come to see as intolerable the meanness, corruption, and partisan dysfunction so much in evidence at the opposite end of Pennsylvania Avenue. We need not wax sentimental over the days when Lyndon Johnson and Everett Dirksen presided over the Senate to conclude that Mitch McConnell and Chuck Schumer represent something other than progress. If Congress continues to behave as contemptibly as it has in recent years, it will, by default, allow the conditions that have produced Trump and his cronies to prevail.

So it's time to take another stab at an approach to governance worthy of a democratic republic. Where to begin? I submit that Rabbit Angstrom's question offers a place to start: What's the point of being an American?

Authentic progressives and principled conservatives will offer different answers to Rabbit's query. My own answer is rooted in an abiding conviction that our problems are less quantitative than qualitative. Rather than simply more—yet more wealth, more freedom, more attempts at global leadership—the times call for different. In my view, the point of being an American is to participate in creating a society that strikes a balance between wants and needs, that exists in harmony with nature and the rest of humankind, and that is rooted in an agreed upon conception of the common good.

My own prescription for how to act upon that statement of purpose is unlikely to find favor with most readers of *TomDispatch*. But therein lies the basis for an interesting debate, one that is essential to prospects for stemming the accelerating decay of American civic life.

Initiating such a debate, and so bringing into focus core issues, will remain next to impossible, however, without first clearing away the accumulated debris of the post–Cold War era. Preliminary steps in that direction, listed in no particular order, ought to include the following:

First, abolish the Electoral College. Doing so will preclude any further occurrence of the circumstances that twice in recent decades cast doubt on the outcome of national elections and thereby did far more than any foreign interference to undermine the legitimacy of American politics.

Second, rollback gerrymandering. Doing so will help restore competitive elections and make incumbency more tenuous.

Third, limit the impact of corporate money on elections at all levels, if need be by amending the Constitution.

Fourth, mandate a balanced federal budget, thereby demolishing the pretense that Americans need not choose between guns and butter.

Fifth, implement a program of national service, thereby eliminating the all-volunteer military and restoring the tradition of the citizen-soldier. Doing so will help close the gap between the military and society and enrich the prevailing conception of citizenship. It might even encourage members of Congress to think twice before signing off on wars that the commander in chief wants to fight.

Sixth, enact tax policies that will promote greater income equality.

Seventh, increase public funding for public higher education, thereby ensuring that college remains an option for those who are not well-to-do.

Eighth, beyond mere "job" creation, attend to the growing challenges of providing meaningful work—employment that is both rewarding and reasonably remunerative—for those without advanced STEM degrees.

Ninth, end the thumb-twiddling on climate change and start treating it as the first-order national security priority that it is.

Tenth, absent evident progress on the above, create a new party system, breaking the current duopoly in which Republicans and Democrats tacitly collaborate to dictate the policy agenda and restrict the range of policy options deemed permissible.

These are not particularly original proposals and I do not offer them as a panacea. They may, however, represent preliminary steps toward devising some new paradigm to replace a post–Cold War consensus that, in promoting transnational corporate greed, mistaking libertinism for liberty, and embracing militarized neo-imperialism as the essence of statecraft, has paved the way for the presidency of Donald Trump.

We can and must do better. But doing so will require that we come up with better and truer ideas to serve as a foundation for American politics.

37
How We Got Donald Trump

(And How We Might Have Avoided Him)

January 30, 2018

The present arrives out of a past that we are too quick to forget, misremember, or enshroud in myth. Yet like it or not, the present is the product of past choices. Different decisions back then might have yielded very different outcomes in the here and now. Donald Trump ascended to the presidency as a consequence of myriad choices that Americans made (or had made for them) over the course of decades. Although few of those were made with Trump in mind, he is the result.

Where exactly did Trump come from? How are we to account for his noxious presence as commander in chief and putative leader of the free world? The explanations currently on offer are legion. Some blame the nefarious Steve Bannon, others Hillary Clinton and her lackluster campaign. Or perhaps the fault lies with the Bernie Sanders insurgency, which robbed Clinton of the momentum she needed to win, or with Little Marco, Lyin' Ted, and Low Energy Jeb, and the other pathetic Republicans whom Trump trampled underfoot en route to claiming the nomination. Or perhaps the real villains are all those "deplorables"—the angry and ignorant white males whose disdain for immigrants, feminists, anyone LGBTQ, and people of color Trump stoked and manipulated to great effect.

All such explanations, however, suggest that the relevant story began somewhere around June 2015 when Trump astonished the political world by announcing his intention to seek the presidency. My aim here is to suggest that the origins of the real story are to be found much earlier. The conditions that enabled Trump to capture the presidency stemmed from acts of commission and omission that occurred well before he rode down that escalator at Trump Tower to offer his services to the nation.

The sad part is that at each step along the way, other alternatives were available. Had those alternatives been exercised, a Trump presidency would have remained an absurd fantasy rather than becoming an absurd and dangerous reality. Like the Cuban Missile Crisis or the Vietnam War or 9/11, Trump qualifies as a completely avoidable catastrophe with roots deep in the past.

So who's at fault? Ultimately, we—the American people—must accept a considerable share of the responsibility. This is one buck that can't be passed.

Coulda, Woulda, Shoulda

So what follows is a review of roads taken (and not) ultimately leading to the demoralizing presidency of Donald Trump, along with a little speculation on how different choices might have resulted in a decidedly different present.

1989: *The Fall of the Berlin Wall.* As the Cold War wound down, members of Washington's smart set, Republicans and Democrats alike, declared that the opportunities now presenting themselves went beyond the merely stupendous. Indeed, history itself had ended. With the United States as the planet's sole superpower, liberal democratic capitalism was destined to prevail everywhere. There would be no way except the American Way. In fact, however, the passing of the Cold War should have occasioned a moment of reflection regarding the sundry mistakes and moral compromises that marred US policy from the 1940s through the 1980s. Unfortunately, policy elites had no interest in second thoughts—and certainly not in remorse or contrition. In the 1990s, rampant victory disease fueled extraordinary hubris and a pattern of reckless behavior informed by an assumption that the world would ultimately conform to the wishes of the "indispensable nation." In the years to come, an endless sequence of costly mishaps would ensue from Mogadishu to Mosul. When, in due time, Trump announced his intention to dismantle the establishment that had presided over those failures, many Americans liked what he had to say, even if he spoke from a position of total ignorance.

1992: *President H. Ross Perot.* In the first post–Cold War presidential election, H. Ross Perot, a wealthy entrepreneur and political novice, mounted an independent challenge to the Republican and Democratic nominees. Both parties, Perot charged, were in bed with lobbyists, insiders, and special interests. Both were enthusiastically presiding over the deindustrialization of a once dominant American economy. The rich were getting richer, the national debt was growing, and ordinary citizens were getting screwed, he contended. His charges were not without merit. Yet when Perot lost, Washington was back to business as usual. We cannot know what a Perot presidency would have produced. Yet such a victory—the American electorate, in effect, repudiating the two established parties—might have created powerful incentives for both Republicans and Democrats to clean up their acts and find ways of governing more effectively. Had they done so, Trump's later vow to "drain the swamp" of corruption and self-dealing would have been beside the point.

1993: *Gays in the Military.* Bill Clinton ran for the presidency as a centrist. Even so, once elected, he immediately announced his intention to remove restrictions on gays serving in the armed forces. This was, to put it mildly, anything but the act of a centrist. Outraged senior military officers made clear their intention to defy the new commander in chief. Although Clinton quickly backpedaled, the episode infuriated both cultural traditionalists and progressives. Within twenty years, a different generation of senior officers decided that gays serving in the military was no big deal. The issue instantly vanished. Yet the controversy left behind a residue of bitterness, especially on the right, that worked in Trump's favor. Had the generals of 1993 suppressed their insubordinate inclinations, they might have ever so slightly turned down the heat on the culture wars. When the heat is high, it's the tub-thumpers and noisy haranguers who benefit.

1998: *The Lewinsky Scandal.* When President Clinton's sexual encounters with a young White House intern became known, Hillary

Clinton stood by her man. The First Lady's steadfast loyalty helped her husband avoid being thrown out of office, providing cover for other feminists to continue supporting the president. Imagine if she had done otherwise, declaring his conduct unacceptable. The pressure on him to resign coming from those who had been among his strongest supporters would have been intense. Certainly, had evidence of infidelity, compounded by prior allegations of abuse toward women, forced President Clinton from office, Trump would never have had a chance of being elected president. In all likelihood he would never even have considered running.

2000: *Cheney Picks a Veep.* When George W. Bush wrapped up the Republican nomination in 2000, he tagged Dick Cheney, his father's defense secretary, with the task of identifying a suitable running mate. After surveying the field, Cheney decided that he himself was the man for the job. As vice president, Cheney wasted no time in stacking the upper ranks of the administration with like-minded allies keen to wield American military muscle to smite "evildoers" and expand America's empire. Bush had promised, if elected, to pursue a "humble" foreign policy and forego nation-building. Had he not surrounded himself with Cheney and bellicose companions like Donald Rumsfeld and Paul Wolfowitz, he might possibly have stuck to that course, even after 9/11. Instead, urged on by the uber-hawks in his own administration, he embarked upon a misguided Global War on Terrorism. No single action played a greater role in paving the way for Trump to become president.

2000: *The Supremes Pick a President.* If, in choosing a president on our behalf, the Supreme Court had given the nod to Al Gore instead of George Bush, might they have averted that never-ending, never-contracting War on Terrorism? No doubt the 9/11 attacks would still have occurred and some US military action would have ensued. But Gore did not share the obsession with Saddam Hussein that infected members of the Bush-Cheney axis. Arguably, a President Gore would have been less likely than President Bush to insist on invading a country that had played no part in the al-Qaeda conspiracy. Had the US not embarked upon a preventive war against Iraq—had this original sin of the post-9/11 era not occurred—a Trump presidency would have been far less likely.

2003: *Congress Rolls Over.* To its perpetual disgrace, Congress assented to Bush's demands to invade Iraq. It did so less because its members, including presidential aspirants like Senators Hillary Clinton and John Kerry, were persuaded that Iraq posed a threat to national security (it did not) than because they sought to insulate themselves from the political consequences of opposing a president hell-bent on war. For decades, Congress had allowed presidents to encroach upon its constitutional responsibility to declare war, but this would be the last straw. Supine legislators became complicit in a disaster that to this day continues to unfold. A Congress with gumption might have averted that disaster, recovered its cojones, and left us with a legislative branch willing and able to fulfill its constitutional responsibilities.

2003: *GM Kills the EV1 Electric Automobile.* In the 1990s, General Motors produced the first viable electric car. Drivers loved it, but GM doubted its potential profitability. Shareholders were more likely to make money if the company focused on manufacturing vehicles powered by gasoline engines. So in 2003, GM executives killed the EV1. The effect was to postpone by at least a decade the development of a mass-produced electric car. Had GM persisted, it's just possible that the EV1 might have jump-started the transition to a post–fossil fuel economy and offered humanity a leg up on climate change. Instead, politicians spent years bickering about whether climate change was even real. More than a few Republicans made political hay by denouncing those waging a "war on coal" or inhibiting crucially needed oil exploration—bogus charges that Trump adroitly exploited for his own purposes. Perhaps if the EV1 had fulfilled its potential, anyone mounting a presidential campaign while denouncing global warming as a hoax would have been laughed out of town instead of capturing the White House.

2009: *Obama Bails Out Wall Street.* President Obama entered the Oval Office with the US economy in free fall. His administration took prompt action to prevent systemic collapse—that is, it bailed out Wall Street. Meanwhile the little guy got clobbered, with millions of Americans losing their jobs and homes. A billionaire complaining about the system being "rigged" might otherwise have tested the outer limits of irony, but for Trump the government's handling of the Great Recession was a gift from the gods.

2010: *Presidential Twitter Accounts.* Huge numbers of Americans have willingly surrendered their lives to social media. I'm guessing that there are more vegans and curling aficionados in the United States today than there are nonsubscribers to Facebook. So it was perhaps inevitable that politicians would hoist themselves onto the social media bandwagon, keen to use direct, unmediated electronic communications as a way of mobilizing their followers. Yet the resulting impact on American politics has been entirely negative. The space available for reasoned exchanges has shrunk. Political discourse has become increasingly corrosive, its apparent purpose less to inform than to obfuscate, trivialize, and create division. This development was probably inevitable and will no doubt prove irreversible. Even so, it was *not* inevitable that the presidency itself should succumb to this phenomenon. In 2010, when Obama "made history" by sending the first presidential tweet, it was as if the pope had begun spending his idle hours hanging out at some corner saloon. Even if only in barely measurable increments, the dignity and decorum associated with the presidency began to fade and with it the assumption that crude or boorish behavior would automatically disqualify someone for high office. Trump, a first-class boor and maestro of Twitter, was quick to take notice.

2010: *Mitch McConnell Chooses Party Over Country.* With the nation still in the midst of a devastating economic crisis, Republican Senate leader McConnell declared on behalf of his party that the denial of a second term to President Obama was "the single most important thing we want to achieve." To hell with the country, the GOP wanted Obama gone. McConnell's troops fell obediently into line and the last vestiges of bipartisanship disappeared from Washington. Of course, the president won reelection in 2012 anyway, but in effect McConnell refused to recognize the result. So when Obama exercised a president's prerogative to nominate someone to fill a Supreme Court vacancy, McConnell ensured that the nominee would not even receive the courtesy of a hearing. An environment rife with hyper-partisanship presented the perfect situation for a political outsider skilled in the "art of the deal" to offer himself as the antidote to persistent gridlock. Congratulations, Mitch! You won after all!

And So . . . ?

It's time to look in the mirror, folks. Blaming Trump for being Trump simply won't do. Like Lenin or Franco or Perón or dozens of other demagogues, Trump merely seized the opportunity that presented itself. Our president is a product and beneficiary of several decades' worth of vainglory, cynicism, epic folly, political cowardice, missed opportunities, and a public not given to paying attention. In present-day Washington, no one can deny that the chickens have come home to roost. The biggest fowl of them all has taken up residence in the White House and, in a very real sense, we all put him there.

38
After Trump

The Donald in the Rearview Mirror

September 11, 2018

onald Trump's tenure as the forty-fifth US president may last another few weeks, another year, or another sixteen months. However unsettling the prospect, the leaky vessel that is the S.S. Trump might even manage to stay afloat for a second term. Nonetheless, recent headline-making revelations suggest that, like some derelict ship that's gone aground, the Trump presidency may already have effectively run its course. What, then, does this bizarre episode in American history signify?

Let me state my own view bluntly: forget the atmospherics. Despite the lies, insults, name calling, and dog whistles, *almost nothing of substance has changed.* Nor will it.

To a far greater extent than Trump's perpetually hyperventilating critics are willing to acknowledge, the United States remains on a trajectory that does not differ appreciably from what it was prior to POTUS #45 taking office. Post-Trump America, just now beginning to come into view, is shaping up to look remarkably like pre-Trump America.

I understand that His Weirdness remains in the White House. Yet for all practical purposes, Trump has ceased to govern. True, he continues to rant and issue bizarre directives, which his subordinates implement, amend, or simply disregard as they see fit. Except in a ceremonial sense, the office of the presidency presently lies vacant. Call it an abdication-in-place. It's as if British King Edward VIII, having abandoned his throne for "the woman I love," continued to hang around Buckingham Palace fuming about the lack of respect given

Wallis and releasing occasional bulletins affirming his admiration for Adolf Hitler.

In Trump's case, it's unlikely he ever had a more serious interest in governing than Edward had in performing duties more arduous than those he was eventually assigned as Duke of Windsor. Nonetheless, the sixty-plus million Americans who voted for Trump did so with at least the expectation that he was going to shake things up.

And bigly. Remember, he was going to "lock her up." He would "drain the swamp" and "build a wall," with Mexico volunteering to foot the bill. Without further ado, he would end "this American carnage." Meanwhile, "America First" would form the basis for US foreign policy. Once Trump took charge, things were going to be different, as he and he alone would "make America great again."

Yet the cataclysm that Trump's ascendency was said to signify has yet to occur. Barring a nuclear war, it won't.

If you spend your days watching CNN or MSNBC or reading columnists employed by the *New York Times* and the *Washington Post*, you might conclude otherwise. But those are among the institutions that, on November 8, 2016, suffered a nervous breakdown from which they have yet to recover. Nor, it now seems clear, do they wish to recover as long as Trump remains president. To live in a perpetual state of high dudgeon, denouncing his latest inanity and predicting the onset of fascism, is to enjoy the equivalent of a protracted psychic orgasm, one induced by mutual masturbation.

Yet if you look beyond the present to the fairly recent past, it becomes apparent that change on the scale that Trump was promising *had* actually occurred, even if well before he himself showed up on the scene. The consequences of that Big Change are going to persist long after he is gone. It's those consequences that now demand our attention, not the ongoing Gong Show jointly orchestrated by the White House and journalists fancying themselves valiant defenders of Truth.

Trump himself is no more than a pimple on the face of this nation's history. It's time to step back from the mirror and examine the face in full. Pretty it's not.

The Way We Were

Compare the America that welcomed young Donald Trump into the world in 1946 with the country that, some seventh years later, elected him president. As the post–World War II era was beginning, three large facts—so immense that they were simply taken for granted—defined America.

First, the United States made everything and made more of it than anyone else. In postwar America, wealth derived in large measure from the manufacture of stuff: steel, automobiles, refrigerators, shoes, socks, blouses, baseballs, you name it. "Made in the USA" was more than just a slogan. With so much of the industrialized world in ruins, the American economy dominated and defined everyday economic reality globally.

Second, back then while the mighty engine of industrial capitalism was generating impressive riches, it was also distributing the benefits on a relatively equitable basis. Postwar America was the emblematic middle-class country, the closest approximation to a genuinely classless and democratic society the world had ever seen.

Third, having had their fill of fighting from 1941 to 1945, Americans had a genuine aversion to war. They may not have been a peace-loving people, but they knew enough about war to see it as a great evil. Avoiding its further occurrence, if at all possible, was a priority, although one not fully shared by the new national security establishment just then beginning to flex its muscles in Washington.

Now, by twenty-first-century standards, many, perhaps nearly all, Americans of that era were bigots of one sort or the other. Racism, sexism, and homophobia flourished, lamented by some, promoted by others, tolerated by the vast majority. An anti-communist political hysteria, abetted by cynical politicians, also flourished. Americans worked themselves into a tizzy over the putative threat posed by small numbers of homegrown subversives. And they fouled the air, water, and soil with abandon. Add to this list violence, crime, corruption, sexual angst, and various forms of self-abuse. Taken as a whole, American society, as it existed when Trump was growing up, was anything but perfect. Yet, for all that, postwar Americans were the envy of the world. And they knew it.

By 2016, when Trump was elected president, America had become an altogether different country. Without actually disappearing, racism, sexism, and homophobia had—at least for the moment—gone underground. Attitudes toward people of color, women, and LGBTQ folks that a half-century earlier had been commonplace were now taboo in polite society. Hysteria about communists had essentially disappeared, only to be replaced by hysteria over Islamic terrorists. Pollution, of course, persisted, as did violence, crime, corruption, and sexual angst. New and more imaginative forms of self-destructive behavior had made their appearance.

Yet little of that turned out to be central. What had truly changed in the decades since Trump was a babe in arms were those three taken-for-granted facts that had once distinguished the United States. New realities emerged to invert them.

By 2016, the US was no longer by any stretch of the imagination the place that made everything, though it bought everything, often made elsewhere. It had long since become the ultimate consumer society, with Americans accustomed to acquiring and enjoying more than they produced or could afford. Accounts no longer balanced. The government lived on credit, assuming that the bills would never come due. So, too, did many citizens.

By 2016, the US had long since become a deeply unequal society of haves and have-nots. Finance capitalism, the successor to industrial capitalism, was creating immense fortunes without even pretending to distribute the benefits equitably. Politicians still routinely paid tribute to the Great American Middle Class. Yet the hallmarks of postwar middle-class life—a steady job, a paycheck adequate to support a family, the prospect of a pension—were rapidly disappearing. While Americans still enjoyed freedom of a sort, many of them lacked security.

By 2016, Americans had also come to accept war as normal. Here was "global leadership" made manifest. So US troops were now always out there somewhere fighting, however obscure the purpose of their exertions and however dim their prospects of achieving anything approximating victory. The 99 percent of Americans who were not soldiers learned to tune out those wars, content merely to "support the troops," an obligation fulfilled by offering periodic expressions of reverence on public occasions. Thank you for your service!

The Way We Are

But note: Trump played no role in creating this America or consigning the America of 1946 to oblivion. As a modern equivalent of P. T. Barnum, he did demonstrate considerable skill in exploiting the opportunities on offer as the strictures of postwar America gave way. Indeed, he parlayed those opportunities into fortune, celebrity, lots of golf, plenty of sex, and eventually the highest office in the land. Only in America, as we used to say.

In 1946, it goes without saying, he would never have been taken seriously as a would-be presidential candidate. By 2016, his narcissism, bombast, vulgarity, and talent for self-promotion nicely expressed the underside of the prevailing zeitgeist. His candidacy was simultaneously preposterous, yet strangely fitting.

By the twenty-first century, the values that Trump embodies had become as thoroughly and authentically American as any of those specified in the oracular pronouncements of Jefferson, Lincoln, or Roosevelt. Trump's critics may see him as an abomination. But he is also one of us.

The real news is that the essential traits that define America today—those things that make this country so different from what it seemed to be in 1946—will surely survive the Trump presidency. If anything, he and his cronies deserve at least some credit for sustaining just those traits.

Candidate Trump essentially promised Americans a version of 1946 redux. He would revive manufacturing and create millions of well-paying jobs for working stiffs. By cutting taxes, he would put more money in the average Joe or Jill's pocket. He would eliminate the trade deficit and balance the federal budget. He would end our endless wars and bring the troops home where they belong. He would oblige America's allies, portrayed as a crew of freeloaders, to shoulder their share of the burden. He would end illegal immigration. He would make the United States once more the God-fearing Christian country it was meant to be.

How seriously Trump expected any of those promises to be taken is anyone's guess. But this much is for sure: they remain almost entirely unfulfilled.

True, domestic manufacturing has experienced a slight uptick, but globalization remains an implacable reality. Unless you've got a STEM degree, good jobs are still hard to come by. Ours is increasingly a "gig" economy, which might be cool enough when you're twenty-five, but less so when you're in your sixties and wondering if you'll ever be able to retire.

While Trump and a Republican Congress delivered on their promise of tax "reform," its chief beneficiaries will be the rich—further confirmation, if it were needed, that the American economy is indeed rigged in favor of a growing class of plutocrats. Trade deficit? It's headed for a ten-year high. Balanced budget? You've got to be joking. The estimated federal deficit next year will exceed a trillion dollars, boosting the national debt past $21 trillion. (Trump had promised to eliminate that debt entirely.)

And, of course, the wars haven't ended. Here is Trump, just last month, doing his best George McGovern imitation: "I'm constantly reviewing Afghanistan and the whole Middle East," he asserted. "We never should have been in the Middle East. It was the single greatest mistake in the history of our country." Yet Trump has perpetuated and, in some instances, expanded America's military misadventures in the Greater Middle East, while essentially insulating himself from personal responsibility for their continuation.

As commander in chief, he's a distinctly hands-off kind of guy. Despite being unable to walk, President Franklin Roosevelt visited GIs serving in combat zones more often than Trump has. If you want to know why we are in Afghanistan and how long US forces will stay there, ask Defense Secretary James Mattis or some general, but don't, whatever you do, ask the president.

On Not Turning America's Back on the World

And then there is the matter of Trump's "isolationism." Recall that when he became president, foreign policy experts across Washington warned that the United States would now turn its back on the world and abandon its self-assigned role as keeper of order and defender of democracy. Now, nearing the midpoint of Trump's first (and hopefully last) term, the United States remains formally committed to defending the territorial integrity of each and every NATO member state, numbering twenty-nine in all. Add to that an obligation to defend nations as varied as Japan, South Korea, and, under the terms of the Rio Pact of 1947, most of Latin America. Less formally but no less substantively, the US ensures the security of Israel, Saudi Arabia, and various other Persian Gulf countries.

As for obliging those allies to pony up more for the security we have long claimed to provide, that's clearly not going to happen any time soon. Our European allies have pocketed both Trump's insults and his assurances that the United States will continue to defend them, offering in return the vaguest of promises that, sometime in the future, they might consider investing more in defense.

By the by, US forces under Trump's ostensible command are today present in more than 150 countries worldwide. Urged on by the president, Congress has passed a bill that boosts the Pentagon budget to $717 billion, an $82 billion increase over the prior year. Needless to say, no adversary or plausible combination of adversaries comes anywhere close to matching that figure.

To call this isolationism is comparable to calling Trump svelte.

As for the promised barrier, that "big, fat, beautiful wall," to seal the southern border, it has advanced no further than the display of several possible prototypes. No evidence exists to suggest that Mexico will, as Trump insisted, pay for its construction, nor that Congress will appropriate the necessary funds, estimated at somewhere north of $20 billion, even with Republicans still controlling both houses of Congress. And in truth, whether it is built or not, the US-Mexico border will remain what it has been for decades: heavily patrolled but porous, a conduit for desperate people seeking safety and opportunity, but also for criminal elements trafficking in drugs or human beings.

The point of this informal midterm report card is not to argue that Trump has somehow failed. It is rather to highlight his essential irrelevance.

Trump is not the disruptive force that anti-Trumpers accuse him of being. He is merely a noxious, venal, and ineffectual blowhard, who has assembled a team of associates who are themselves, with few exceptions, noxious, venal, or ineffectual.

The upshot of it all is, if you were basically okay with where America was headed prior to November 2016, just take a deep breath and think of Trump as the political equivalent of a kidney stone—not fun, but sooner or later, it will pass. And when it does, normalcy will return. Soon enough you'll forget it ever happened.

If, on the other hand, you were not okay with where America was headed in 2016, it's past time to give up the illusion that Donald Trump is going to make things right. Eventually a pimple dries up and disappears, often without leaving a trace. Such is the eventual destiny of Donald Trump as president.

In the meantime, of course, there are any number of things about Trump to raise our ire. Climate change offers a good example. And yet climate change may be the best illustration of Trump's insignificance. Under President Obama, the United States showed signs of mounting a belated effort to address global warming. The Trump administration wasted little time in reversing course, reverting to the science-denying position to which Republicans adhered long before Trump himself showed up.

No doubt future generations will find fault with Trump's inaction in the face of this crisis. Yet when Miami is underwater and California wildfires rage throughout the year, Trump himself won't be the only—or even the principal—culprit charged with culpable neglect.

The nation's too-little, too-late response to climate change for which a succession of presidents share responsibility illustrates the great and abiding defect of contemporary American politics. When all is said and done, presidents don't shape the country; the country shapes the presidency—or at least it defines the parameters within which presidents operate. Over the course of the last few decades, those parameters have become increasingly at odds with the collective well-being of the American people, not to mention of the planet as a whole.

Yet Americans have been obdurate in refusing to acknowledge that fact.

Americans today are deeply divided. There exists no greater symbol of that division than Trump himself—the wild enthusiasm he generates in some quarters, and the antipathy verging on hatred he elicits in others.

The urgent need of the day is to close that divide, which is as broad as it is deep, touching on culture, the political economy, America's role in the world, and the definition of the common good. I submit that these matters lie beyond any president's purview, but especially this one's.

Trump is not the problem. Think of him instead as a summons to address the real problem, which in a nation ostensibly of, by, and for the people is the collective responsibility of the people themselves. For Americans to shirk that responsibility further will almost surely pave the way for more Trumps—or someone worse—to come.

39

The Real Cover-Up

Putting Donald Trump's Impeachment in Context

October 8, 2019

There is blood in the water and frenzied sharks are closing in for the kill. Or so they think.

From the time of Trump's election, American elites have hungered for this moment. At long last, they have the forty-fifth president of the United States cornered. In typically ham-handed fashion, Trump has given his adversaries the very means to destroy him politically. They will not waste the opportunity. Impeachment now—finally, some will say—qualifies as a virtual certainty.

No doubt many surprises lie ahead. Yet the Democrats controlling the House of Representatives have passed the point of no return. The time for prudential judgments—the Republican-controlled Senate will never convict, so why bother?—is gone for good. To back down now would expose the president's pursuers as spineless cowards. The *New York Times*, the *Washington Post*, CNN, and MSNBC would not soon forgive such craven behavior.

So, as President Woodrow Wilson, speaking in 1919, put it, "The stage is set, the destiny disclosed. It has come about by no plan of our conceiving, but by the hand of God." Of course, the issue back then was a notably weighty one: whether to ratify the Versailles Treaty. That it now concerns what Congressman Adam Schiff (D-CA) referred to as a "Mafia-like shakedown" orchestrated by one of Wilson's successors tells us something about the trajectory of American politics over the course of the last century and it has not been a story of ascent.

The effort to boot the president from office is certain to yield a memorable spectacle. The rancor and contempt that have clogged American politics like a backed-up sewer since the day of Trump's election will now find release. Watergate will pale by comparison. The uproar triggered by Bill Clinton's "sexual relations" will be nothing by comparison. A de facto collaboration between Trump, those who despise him, and those who despise his critics all but guarantees that this story will dominate the news, undoubtedly for months to come.

As this process unspools, what politicians like to call "the people's business" will go essentially unattended. So while Congress considers whether or not to remove Trump from office, gun-control legislation will languish, the deterioration of the nation's infrastructure will proceed apace, needed healthcare reforms will be tabled, the military-industrial complex will waste yet more billions, and the national debt, already at $22 trillion—larger, that is, than the entire economy—will continue to surge. The looming threat posed by climate change, much talked about of late, will proceed all but unchecked. For those of us preoccupied with America's role in the world, the obsolete assumptions and habits undergirding what's still called "national security" will continue to evade examination. Our endless wars will remain endless and pointless.

By way of compensation, we might wonder what benefits impeachment is likely to yield. Answering that question requires examining four scenarios that describe the range of possibilities awaiting the nation.

The first and most to be desired (but least likely) is that Trump will tire of being a public piñata and just quit. With the thrill of flying in Air Force One having worn off, being president can't be as much fun these days. Why put up with further grief? How much more entertaining for Trump to retire to the political sidelines where he can tweet up a storm and indulge his penchant for name-calling. And think of the "deals" an ex-president could make in countries like Israel, North Korea, Poland, and Saudi Arabia on which he's bestowed favors. Cha-ching! As of yet, however, the president shows no signs of taking the easy (and lucrative) way out.

The second possible outcome sounds almost as good but is no less implausible: a sufficient number of Republican senators rediscover their moral compass and "do the right thing," joining with Democrats to create the two-thirds majority needed to convict Trump and send him packing. In the Washington of that classic twentieth-century film director Frank Capra, with Jimmy Stewart holding forth on the Senate floor and a moist-eyed Jean Arthur cheering him on from the gallery, this might have happened. In the real Washington of "Moscow Mitch" McConnell, think again.

The third somewhat seamier outcome might seem a tad more likely. It postulates that McConnell and various GOP senators facing reelection in 2020 or 2022 will calculate that turning on Trump just might offer the best way of saving their own skins. The president's loyalty to just about anyone, wives included, has always been highly contingent, the people streaming out of his administration routinely making the point. So why should senatorial loyalty to the president be any different? At the moment, however, indications that Trump loyalists out in the hinterlands will reward such turncoats are just about nonexistent. Unless that base were to flip, don't expect Republican senators to do anything but flop.

That leaves outcome number four, easily the most probable: while the House will impeach, the Senate will decline to convict. Trump will therefore stay right where he is, with the matter of his fitness for office effectively deferred to the November 2020 elections. Except as a source of sadomasochistic diversion, the entire agonizing experience will, therefore, prove to be a colossal waste of time and blather.

Furthermore, Trump might well emerge from this national ordeal with his reelection chances enhanced. Such a prospect is belatedly insinuating itself into public discourse. For that reason, certain anti-Trump pundits are already showing signs of going wobbly, suggesting, for instance, that censure rather than outright impeachment might suffice as punishment for the president's various offenses. Yet censuring Trump while allowing him to stay in office would be the equivalent of letting Harvey Weinstein off with a good tongue-lashing so that he can get back to making movies. Censure is for wimps.

Besides, as Trump campaigns for a second term, he would almost surely wear censure like a badge of honor. Keep in mind that Congress's approval ratings are considerably worse than his. To more than a few members of the public, a black mark awarded by Congress might look like a gold star.

Not Removal But Restoration

So if Trump finds himself backed into a corner, Democrats aren't necessarily in a more favorable position. And that ain't the half of it. Let me suggest that, while Trump is being pursued, it's you, my fellow Americans, who are really being played. The unspoken purpose of impeachment is not removal, but restoration. The overarching aim is not to replace Trump with Mike Pence—the equivalent of exchanging Groucho for Harpo. No, the object of the exercise is to return power to those who created the conditions that enabled Trump to win the White House in the first place.

Just recently, for instance, Hillary Clinton declared Trump to be an "illegitimate president." Implicit in her charge is the conviction—no doubt sincere—that people like Trump are not supposed to *be* president. People like Hillary Clinton—people possessing credentials like hers and sharing her values—should be the chosen ones. Here we glimpse the true meaning of legitimacy in this context. Whatever the vote in the Electoral College, Trump doesn't *deserve* to be president and never did.

For many of the main participants in this melodrama, the actual but unstated purpose of impeachment is to correct this great wrong and thereby restore history to its anointed path.

In a recent column in the *Guardian*, Professor Samuel Moyn makes the essential point: Removing from office a vulgar, dishonest, and utterly incompetent president comes nowhere close to capturing what's going on here. To the elites most intent on ousting Trump, far more important than anything he may say or do is what he signifies. He is a walking, talking repudiation of everything they believe and, by extension, of a future they had come to see as foreordained.

Moyn styles these anti-Trump elites as "centrists," members of the post–Cold War political mainstream that allowed ample room for nominally conservative Bushes and nominally liberal Clintons, while leaving just enough space for Obama's promise of hope and (not-too-much) change.

These centrists share a common worldview. They believe in the universality of freedom as defined and practiced within the United States. They believe in corporate capitalism operating on a planetary scale. They believe in American primacy, with the United States presiding over a global order as the sole superpower. They believe in "American global leadership," which they define as primarily a military enterprise. And perhaps most of all, while collecting degrees from Georgetown, Harvard, Oxford, Wellesley, the University of Chicago, and Yale, they came to believe in a so-called meritocracy as the preferred mechanism for allocating wealth, power, and privilege. All of these together comprise the sacred scripture of contemporary American political elites. And if Trump's antagonists have their way, his removal will restore that sacred scripture to its proper place as the basis of policy.

"For all their appeals to enduring moral values," Moyn writes, "the centrists are deploying a transparent strategy to return to power." Destruction of the Trump presidency is a necessary precondition for achieving that goal. "Centrists simply want to return to the status quo interrupted by Trump, their reputations laundered by their courageous opposition to his mercurial reign, and their policies restored to credibility." Precisely.

High Crimes and Misdemeanors

For such a scheme to succeed, however, laundering reputations alone will not suffice. Equally important will be to bury any recollection of the catastrophes that paved the way for an über-qualified centrist to lose to an indisputably unqualified and unprincipled political novice in 2016.

Holding promised security assistance hostage unless a foreign leader agrees to do you political favors is obviously and indisputably wrong. Trump's antics regarding Ukraine may even meet some definition of criminal. Still, how does such misconduct compare to the calamities engineered by the "centrists" who preceded him? Consider, in particular, the

George W. Bush administration's decision to invade Iraq in 2003 (along with the spin-off wars that followed). Consider, too, the reckless economic policies that produced the Great Recession of 2007–2008. As measured by the harm inflicted on the American people (and others), the offenses for which Trump is being impeached qualify as mere misdemeanors.

Honest people may differ on whether to attribute the Iraq War to outright lies or monumental hubris. When it comes to tallying up the consequences, however, the intentions of those who sold the war don't particularly matter. The results include thousands of Americans killed; tens of thousands wounded, many grievously, or left to struggle with the effects of PTSD; hundreds of thousands of non-Americans killed or injured; millions displaced; trillions of dollars expended; radical groups like ISIS empowered (and in its case even formed inside a US prison in Iraq); and the Persian Gulf region plunged into turmoil from which it has yet to recover. How do Trump's crimes stack up against these?

The Great Recession stemmed directly from economic policies implemented during the administration of President Bill Clinton and continued by his successor. Deregulating the banking sector was projected to produce a bonanza in which all would share. Yet, as a direct result of the ensuing chicanery, nearly nine million Americans lost their jobs, while overall unemployment shot up to 10 percent. Roughly four million Americans lost their homes to foreclosure. The stock market cratered and millions saw their life savings evaporate. Again, the question must be asked: How do these results compare to Trump's dubious dealings with Ukraine?

Trump's critics speak with one voice in demanding accountability. Yet virtually no one has been held accountable for the pain, suffering, and loss inflicted by the architects of the Iraq War and the Great Recession. Why is that? As another presidential election approaches, the question not only goes unanswered, but unasked.

To win reelection, Trump, a corrupt con man (who jumped ship on his own bankrupt casinos, money in hand, leaving others holding the bag) will cheat and lie. Yet, in the politics of the last half-century, these do not qualify as novelties. (Indeed, apart from being the son of a sitting

US vice president, what made Hunter Biden worth fifty Gs per month to a gas company owned by a Ukrainian oligarch? I'm curious.) That the president and his associates are engaging in a cover-up is doubtless the case. Yet another cover-up proceeds in broad daylight on a vastly larger scale. "Trump's shambolic presidency somehow seems less unsavory," Moyn writes, when considering the fact that his critics refuse "to admit how massively his election signified the failure of their policies, from endless war to economic inequality." Just so.

What are the real crimes? Who are the real criminals? No matter what happens in the coming months, don't expect the Trump impeachment proceedings to come within a country mile of addressing such questions.

40

A Good Deed from the Wicked Witch?

Actually Ending the War in Afghanistan

November 24, 2020

Let's open up and sing, and ring the bells out
Ding-dong! the merry-oh sing it high, sing it low
Let them know the wicked witch is dead!

Within establishment circles, Trump's failure to win reelection has prompted merry singing and bell-ringing galore. If you read the *New York Times* or watch MSNBC, the song featured in the 1939 movie *The Wizard of Oz* nicely captures the mood of the moment.

As a consequence, expectations for Biden and Harris to put America back on the path to the Emerald City after a dispiriting four-year detour are sky high. The new administration will defeat COVID-19, restore prosperity, vanquish racism, reform education, expand healthcare coverage, tackle climate change, and provide an effective and humane solution to the problem of undocumented migrants. Oh, and Biden will also return the United States to its accustomed position of global leadership. And save America's soul to boot.

So we are told.

That these expectations are deemed even faintly credible qualifies as passing strange. After all, the outcome of the 2020 presidential election turned less on competing approaches to governance than on the character of the incumbent. It wasn't Joe Biden as principled standard-bearer of enlightened twenty-first-century liberalism who prevailed. It was Joe Biden, a retread centrist pol who emerged as the last line of defense shielding America and the world from four more years of Trump.

So the balloting definitively resolved only a single question: by eighty million to seventy-four million votes, a margin of six million, Americans signaled their desire to terminate Trump's lease on the White House. Yet even if repudiating the president, voters hardly repudiated Trumpism. Republicans actually gained seats in the House of Representatives and appear likely to retain control of the Senate.

On November 3, a twofold transfer of power commenced. A rapt public has fixed its attention on the first of those transfers: Biden's succession to the presidency (and Trump's desperate resistance to the inevitable outcome). But a second, hardly less important transfer of power is also occurring. Once it became clear that Trump was not going to win a second term, control of the Republican Party began reverting from the president to Senate Majority Leader Mitch McConnell. The implications of that shift are immense, as Biden, himself a longtime member of the Senate, no doubt appreciates.

Consider this telling anecdote from former President Obama's just published memoir. Obama had tasked then–Vice President Biden with cajoling McConnell into supporting a piece of legislation favored by the administration. After Biden made his pitch, the hyper-partisan McConnell dourly replied, "You must be under the mistaken impression that I care." End of negotiation.

Perhaps the Democrats will miraculously win both Senate seats in Georgia's January runoff elections and so consign McConnell to the status of minority leader. If they don't, let us not labor under the mistaken impression that he'll support Biden's efforts to defeat COVID-19, restore prosperity, vanquish racism, reform education, expand healthcare coverage, tackle climate change, or provide an effective and humane solution to the problem of undocumented migrants.

It's a given that McConnell isn't any more interested in saving souls than he is in passing legislation favored by Democrats. That leaves restoring American global leadership as the sole remaining arena where President Biden might elicit from a McConnell-controlled GOP something other than unremitting obstructionism.

And that, in turn, brings us face to face with the issue Democrats and Republicans alike would prefer to ignore: the US penchant for war. Since the end of the Cold War and especially since the terror attacks of 9/11, successive administrations have relied on armed force to assert, affirm, or at least shore up America's claim to global leadership. The results have not been pretty. A series of needless and badly mismanaged wars have contributed appreciably—more even than Donald Trump's zany ineptitude—to the growing perception that the United States is now a declining power. That perception is not without validity. Over the past two decades, wars have depleted America's strength and undermined its global influence.

So, as the US embarks on the post-Trump era, what are the prospects that a deeply divided government presiding over a deeply divided polity will come to a more reasoned and prudent attitude toward war? A lot hinges on whether Biden and McConnell can agree on an answer to that question.

An Unexpected Gift for "Sleepy Joe"

As his inevitable exit from the White House approaches, President Trump himself may be forcing the issue.

One of the distinctive attributes of our forty-fifth president is that he never seemed terribly interested in actually tending to the duties of his office. He does not, in fact, possess a work ethic in any traditional sense. He prefers to swagger and strut rather than deliberate and decide. Once it became clear that he wasn't going to win a second term, he visibly gave up even the pretense of governing. Today, he golfs, tweets, and rails. According to news reports, he no longer even bothers to set aside time for the daily presidential intelligence briefing.

As the clock runs out, however, certain Trumpian impulses remain in play. The war in Afghanistan, now in its nineteenth year, offers a notable example. In 2001, President George W. Bush ordered US forces to invade the country, but prematurely turned his attention to a bigger and more disastrous misadventure in Iraq. Obama inherited the Afghanistan War, promised to win it, and ordered a large-scale surge in the US troop presence there. Yet the conflict stubbornly dragged on through his two terms. As for candidate Trump, during campaign 2016, he vowed to end it once and for all. In office, however, he never managed to pull the plug—until now, that is.

Soon after losing the election, the president ousted several senior Pentagon civilians, including Secretary of Defense Mark Esper, and replaced them (for a couple of months anyway) with loyalists sharing his oft-stated commitment to "ending endless wars." Within days of taking office, new Acting Secretary of Defense Christopher Miller issued a letter to the troops, signaling his own commitment to that task.

"We are not a people of perpetual war," he wrote, describing endless war as "the antithesis of everything for which we stand and for which our ancestors fought." The time for accepting the inevitable had now arrived. "All wars must end," he continued, adding that trying harder was not going to produce a better outcome. "We gave it our all," he concluded. "Now, it's time to come home."

Miller avoided using terms like victory or defeat, success or failure, and did not specify an actual timetable for a full-scale withdrawal. Yet Trump had already made his intentions clear: he wanted all US troops out of Afghanistan by the end of the year and preferably by Christmas. Having forgotten or punted on innumerable other promises, Trump appeared determined to make good on this one. It's likely, in fact, that Miller's primary—perhaps only—charge during his abbreviated tour of duty as Pentagon chief is to enable Trump to claim success in terminating at least one war.

So during this peculiar betwixt and between moment of ours, with one administration packing its bags and the next one trying to get its bearings, a question of immense significance to the future course of American statecraft presents itself: Will the United States at long last ring down the curtain on the most endless of its endless wars? Or, under the guise of seeking a "responsible end," will it pursue the irresponsible course of prolonging a demonstrably futile enterprise through another presidency?

As Miller will soon discover, if he hasn't already, his generals don't concur with the commander in chief's determination to "come home." Whether in Afghanistan or Somalia, Iraq, Syria, or Europe, they have demonstrated great skill in foiling his occasional gestures aimed at reducing the US military's overseas profile.

The available evidence suggests that Biden's views align with those of the generals. True, the conduct and legacy of recent wars played next to no role in deciding the outcome of the 2020 presidential election (suggesting that many Americans have made their peace with endless war). Still, given expectations that anyone aspiring to high office these days must stake out a position on every conceivable issue and promise something for everyone, candidate Biden spelled out his intentions regarding Afghanistan.

Basically, he wants to have it both ways. So he is on record insisting that "these 'forever wars' have to end," while simultaneously proposing to maintain a contingent of American troops in Afghanistan to "take out terrorist groups who are going to continue to emerge." In other words, Biden proposes to declare that the longest war in US history has ended, while simultaneously underwriting its perpetuation.

Such a prospect will find favor with the generals, members of the foreign policy establishment, and media hawks. Yet hanging on in Afghanistan (or other active theaters of war) will contribute nothing to Biden's larger promise to "build back better." Indeed, the staggering expenses that accompany protracted wars will undermine his prospects of making good on his domestic reform agenda. It's the dilemma that Lyndon Johnson faced in the mid-1960s: You can have your Great Society, Mr. President, or you can have your war in Vietnam, but you can't have both.

Biden will face an analogous problem. Put simply, his stated position on Afghanistan is at odds with the larger aspirations of his presidency.

At Long Last an Exit Strategy?

As a practical matter, the odds of Trump actually ending the US military presence in Afghanistan between now and his departure from office are nil. The logistical challenges are daunting, especially given that the pickup team now running the Pentagon is made up of something other than all-stars. And the generals will surely drag their feet, while mobilizing allies not just in the punditocracy but in the Republican Party itself.

As a practical matter, Acting Secretary Miller has already bowed to reality. The definition of success now is, it seems, to cut the force there roughly in half, from 4,500 to 2,500, by Inauguration Day, with the remainder of US troops supposedly coming out of Afghanistan by May 2021 (months after both Trump and Miller will be out of a job).

So call it Operation Half a Loaf. But half is better than none. Even if Trump won't succeed in reducing US troop strength in Afghanistan to zero, I'm rooting for him anyway. As, indeed, Biden should be—because if Trump makes headway in shutting down America's war there, Biden will be among the principal beneficiaries.

Whatever his actual motives, Trump has cracked open a previously shut door to an exit strategy. Through that door lies the opportunity of turning the page on a disastrous era of American statecraft dominated by a misplaced obsession with events in the Greater Middle East.

Twin convictions shaped basic US policy during this period: the first was that the United States has vital interests at stake in this region, even in utterly remote parts of it like Afghanistan; the second, that the United States can best advance those interests by amassing and employing military power. The first of those convictions turned out to be wildly misplaced, the second tragically wrongheaded. Yet pursuant to those very mistaken beliefs, successive administrations have flung away lives, treasure, and influence with complete abandon. The American people have gained less than nothing in return. In fact, in terms of where taxpayer dollars were invested, they've lost their shirts.

Acting Secretary Miller's charge to the troops plainly acknowledges a bitter truth to which too few members of the Washington establishment have been willing to admit: the time to move on from this misguided project is now. To the extent that Trump's lame-duck administration begins the process of extricating the United States from Afghanistan, he will demonstrate the feasibility of doing so elsewhere as well. Tired arguments for staying the course could then lose their persuasive power.

Doubtless, after all these disastrous years, there will be negative consequences to leaving Afghanistan. Ill-considered and mismanaged wars inevitably yield poisonous fruit. There will be further bills to pay. Still, ending the US war there will establish a precedent for ending our military involvement in Iraq, Syria, and Somalia as well. Terminating direct US military involvement across the Greater Middle East and much of Africa will create an opportunity to reconfigure US policy in a world that has changed dramatically since the United States recklessly embarked upon its crusade to transform great swathes of the Islamic world.

Biden himself should welcome such an opportunity. Admittedly, McConnell, no longer fully subservient to President Trump, predicts that withdrawing from Afghanistan will produce an outcome "reminiscent of the humiliating American departure from Saigon in 1975." In reality, of course, failure in Vietnam stemmed not from the decision to leave, but from an erroneous conviction that it was incumbent upon Americans to decide the destiny of the Vietnamese people. The big mistake occurred not in 1975 when American troops finally departed, but a decade earlier when President Johnson decided that it was incumbent upon the United States to Americanize the war.

As Americans learned in Vietnam, the only way to end a war gone wrong is to leave the field of battle. If that describes Trump's intentions in Afghanistan, then we may finally have some reason to be grateful for his service to our nation. With time, Biden and McConnell might even come to see the wisdom of doing so.

And then, of course, they can bicker about the shortest path to the Emerald City.

V

JOE GRABS THE TILLER

41
Beyond Donald Trump

When Poisons Curdle

February 11, 2021

When Martin Luther King preached his famous sermon "Beyond Vietnam" at Riverside Church in New York City in April 1967, I don't recall giving his words a second thought. Although at the time I was just up the Hudson River attending West Point, his call for a "radical revolution in values" did not resonate with me. By upbringing and given my status as a soldier in the making, radical revolutions were not my thing. To grasp the profound significance of "the giant triplets of racism, extreme materialism, and militarism" to which he called his listeners' attention was beyond my intellectual capacity. I didn't even try to unpack their meaning.

In that regard, the ensuing decades have filled a void in my education. I long ago concluded that Dr. King was then offering the essential interpretive key to understanding our contemporary American dilemma. The predicament in which we find ourselves today stems from our reluctance to admit to the crippling interaction among the components of the giant triplets he described in that speech. True, racism, extreme materialism, and militarism each deserve—and separately sometimes receive—condemnation. But it's the way that the three of them sustain one another that accounts for our nation's present parlous condition.

Let me suggest that King's prescription remains as valid today as when he issued it more than half a century ago—hence, my excuse for returning to it so soon after citing it in a previous *TomDispatch*. Sadly, however, neither the American people nor the American ruling class seem any more inclined to take that prescription seriously today than I was in 1967. We persist in rejecting Dr. King's message.

Martin Luther King is enshrined in American memory as a great civil rights leader and rightly so. Yet as his Riverside Church address made plain, his life's mission went far beyond fighting racial discrimination. His real purpose was to save America's soul, a self-assigned mission that was either wildly presumptuous or deeply prophetic.

In either case, his Riverside Church presentation was not well received at the time. Even in quarters generally supportive of the civil rights movement, press criticism was widespread. King's detractors chastised him for straying out of his lane. "To divert the energies of the civil rights movement to the Vietnam issue is both wasteful and self-defeating," the *New York Times* insisted. Its editorial board assured their readers that racism and the ongoing war were distinct and unrelated: "Linking these hard, complex problems will lead not to solutions but to deeper confusion." King needed to stick to race and let others more qualified tend to war.

The *Washington Post* agreed. King's ill-timed and ill-tempered presentation had "diminished his usefulness to his cause, to his country, and to his people." According to the *Post's* editorial board, King had "done a grave injury to those who are his natural allies" and "an even greater injury to himself." His reputation had suffered permanent damage. "Many who have listened to him with respect will never again accord him the same respect."

Life magazine weighed in with its own editorial slap on the wrist. To suggest any connection between the war in Vietnam and the condition of Black citizens at home, according to *Life*, was little more than "demagogic slander." The ongoing conflict in Southeast Asia had "nothing to do with the legitimate battle for equal rights here in America."

How could King not have seen that? In retrospect, we may wonder how ostensibly sophisticated observers could have overlooked the connection between racism, war, and a perverse value system that obsessively elevated and celebrated the acquisition and consumption of mere things.

More Than the Sum of Its Parts

In recent months, more than a few stressed-out observers of the American scene have described 2020 as this nation's Worst. Year. Ever. Only those with exceedingly short memories will buy such hyperbole.

As recently as the 1960s, dissent and disorder occurred on a far larger scale and a more sustained basis than anything that Americans have endured of late. No doubt Covid-19 and Donald Trump collaborated to make 2020 a year of genuine misery and death, with last month's assault on the Capitol adding a disconcerting exclamation point to the nightmare.

But recall the headline events following King's Riverside Church presentation. The year 1968 began with the Tet Offensive in Vietnam, which obliterated official claims that the United States was "winning" the war there. Next came North Korea's audacious seizure of a US Navy ship, the USS *Pueblo*, a national humiliation. Soon after, President Lyndon Johnson's surprise decision not to run for reelection turned the race for the presidency upside down.

In April, an assassin murdered Dr. King, an event that triggered rioting on a scale dwarfing 2020's disturbances in Minneapolis, Minnesota, Portland, Oregon, and Kenosha, Wisconsin. (Mere days after the assassination, as I arrived in Washington for—of all things—a rugby tournament, fires were still burning and the skies were still black with smoke.) That June, not five years after his brother was shot and killed, Senator Robert Kennedy, his effort to win the Democratic presidential nomination just then gaining momentum, fell to an assassin's bullet, his death stunning the nation and the world. The chaotic and violent Democratic National Convention, held in Chicago that August and broadcast live, suggested that the country was on the verge of coming apart at the seams. By year's end, Richard Nixon, back from the political wilderness, was preparing to assume the reins as president—a prospect that left intact the anger and division that had been accumulating over the preceding twelve months.

True enough, the total number of American deaths caused by COVID-19 in 2020 greatly exceeds those from a distant war and domestic violence in 1968. Even so—and even without the menacing presence of Donald Trump looming over the political scene—the stress to which the nation was subjected in 1968 was at least as great as what occurred last year.

The point of making such a been there, done that comparison is not to suggest that, with Trump exiled to Mar-a-Lago, Americans can finally begin to relax, counting on Joe Biden to "build back better" and restore a semblance of normalcy to the country. Rather the point is that the evils afflicting our nation are deep-seated, persistent, and lie beyond the power of any mere president to remedy.

America's Twenty-First-Century Racist Wars

A devotion to life, liberty, and the pursuit of happiness defines the essence of the American way of life. So the founders declared and so we are schooled to believe. Well, yes, replied Dr. King in 1967, but racism, materialism, and militarism have likewise woven themselves into the fabric of American life. As much as we may prefer to pretend otherwise, those giant triplets define who we are as much as Jefferson's Declaration or the framers' Constitution do.

For various reasons, Trump not least among them, racism today again ranks atop the hierarchy of issues commanding national attention. Political progressives, champions of diversity, cultural elites, and even multinational corporations attentive to the bottom line profess their commitment to ending racism (as they define it) finally and forever. Some not-trivial portion of the rest of the population—the white nationalists chanting "You will not replace us," for example—hold to another view. The elimination of racism, assuming such a goal is even plausible, will surely entail a further protracted struggle.

By 1967, King had concluded that winning that fight required expanding the scope of analysis. Hence, the imperative of speaking out against the Vietnam War, which until that moment he had hesitated to do. For King, it had become "incandescently clear" that the ongoing war was poisoning "America's soul." Racism and war were intertwined. They fed upon one another.

By now, it should be incandescently clear that our own forever wars of the twenty-first century, fought on a distinctly lesser scale than Vietnam, though over an even longer period of time, have had a similar effect. The places that the United States bombs, invades, and/or occupies typically fall into the category of what President Trump once disparaged as "shithole countries." The inhabitants tend to be impoverished, non-white, non–English speaking, and, by American standards, often not especially well educated. They subscribe to customs and religious traditions that many Americans view as primitive if not altogether alien.

That the average GI should deem the lives of Afghans or Iraqis of lesser value than the life of an American may be regrettable, but given our history it can hardly be surprising. A persistent theme of American wars going back to the colonial era is that, once the shooting starts, difference signifies inferiority.

Although no high-ranking government official and no senior military officer will admit it, racism permeates our post-9/11 wars. And as is so often the case, poisons generated abroad have a curious knack for finding their way home.

With few exceptions, Americans prefer to ignore this reality. Implicit in the thank-you-for-your-service air kisses so regularly lofted toward the troops is an illusion that wartime service correlates with virtue, as if combat were a great builder of character. Last month's assault on the Capitol should finally have made it impossible to sustain that illusion.

In fact, as a consequence of our post-9/11 "forever wars," the virus of militarism has infected many quarters of American society, perhaps even more so in our day than in King's. Among the evident results: the spread of racist and extreme right-wing ideologies within the ranks of the armed services; the conversion of police forces into quasi-military entities with a penchant for using excessive force against people of color; and the emergence of well-armed militia groups posing as "patriots" while conspiring to overturn the constitutional order.

It's important, of course, not to paint such a picture with too broad a brush. Not every soldier is a neo-Nazi—not even close. Not every cop is a shoot-first, then-knock racist thug. Not every defender of the Second

Amendment conspires to "stop the steal" and reinstall Trump in the Oval Office. But bad soldiers, bad cops, and traitors who wrap themselves in the flag exist in disturbingly large numbers. Certainly, were he alive today, Martin Luther King would not flinch from pointing out that the American penchant for war in recent decades has yielded a host of perverse results here at home.

Then there's King's third triplet, hidden in plain sight: the "extreme materialism" of a people intent on satisfying appetites that are quite literally limitless in a society that has become ever more economically unequal. Americans have always been the people of more. Enough is never enough. True in 1776, this remains true today.

A nation in which "machines and computers, profit motives and property rights" take precedence over people, King warned in 1967, courts something akin to spiritual death. King's primary concern was not the distribution of material wealth, but the obsessive importance attributed to accumulating and possessing it.

Embracing *equity* as a major theme, the Biden administration holds to a different view. Its stated aim is to enable the "underserved and left behind" to catch up, with priority attention given to "communities of color and other underserved Americans." In short: more for some, but not for others.

Such an effort will inevitably produce a backlash. Given a culture that deems billionaires the ultimate fulfillment of the American dream, the only politically acceptable program is one that holds out the promise of more for all. Since its very first days, the purpose of the American experiment has been to satisfy this demand for *more,* even if perpetuating that effort today inflicts untold damage on the natural environment.

Prophetic Deficit

In his Riverside Church sermon, King mused that "the world now demands a maturity of America that we may not be able to achieve." In the decades since, has our nation "matured" in any meaningful sense? Or have the habits of consumption that defined our way of life in 1967 only become more entrenched, even as Information Age manipulations to which Americans willingly submit reinforce those habits further?

Maturity suggests wisdom and judgment. It implies experience put to good use. Does that describe the America of our time? Again, it's important to avoid painting with too broad a brushstroke. But ours is a country in which seventy-four million Americans voted to give Donald Trump a second term, a larger total than *any* prior presidential candidate ever received. And ours is a country in which millions believe that a cabal of Satan-worshiping pedophiles controls the apparatus of government.

Whether wittingly or not, when Biden committed himself in 2020 to saving "the soul of America," he was echoing King in 1967. But saving the nation's soul requires more than simply replacing Trump in the Oval Office, issuing a steady stream of executive orders, and reciting speeches off a teleprompter (something that Biden does with evident difficulty).

Saving that soul requires moral imagination, a quality not commonly found in American politics. George Washington probably possessed it. Lincoln surely did. For a brief moment when delivering his farewell address, President Eisenhower spoke in a prophetic voice. So, too, did Carter in his widely derided but enduringly profound "malaise speech" of 1979. But as this mere handful of examples suggests, the rough and tumble of political life only rarely accommodates prophets.

While Biden may be a decent enough fellow, at no point in his long but not especially distinguished political career has he ever been mistaken for possessing prophetic gifts. Much the same can be said about the highly credentialed political veterans with whom he has surrounded himself: Kamala Harris, Antony Blinken, Lloyd Austin, Jake Sullivan, Janet Yellen, and the rest. When it comes to diversity, they check all the necessary boxes. Yet none of them gives even the slightest indication of grasping the plight of a nation held in the grip of King's giant triplets.

As a devout Christian and a preacher of surpassing eloquence, King knew that salvation begins with an admission of sinfulness, followed by repentance. Only then does redemption become a possibility.

Only by acknowledging the evil caused by the simultaneous presence of racism and materialism and militarism at the heart of this country will it be remotely possible for the United States to take even the first few halting steps toward redemption. We await the prophetic voice that will awaken the American people to this imperative.

42

On Shedding
an Obsolete Past

Biden Defers to the Blob

March 11, 2021

You may have noticed: the Blob is back. Beneath a veneer of gender and racial diversity, the Biden national security team consists of seasoned operatives who earned their spurs in Washington long before Trump showed up to spoil the party. So, if you're looking for fresh faces at the departments of state or defense, the National Security Council or the various intelligence agencies, you'll have to search pretty hard. Ditto, if you're looking for fresh insights. In Washington, members of the foreign policy establishment recite stale bromides, even as they divert attention from a dead past to which they remain devoted.

The boss shows them how it's done.

Just two weeks into his presidency, Biden visited the State Department to give American diplomats their marching orders. In his formal remarks, the president committed his administration to "diplomacy rooted in America's most cherished democratic values: defending freedom, championing opportunity, upholding universal rights, respecting the rule of law, and treating every person with dignity."

His language allowed no room for quibbles or exemptions. In our world, some things can be waived—SAT scores for blue-chip athletes being recruited to play big-time college ball, for example. Yet cherished values presumably qualify as sacrosanct. To take Biden at his word, his administration will honor this commitment not some of the time, but consistently; not just when it's convenient to do so, but without exception.

Less than a month later, the president received a ready-made opportunity to demonstrate his fealty to those very values. The matter at hand concerned Saudi Arabia, more specifically the release of an intelligence report fingering Mohammad bin Salman, aka MBS, the Saudi crown prince and de facto ruler of that country, for ordering the 2018 murder and dismemberment of Jamal Khashoggi, a journalist employed by the *Washington Post*. The contents of the report surprised no one. The interesting question was how the new president would respond.

Months earlier, during the election campaign, Biden had described Saudi Arabia, a longtime US ally, as a "pariah state" that possessed "no redeeming value." Previously, Trump had cozied up to the Saudi royals—they were his kind of people. As far as candidate Biden was concerned, the time for romancing Riyadh had ended. Never again, he vowed, would Washington "check its principles at the door just to buy oil or sell weapons."

Let it be said that a preference for lucre rather than principles succinctly describes traditional US-Saudi relations going back several decades. While President Trump treated the "friendship" between the two countries as cause for celebration, other American leaders gingerly tiptoed around the role allotted to arms and oil. In diplomacy, some things were better left unsaid. So, to hear candidate Biden publicly acknowledge the relationship's tawdry essence was little short of astonishing.

While a member of the Senate and during his eight years as vice president, he had hardly gone out of his way to pick fights with the Kingdom. Were Biden to replace Trump, however, things were going to change. Big time.

Threading the Needle

As it turned out, not so much. Once inaugurated, Biden found ample reason for checking American principles at the door. Shelving further references to Saudi Arabia as a pariah, he tweaked Washington's relationship with the Kingdom, while preserving its essence.

The term chosen to describe the process is *recalibrate*. In practical terms, recalibration means that the US government is sanctioning a few dozen Saudi functionaries for their involvement in the Khashoggi assassination, while giving Mohammad bin Salman himself a pass. MBS's sanctioned henchmen would do well to cancel any planned flights into New York's JFK airport or Washington's Dulles, where the FBI will undoubtedly be waiting to take them into custody. That said, unless they fall out of favor with the crown prince himself, the assassins will literally get away with murder.

Recalibration also means that the United States is "pausing"—not terminating—further arms sales to Saudi Arabia. The purpose of the pause, Secretary of State Antony Blinken has explained, is "to make sure that what is being considered is something that advances our strategic objectives and advances our foreign policy." Translation? Don't expect much to happen.

Inside the Beltway, lobbyists for US arms merchants are undoubtedly touching base with members of Congress whose constituencies benefit from exporting weapons to that very country. Said lobbyists need not burn the midnight oil, however. Mr. Khashoggi's demise has complicated but will not derail the US-Saudi relationship. Given time, some version of the status quo will be restored.

Just one more example of American hypocrisy? Within the Blob, a different view pertains. Consider the perspective of former senior official and longtime Middle Eastern hand Dennis Ross. "This is the classic example of where you have to balance your values and your interests," Mr. Ross told the *New York Times*. Biden, he added approvingly, is now "trying to thread the needle." Mustering the wisdom acquired from decades of service deep inside the Blob, Ross pointed out that "there isn't an issue in the Middle East where we don't need them to play a role—on Iran, on competing with the Chinese." Ultimately, it's that simple: The United States *needs* Saudi Arabia.

As a respected member of the foreign policy establishment, Ross speaks with the authority that gets you quoted in the *Times*. Informing his perspective is a certain iron logic, time-tested and seemingly endorsed by history itself. Take that logic at face value and Washington needs Saudi Arabia because it needs to police the Persian Gulf and its environs, as required by the decades-old, never-to-be-questioned Carter Doctrine. The United States needs Saudi Arabia because the Kingdom already plays a not-inconsequential role in the drama accompanying energy-hungry China's emergence as a great power. And let's face it: the United States also needs Saudi Arabia because of all that oil (even though this country no longer actually uses that oil itself) and because MBS's insatiable appetite for arms helps to sustain the military-industrial complex.

So the pieces all fit into a coherent whole, thereby validating a particular conception of history itself. The United States *needs* Saudi Arabia for the same reason that it *needs* to remain part of NATO, *needs* to defend various other allies, *needs* to maintain a sprawling worldwide constellation of bases, *needs* to annually export billions of dollars' worth of weaponry, *needs* to engage in endless wars, and *needs* to spend a trillion-plus dollars annually pursuant to what is usually described as "national security." More broadly, the United States needs to do all these things because it *needs* to lead a world that cannot do without its leadership. The trajectory of events going back more than a century now, encompassing two world wars, the Cold War, and the forever wars of the post–Cold War era, proves as much. End of discussion.

Second Thoughts?

Not all historians bow to the iron logic to which the Blob subscribes, however. Recent events are prompting a few dissenters to entertain second thoughts. Among them is Professor Martin Conway of Oxford University. Now, Professor Conway is anything but a household name. When it comes to name recognition, he doesn't hold a candle to Dennis Ross, nor is he someone the *New York Times* consults on issues of the day.

So should we attend to Professor Conway's contrarian perspective? Very much so and here's why: Compared to Ross or the sundry Blobbers now in Joe Biden's employ, Conway is not a prisoner of a curated past. He's open to the possibility that the sell-by date attached to that taken-for-granted past may well have expired.

Consider his provocative essay "Making Trump History," recently published online in H-Diplo. (A more accurate title would have been "History as Illuminated by Trump.")

By and large, Conway writes, scholars deem Trump to have been "an insult to the historical narrative," a living, breathing "refutation of deeply held assumptions among historians about how the democratic politics of the U.S. are supposed to work." Their reflexive response is to classify Trump as an outlier, a one-off intruder, a conviction seemingly affirmed by his failure to win a second term. With his departure from the White House, the resumption of normalcy (or at least what passed for the same in Washington) has theoretically become possible. Biden's job is to hasten its return.

Conway entertains another view. He speculates that normalcy may, in fact, be gone for good. And the sooner the rest of us grasp that, he believes, the better.

Conway boldly rejects the media's preferred Manichean account of the so-called Age of Trump. Rather than insulting the traditional Washington narrative, he suggests, Trump simply supplanted it. Wittingly or not, the new president acted in concert with political opportunists in Great Britain, Hungary, Poland, and elsewhere who, in advancing their own ambitions, trampled all over the familiar storyline devised and refined to make *sense* of our age.

As a first step toward grasping what's now underway, Conway urges his fellow historians to "bury their narratives of the twentieth century"—on a par with asking Ohio State or the University of Alabama to give up football. Conway then suggests that a new past he calls a "history of the present" is emerging. And he identifies "three trig points" to begin mapping the "uncharted landscape" that lies ahead.

The first relates to the collapse of barriers that had long confined politics to familiar channels. Today, democratic politics has "burst its banks," Conway writes. The people once assumed to be in charge no longer really are. Presidents, prime ministers, and parliamentarians compete with (and frequently court) "footballers, TV celebrities, and rap artists" who "communicate more directly and effectively with the public." Who do *you* trust? Mitch McConnell or George Clooney? Who has *your* ear? Nancy Pelosi or Oprah Winfrey?

Conway's second trig point references the bond between citizens and the state. The old contract—individual duties performed in exchange for collective benefits—no longer applies. Instead, the "new politics of the bazaar" shortchange the many while benefiting the few (like the mega-wealthy Americans who, during the coronavirus pandemic, have so far raked in an estimated extra $1.3 trillion). Egged on by politicians like Trump or British Prime Minister Boris Johnson, the less privileged have figured this out. Biden's efforts to pass yet another COVID-19-related relief bill responded to but could not conceal the real story: the emergence of an antiestablishment populism.

His final trig point wipes out the old-fashioned "political frontiers of the left and right." In the history of the present, politics emphasize "identity and grievance." Citizens lend their support to causes centered on "emotions, group identity, or aspirations," while rendering once-accepted notions of class and party all but irrelevant. "Institutional structures, ideological traditions, and indeed democratic norms" are being "replaced by a less disciplined and more open politics." Passions govern, imparting to the History of the Present unprecedented levels of volatility.

Conway doesn't pretend to know where all this will lead, other than suggesting that the implications are likely to be striking and persistent. But let me suggest the following: For all their rote references to new challenges in a new era, President Biden and the members of his crew are clueless as to what the onset of Conway's history of the present portends. Throughout the ranks of the establishment, the reassuringly familiar narratives of the twentieth century retain their allure. Among other things, they obviate the need to think.

Wrong Thread, Wrong Needle

Nowhere is this more emphatically the case than in quarters where members of the Blob congregate and where the implications of Conway's analysis may well have the most profound impact. Conway's primary concern is with developments within what used to be called the West.

330 On Shedding an Obsolete Past

That said, the History of the Present will profoundly impact relations *between* the West (which, these days, really means the United States) and the rest of the world. And that brings us right back to President Biden's awkward effort to "thread the needle" regarding Saudi Arabia.

Someday, when a successor to BuzzFeed posts an official ranking of twenty-first century crimes, the vicious murder and dismemberment of Jamal Khashoggi in the Saudi consulate in Istanbul won't even make it anywhere near the first tier. His assassination will, for instance, certainly trail well behind the George W. Bush administration's disastrous 2003 invasion of Iraq, not to speak of various other US military actions from Afghanistan to Somalia undertaken as part of the so-called Global War on Terror.

Whether explicitly or implicitly, President Bush and his successors cited those very "narratives of the twentieth century" to which Professor Conway refers to justify their interventions across the Greater Middle East. The most important—indeed beloved—narrative celebrates the US role in ensuring freedom's triumph over evil in the form of various totalitarian ideologies.

Attach all the caveats and exceptions you want: Hiroshima, Vietnam, CIA-engineered coups, the Bay of Pigs, the Iran-Contra scandal, and so on and so forth. Yet even today, most Americans believe and virtually anyone responsible for formulating and implementing basic US global policy affirms that the United States is a force for good in the world. As such, America is irreplaceable, indispensable, and essential. Hence, the unique prerogatives that it confers on itself are justified. Such thinking, of course, sustains the conviction that, even today, alone among nations, the United States is able to keep its interests and "its most cherished democratic values" in neat alignment.

By discarding the narratives of the twentieth century, Conway's history of the present invites us to see this claim for what it is—a falsehood of Trumpian dimensions, one that, in recent decades, has wreaked untold havoc while distracting policymakers from concerns far more urgent than engaging in damage control on behalf of Mohammad bin Salman. A proper appreciation of the history of the present will only begin with the realization that the United States needs neither MBS, nor Saudi Arabia, nor for that matter a sprawling and expensive national security apparatus to police the Persian Gulf.

What this country does need is to recognize that the twentieth century is gone for good. Developments ranging from the worsening threat posed by climate change to the shifting power balance in East Asia, not to mention the transformation of American politics ushered in by Donald Trump, should have made this patently obvious. If Professor Conway is right—and I'm convinced that he is—then it's past time to give the narratives of the twentieth century a decent burial. Doing so may be a precondition for our very survival.

Sadly, Joe Biden and his associates appear demonstrably incapable of exchanging the history that they know for a history on which our future may well depend. As a result, they will cling to an increasingly irrelevant past. Under the guise of correcting Trump's failures, they will perpetuate their own.

43
America's Longest War Winds Down

No Bang, No Whimper, No Victory

March 28, 2021

"Ours is the cause of freedom. We've defeated freedom's enemies before, and we will defeat them again . . . . We know our
cause is just and our ultimate victory is assured . . . . My fellow
Americans, let's roll."

—**George W. Bush**, November 8, 2001

In the immediate wake of 9/11, it fell to President George W. Bush to
explain to his fellow citizens what had occurred and frame the nation's
response to that singular catastrophe. Bush fulfilled that duty by in-
augurating the Global War on Terrorism, or GWOT. Both in terms of
what was at stake and what the United States intended to do, the president explicitly compared that new conflict to the defining struggles of
the twentieth century. However great the sacrifices and exertions that
awaited, one thing was certain: the GWOT would ensure the triumph
of freedom, as had World War II and the Cold War. It would also affirm
American global primacy and the superiority of the American way of life.

The twentieth anniversary of the terrorist attack on the World
Trade Center and the Pentagon now approaches. On September 11,
2021, Americans will mark the occasion with solemn remembrances,
perhaps even setting aside, at least momentarily, the various trials that,
in recent years, have beset the nation.

Twenty years to the minute after the first hijacked airliner slammed into the North Tower of the World Trade Center, bells will toll. In the ensuing hours, officials will lay wreathes and make predictable speeches. Priests, rabbis, and imams will recite prayers. Columnists and TV commentators will pontificate. If only for a moment, the nation will come together.

It's less likely that the occasion will prompt Americans to reflect on the sequence of military campaigns over the two decades that followed 9/11. This is unfortunate. Although barely noticed, those campaigns—the term GWOT long ago fell out of favor—give every sign of finally winding down, ending not with a promised victory but with something more like a shrug. On that score, the Afghanistan War serves as Exhibit A.

President Bush's assurances of ultimate triumph now seem almost quaint—the equivalent of pretending that the American Century remains alive and well by waving a foam finger and chanting, "We're number one!" In Washington, the sleeping dog of military failure snoozes undisturbed. Senior field commanders long ago gave up on expectations of vanquishing the enemy.

While politicians ceaselessly proclaim their admiration for "the troops," in a rare show of bipartisanship they steer clear of actually inquiring about what US forces have achieved and at what cost. As for distracted and beleaguered ordinary Americans, they have more pressing things to worry about than distant wars that never panned out as promised.

Into the Graveyard of Empires

In his January 2001 farewell address, welcoming the dawn of the third millennium, President Bill Clinton asserted with sublime assurance that, during his eight years in office, the United States had completed its "passage into the global information age, an era of great American renewal." In fact, that new century would bring not renewal but a cascade of crises that have left the average citizen reeling.

First came 9/11 itself, demolishing assurances that history had rendered a decisive verdict in America's favor. The several wars that followed were alike in this sense: once begun, they dragged on and on.

More or less contemporaneously, the "rise" of China seemingly signaled that a centuries-old era of Western global dominion was ending. After all, while the United States was expending vast sums on futile military endeavors, the People's Republic was accumulating global market share at a striking rate. Meanwhile, on the domestic front, a populist backlash against neoliberal and postmodern nostrums vaulted an incompetent demagogue into the White House.

As the worst pandemic in a century then swept across the planet, killing more Americans than died fighting World War II, the nation's chosen leader dithered and dissembled, depicting himself as the real victim of the crisis. Astonishingly, that bogus claim found favor with tens of millions of voters. In a desperate attempt to keep their hero in office for another four (or more) years, the president's most avid supporters mounted a violent effort to overturn the constitutional order. Add to the mix recurring economic cataclysms and worries about the implications of climate change and Americans have good reason to feel punch-drunk.

It's hardly surprising that they have little bandwidth left for reflecting on the war in Afghanistan as it enters what may be its final phase. After all, overlapping with the more violent and costly occupation of Iraq, the conflict in Afghanistan never possessed a clear narrative arc. Lacking dramatic duels or decisive battles, it was the military equivalent of white noise, droning in the background all but unnoticed. Sheer endlessness emerged as its defining characteristic.

The second President Bush launched the Afghan War less than a month after 9/11. Despite what seemed like a promising start, he all but abandoned that effort in his haste to pursue bigger prey, namely Saddam Hussein. In 2009, Obama inherited that by-now-stalemated Afghan conflict and vowed to win and get out. He would do neither. Succeeding Obama in 2017, Trump doubled down on the promise to end the war completely, only to come up short himself.

Now, taking up where Trump left off, Biden has signaled his desire to ring down the curtain on America's longest-ever armed conflict and so succeed where his three immediate predecessors failed. Doing so won't be easy. As the war dragged on, it accumulated complications, both within Afghanistan and regionally. The situation remains fraught with potential snags.

While in office, Trump committed to a complete withdrawal of US troops from Afghanistan by May first of this year. Although Biden recently acknowledged that meeting such a deadline would be "tough," he also promised that any further delay will extend no more than a few months. So it appears increasingly likely that a conclusion of some sort may finally be in the offing. Prospects for a happy ending, however, range between slim and nonexistent.

One thing seems clear: whether Washington's ongoing efforts to broker a peace deal between the Taliban and the Afghan government succeed, or whether the warring parties opt to continue fighting, time is running out on the US military mission there. In Washington, the will to win is long gone, while patience with the side we profess to support wastes away and determination to achieve the minimalist goal of avoiding outright defeat is fading fast. Accustomed to seeing itself as history's author, the United States finds itself in the position of a supplicant, hoping to salvage some tiny sliver of grace.

What then does this longest war in our history signify? Even if the issue isn't one that Americans now view as particularly urgent, at least a preliminary answer seems in order, if only because the US troops who served there—more than three-quarters of a million in all—deserve one.

And there's also this: A war that drags on inconclusively for twenty years is not like a ball game that goes into extra innings. It's a failure of the first order that those who govern and those who are governed should face squarely. To simply walk away, as Americans may be tempted to do, would be worse than irresponsible. It would be obscene.

A Fresh Bite of a Poisonous Imperial Apple

Assessing the significance of Afghanistan requires placing it in a larger context. As the first war of the post-9/11 era, it represents a particularly instructive example of imperialism packaged as uplift.

The European powers of the nineteenth and early twentieth centuries pioneered a line of self-regarding propaganda that imparted a moral gloss to their colonial exploitation throughout much of Asia and Africa. When the United States invaded and occupied Cuba in 1898 and soon after annexed the entire Philippine archipelago, its leaders devised similar justifications for their self-aggrandizing actions.

The aim of the American project in the Philippines, for example, was "benevolent assimilation," with Filipino submission promising eventual redemption. The proconsuls and colonial administrators Washington dispatched to implement that project may even have believed those premises. The recipients of such benefactions, however, tended to be unpersuaded. As Filipino leader Manuel Quezon famously put it, "Better a government run like hell by the Filipinos than one run like heaven by the Americans." A patriotic nationalist, Quezon preferred to take his chances with self-determination, as did many other Filipinos unimpressed with American professions of benign intentions.

This gets to the core of the problem, which remains relevant to the US occupation of Afghanistan in the present century. In 2001, American invaders arrived in that country bearing a gift labeled "Enduring Freedom"—an updated version of benign assimilation—only to find that substantial numbers of Afghans had their own ideas about the nature of freedom or refused to countenance infidels telling them how to run their affairs. Certainly, efforts to disguise Washington's imperial purposes by installing Hamid Karzai, a photogenic, English-speaking Afghan, as the nominal head of a nominally sovereign government in Kabul fooled almost no one. And once Karzai, the West's chosen agent, himself turned against the entire project, the jig should have been up.

The US war in Afghanistan has to date claimed the lives of more than 2,300 US troops, while wounding another twenty thousand. Staggeringly larger numbers of Afghans have been killed, injured, or displaced. The total cost of that American war long ago exceeded $2 trillion. Yet, as documented by "The Afghanistan Papers" published last year by the *Washington Post*, the United States and its allies haven't defeated the Taliban, created competent Afghan security forces, or put in place a state apparatus with the capacity to govern effectively. Despite almost twenty years of effort, they haven't come close. Neither have the US and its NATO coalition partners persuaded the majority of Afghans to embrace the West's vision of a suitable political order. When it comes to the minimum preconditions for mission accomplishment, in other words, the United States and its allies are batting 0 for 4.

Intensive and highly publicized American attempts to curb Afghan corruption have failed abysmally. So, too, have well-funded efforts to reduce opium production. With the former a precondition for effective governance and the latter essential to achieving some semblance of aboveboard economic viability, make that 0 for 6, even as the momentum of events at this moment distinctly favors the Taliban. With 75 percent of government revenues coming from foreign donors, the Islamic Republic of Afghanistan is effectively on the international dole and has no prospect of becoming self-sufficient anytime soon.

Whether the US-led effort to align Afghanistan with Western values was doomed from the start is impossible to say. At the very least, however, that effort was informed by remarkable naivete. Assessing the war a decade ago—ten years after it began—General Stanley Mc-Chrystal, former commander of all coalition forces there, lamented that "we didn't know enough and we still don't know enough" about Afghanistan and its people. "Most of us—me included—had a very superficial understanding of the situation and history, and we had a frighteningly simplistic view of recent history, the last fifty years." Implicit in that seemingly candid admission is the suggestion that knowing more would have yielded a better outcome, that Afghanistan should have been "winnable."

For the thwarted but unreconstructed imperialist, consider this the last line of retreat: success could have been ours if only decision makers had done things differently. Anyone familiar with the should-have-beens trotted out following the Vietnam War in the previous century—the US should have bombed more (or less), invaded the North, done more to win hearts and minds, etc.—will recognize those claims for what they are: dodges. As with Vietnam, to apply this if-only line of reasoning to Afghanistan is to miss that war's actual significance.

Minor War, Major Implications

As American wars go, Afghanistan ranks as a minor one. Yet this relatively small but very long conflict stands at the center of a distinctive and deeply problematic era in American history that dates from the end of the Cold War some forty years ago. Two convictions defined that era. According to the first, by 1991 the United States had achieved something akin to unquestioned global military supremacy. Once the Soviets left the playing field, no opponent worthy of the name remained. That appeared self-evident.

According to the second conviction, circumstances now allowed—even cried out for—putting the US military to work. Reticence, whether defined as deterrence, defense, or containment, was for wusses. In Washington, the temptation to employ armed force to overthrow "evil" became irresistible. Not so incidentally, periodic demonstrations of US military might would also warn potential competitors against even contemplating a challenge to American global primacy.

Lurking in the background was this seldom acknowledged conviction: in a world chockablock full of impoverished, ineptly led nations, most inhabited by people implicitly classified as backward, someone needed to take charge, enforce discipline, and provide at least a modicum of decency. That the United States alone possessed the power and magnanimity to play such a role was taken for granted. After all, who was left to say nay?

So, with the passing of the Cold War, a new chapter in the history of American imperialism commenced, even if in policy circles that i-word was strictly verboten. Among the preferred euphemisms, *humanitarian intervention*, sometimes justified by a recently discovered *responsibility to protect*, found particular favor. But this was mostly theater, an updating of Philippine-style benevolent assimilation designed to mollify twenty-first-century sensibilities.

In actual practice, it fell to the president of the United States, commonly and without irony referred to as "the most powerful man in the world," to decide where US bombs were to fall and US troops arrive. When American forces flexed their muscles in faraway places, ranging from Panama, Iraq, Somalia, Haiti, Bosnia, Kosovo, Serbia, Afghanistan, Sudan, and the Philippines to Afghanistan (again), Iraq (again), Libya, various West African countries, Somalia (again), Iraq (for a third time), or Syria, authorization by the United Nations Security Council or Congress ranked as somewhere between incidental and unnecessary. For military actions that ranged from full-scale invasions to assassinations to a mere show of force, whatever justification the "leader of the free world" chose to offer was deemed sufficient.

Military action undertaken at the behest of the commander in chief became the unspoken but definitive expression of American global leadership. That Bush the father, Clinton, Bush the son, Obama, and Trump would all wield extra-constitutional authority to—so the justification went—advance the cause of peace and freedom worldwide only testified to the singularity of the United States. In this way, an imperial presidency went hand in hand with imperial responsibilities and prerogatives.

At first imperceptibly, but more overtly with the passage of time, military adventurism undertaken by imperial presidents fostered a pattern of hypocrisy, dishonesty, cynicism, waste, brutality, and malaise that have today become pervasive. In certain quarters, the tendency persists to blame former President Trump for just about everything that ails this nation, including racism, sexism, inequality, public health crises, and the coarsening of public discourse, not to speak of inattention to environmental degradation and our crumbling infrastructure. Without letting him off the hook, let me suggest that Washington's post–Cold War imperial turn contributed more to our present discontent and disarray than anything Trump did in his four years in the White House.

On that score, the Afghan War made a pivotal and particularly mournful contribution, definitively exposing as delusionary claims of US military supremacy. Even in late 2001, only weeks after President George W. Bush had promised "ultimate victory," the war there had already gone off script. From early on, in other words, there was unmistakable evidence that military activism pursuant to neo-imperial ambitions entailed considerable risk, while exacting costs far outweighing any plausible benefits.

The longest war in US history should by now have led Americans to reflect on the consequences that stem from succumbing to imperial temptations in a world where empire has long since become obsolete. Some might insist that present-day Americans have imbibed that lesson. In Washington, hawks appear chastened, with few calling for President Biden to dispatch US troops to Yemen or Myanmar or even Venezuela, our oil-rich "neighbor," to put things right. For now, the nation's appetite for military intervention abroad appears to be sated.

But mark me down as skeptical. Only when Americans openly acknowledge their imperial transgressions will genuine repentance become possible. And only with repentance will avoiding further occasions to sin become a habit. In other words, only when Americans call imperialism by its name will vows of "never again" deserve to be taken seriously.

In the meantime, our collective obligation is to remember. The siege of ancient Troy, which lasted a decade, inspired Homer to write the *Iliad*. Although the American war in Afghanistan has now gone on almost twice as long, don't expect it to be memorialized in an epic poem. Yet with such poetry out of fashion, perhaps a musical composition of some sort might act as a substitute. Call it—just to suggest a title—"Requiem for the American Century." For one thing should be clear by now: over the course of the nation's longest war, the American Century breathed its last.

44
A Very Long War

From Vietnam to Afghanistan with Detours along the Way

January 23, 2022

In the long and storied history of the United States Army, many young officers have served in many war zones. Few, I suspect, were as sublimely ignorant as I was in the summer of 1970 upon my arrival at Cam Ranh Bay in the Republic of Vietnam.

Granted, during the years of schooling that preceded my deployment there, I had amassed all sorts of facts, some of them at least marginally relevant to the matter at hand. Yet despite the earnest efforts of some excellent teachers, I had managed to avoid acquiring anything that could be dignified with the term education. Now, however haltingly, that began to change. A year later, when my tour of duty ended, I carried home from Vietnam the barest inkling of a question: How had this massive cockup occurred and what did it signify?

Since that question implied rendering judgment on a war in which I had (however inconsequentially) participated, it wasn't one that I welcomed. Even so, the question dogged me. During the ensuing decades, while expending considerable effort reflecting on America's war in Vietnam, I never quite arrived at a fully satisfactory answer. At some level, the entire episode remained incomprehensible to me.

On that score, I suspect that I was hardly alone. No doubt many members of my generation, both those who served and those who protested (or those, like several recent US presidents, who contrived to remain on the sidelines), have long since arrived at fixed conclusions about Vietnam. Yet, for others of us, that war has remained genuinely baffling—a puzzle that defies solution.

Déjà Vu All Over Again

In history, context is everything. Revise that context and the entire story changes, with the 1619 Project a timely but by no means unique example of that phenomenon.

For the successive administrations that took the United States to war in Vietnam, beginning with Harry Truman's and culminating with Lyndon Johnson's, the relevant context that justified our involvement in Southeast Asia was self-evident: the Cold War.

From the late 1940s on, the advertised purpose of basic American policy was to contain the spread of global communism. Across the ranks of the political establishment, anti-communism was tantamount to a religious obligation. For years, that alone sufficed to legitimize our military involvement in Vietnam. Whatever the immediate issue—whether supporting France against the communist Viet Minh there after World War II or midwifing an anti-communist Republic of Vietnam following the French defeat in 1954—stopping the Red Menace rated as a national security priority of paramount importance. In Washington, just about everyone who was anyone agreed.

The actual course of events in Vietnam, however, played havoc with this interpretive framework. Once US combat troops arrived in South Vietnam in 1965, while American bombers tried to pound the communist North into submission, the original rationale for the war became increasingly difficult to sustain. True, the enemy's peasant army displayed a fondness for red flags and uniform accouterments. But so what? The threat posed to the United States itself was nonexistent.

When President Richard Nixon visited "Red" China in 1972, the Cold War morphed into something quite different. With the nation's most prominent anti-communist taking obvious delight in shaking hands with Chairman Mao Zedong in Beijing, the war effort in Vietnam became utterly inexplicable—and so it has remained ever since.

When the Cold War subsequently ended in what was ostensibly a victory of cosmic proportions, any urge to reckon with Vietnam disappeared entirely. After all, in comparison with the fall of the Berlin Wall in 1989, how much did the fall of Saigon in 1975 matter? In

Washington, the answer was clear: not all that much. On an issue that far exceeded the Vietnam War in importance, history had rendered a definitive verdict. Only the churlish would disagree.

Then, quite literally out of the blue, came the events of 9/11. In an instant, the "end of history," inaugurated by the passing of the Cold War, itself abruptly ended. Rather than pausing to consider the possibility that they might have again misconstrued the signs of the times, descendants of the political elite that had contrived the Vietnam War—including several who had found ways to sit out that conflict—devised a new framework for basic US policy. The Global War on Terrorism now became the organizing principle for American statecraft, serving a function comparable to the Cold War during the second half of the prior century.

As had been the case during the early phases of the Cold War, the Manichean mood of that post-9/11 moment favored action over deliberation. So, within weeks of those attacks on the World Trade Center in New York and the Pentagon in Washington, the United States embarked on a new shooting war in—of all places—landlocked, impoverished Afghanistan, famous for being the "graveyard of empires" (including the Soviet one) but not much else.

That war was destined to continue for twenty years. By the time it ended, many observers had long since begun to compare it to Vietnam. The similarities were impossible to miss. Both were wars of doubtful strategic necessity. Both dragged on endlessly. Both concluded in mortifying failure. To capture the essence of the war in Afghanistan, it didn't take long for critics to revive a term that had been widely used to describe Vietnam: each was a *quagmire*. Here was all you needed to know.

So based on outward appearances, the two wars seemed to be siblings. Yet when it came to substance, any relationship between the two rated as incidental. After all, the Vietnam and Afghan Wars occurred in entirely different periods of contemporary history, the one preceding the annus mirabilis of 1989 when that wall in Berlin came down, and the other occurring in its wake.

But here's the thing: in reality, the fall of the Berlin Wall didn't change everything. Among the things it left fully intact was a stubborn resistance to learning in Washington that poses a greater threat to the well-being of the American people than communism or terrorism ever did. To confirm that assertion, look no further than . . . well, yes, the US wars in Vietnam and Afghanistan.

Changing the Frame

You can learn a lot by studying the origins, conduct, and consequences of World War I (1914–1918). And you can learn a lot by studying the origins, conduct, and consequences of World War II (1939–1945). But to arrive at some approximation of definitive historical truth when it comes to twentieth-century Europe, you need to think of those two events as the Thirty Years War of 1914–1945. Only then is the connective tissue between the "Guns of August" and the horrors that were to befall Western civilization three decades later revealed.

Something similar applies to America's wars in Vietnam and Afghanistan. In ways that may not be easily appreciated, the two are intimately related. Bringing to light their kinship—and, by extension, their true significance—requires situating them in a single historical framework. Classifying Vietnam as an episode in the Cold War and Afghanistan as an unrelated part of the Global War on Terrorism confers a certain superficial narrative order on the recent past. But doing so is like pretending that World War I and World War II were unrelated events. It overlooks essential connective tissue.

Instead, to identify a historical frame that encompasses both Vietnam and Afghanistan, consider this proposition: however momentous they were for Europeans, the events of 1989–1991, when the Soviet Union imploded, left the American way of life all but untouched. True, the end of the Cold War had enormous implications for Western and Eastern Europe (soon to merge), for the states of the former Soviet Union (cut loose to pursue their own destinies), and for Russia itself (diminished and humiliated, but still a mammoth successor state to the USSR).

While these events unleashed a torrent of self-congratulation in the US, the passing of the Cold War did not substantively modify the aspirations or expectations of the American people. For decades, the United

States had exerted itself to uphold and enhance the advantageous position it gained in 1945. Its tacit goal was not only to hold the communist world in check but to achieve ideological, economic, political, and military primacy on a global scale, with all but the most cynical American leaders genuinely persuaded that US supremacy served the interests of humankind.

Attach to this outlook whatever label you like: innocence, intractable ignorance, megalomania, naked imperialism, historical myopia, divine will, or destiny. Subsuming them, however, was the concept of American exceptionalism. Whatever your preferred term, here we come to the essence of the American project.

The fall of the Berlin Wall did nothing to dislodge or even modify this strategy. Indeed, the collapse of communism seemingly affirmed the plausibility of preexisting American aspirations and expectations. So, too, did the events of 9/11. Bizarrely but crucially, the attacks on the World Trade Center and the Pentagon only imparted to American exceptionalism a renewed sense that here was the very foundation of the nation's identity. Beginning with the administration of President George W. Bush but continuing to the present moment, the United States regularly doubled down on its quest for a global primacy that was to be achieved largely, though by no means entirely, through the use or threatened use of military power.

We're now in a position to assess the consequences of such an approach. An essential preliminary step toward doing so is to discard the narrative of contemporary history that centers on the Cold War, succeeded, after a brief but blissful interval, by an unrelated Global War on Terrorism. It's time to substitute a narrative describing an American military enterprise that began when the first US combat troops came ashore in South Vietnam and persisted until the last American soldier departed Kabul in defeat some fifty-six years later. While thinking of this conflict as the Fifty-Six Year War may be accurate, it lacks a certain ring to it. So, let's call it the Very Long War (1965–2021), or VLW, instead.

At the outset of the VLW, this country's global preeminence was, of course, self-evident. At home, the constitutional order, however imperfect, appeared sacrosanct. By the time that Very Long War had reached its climax, however, informed observers were debating the international implications of American decline, while speculating anxiously about whether the domestic political order, as it had existed since at least the end of the Civil War, would even survive.

As the episodes that launched, concluded, and defined the essential character of the VLW, the wars in Vietnam and Afghanistan hold the key to understanding its dismal outcome. Whether considered separately or together, they exhibit with unmistakable clarity the grotesque military malpractice that forms the VLW's abiding theme.

Why did the United States fail so ignominiously in Vietnam? Why did it fail again in Afghanistan? The answers to these two questions turn out to be similar.

Begin with the fact that neither the survival of the Republic of Vietnam in the 1960s nor the ouster of the Taliban regime after 9/11 qualified as in any way vital to this country's national interest. Both were wars of choice undertaken in places of (at best) tangential importance to the United States.

Then, add into the mix a near total absence of competent political oversight; deficient generalship, with senior officers struggling to comprehend the nature of the wars they were charged with waging; unwarranted confidence in the utility of advanced military technology; an excessive reliance on firepower that killed, maimed, and displaced noncombatants in striking numbers, thereby alienating the local population; nation-building efforts that succeeded chiefly in spawning widespread corruption; an inability to inculcate in local militaries the capacity and motivation to defend their country; and not least of all, determined enemies who made up for their material shortcomings by outpacing their adversaries in a willingness to fight and die for the cause.

Each one of these factors informed the way the United States fought in Vietnam. A half-century later, each reappeared in Afghanistan.

In terms of their conduct, the two campaigns differed only in one important respect: the role allotted to the American people. Reliance on conscription to raise the force that fought in Vietnam spurred widespread popular opposition to that war. Reliance on a so-called volunteer military to carry the burden of waging the Afghan War allowed ordinary Americans to ignore what was being done in their name, especially when field commanders devised methods for keeping a lid on US casualties.

Bookends

The Very Long War has, in fact, exacted an immense toll, essentially without benefits. Bookended by Vietnam and Afghanistan, the entire enterprise yielded almost nothing of value and contributed significantly to the rise to power of Donald Trump and the wounding of this country's political system. Yet even today, too few Americans are willing to confront the disaster that has befallen the United States as a consequence of our serial misuse of military power.

This represents a grievous failure of imagination.

On that score, just consider for a moment if this country had neither intervened in Vietnam nor responded to 9/11 by invading Afghanistan. What would have happened?

Almost certainly, the North Vietnamese would have succeeded in uniting their divided country with much less bloodshed. And Taliban control of Afghanistan would in all likelihood have continued without interruption in the years following 2001, with the Afghan people left to sort out their own destiny. Yet, despite immense sacrifices by US troops, a vast expenditure of treasure, and quite literally millions of dead in Southeast Asia and Afghanistan, that's exactly how things turned out anyway.

Would the United States be worse off had it chosen not to engage in those twin wars of choice? Would the Soviet Union back in the 1960s and the People's Republic of China more recently have interpreted such self-restraint as evidence of weakness? Or might this country's adversaries have seen the avoidance of needless war as an indication of prudence and sound judgment by a powerful country? And had the follies of war in Vietnam and Afghanistan been avoided, might it not have been possible to avert, or at least diminish, the pathologies currently afflicting this country, including Trumpism and our deepening culture wars? Certainly, that possibility should haunt us all.

Of one thing only can we be certain: it's past time to be done with the Very Long War and the misguided aspirations to global primacy that inspired it. Only if Americans abandon their fealty to the idea of American exceptionalism and the militarism that has sustained it, might it be possible to conclude that the wars in Vietnam and Afghanistan served some faintly useful purpose.

Index

of Iraq," 10-11
comparing to Vietnam, 112-113
damage done by US, 222
Iraqi casualties, 226
Islamic Republic of Iran
	as winner of, 182
length of, 207
list of commanding
	generals, 210-211
not authorized by UN
	Security Council, 148
Obama pledging to end war, 199
reflections on a failed war, 112-116
"Iraqi Freedom," 251
Irma, Hurricane (2017), 159, 190
ISIS, 182, 191, 199, 205, 273.
	see also Islamic State
in Afghanistan, 62
in Iraq, 35, 306
in Libya, 204
presidential candidates in 2016 on,
	119-120, 130, 141, 204, 212
Islamic Republic of Afghanistan, 337
Islamic Republic of Iran. *see* Iran
Islamic State, 11, 119, 197-198,
	204, 211. *see also* ISIS
isolationism, 100-108, 297-298
Israel, 46, 50, 120, 140, 213, 302
	attack on USS *Liberty*, 49
	Israel lobby in US, 130
	and nuclear weapons, 219
	and receipt of US armaments, 219
	US moving embassy to
		Jerusalem, 166
	US obligation to defend, 298
Israeli-Palestinian conflict
	peace needing US, myth of, 166
	"two-state solution," 219

Jackson, Andrew, 277
Jaffe, Greg, 44, 45
Jefferson, Thomas, 7, 92, 101, 282, 319
Jerusalem, US moving

embassy to, 166
Jobs, Steve, 280
John, Gospel of, 51
Johnson, Boris, 328-329
Johnson, Lyndon, 72, 84, 97,
	264, 282, 312, 342
	use of Tonkin Gulf Resolution, 196
Joint Chiefs of Staff (US), 125,
	179, 190, 204, 264, 265
Jones, John (aka Huntley
	Haverstock), 39
Jones, John Paul, 246
Judt, Tony, 109
justice, myth of blind justice, 163-164

Kahn, Herman, 138
Kaplan, Robert, 268
Karzai, Hamid, 336
Katrina, Hurricane (2005),
	159, 171, 190
Kavanaugh, Brett, 163-164, 254
Keillor, Garrison and sexual
	misconduct, 232
Kelly, John, 236
Kelly, Megyn, 136
Kennedy, John F., 17, 50-51, 65, 75,
	84, 111, 116, 128, 161, 231
Kerry, John, 12, 140, 289
Khalilzad, Zalmay, 61
Khashoggi, Jamal, 325-326, 330
Khe Sanh, battle for, 204-205
Kim Il-sung, 84
Kim Jong-Un, 56, 142, 241
King, Martin Luther, Jr., 87-93,
	316-317, 319, 321-322
	murder of in April 1968, 318
Kissinger, Henry, 61
Korean War, 167, 196, 252
Kubrick, Stanley, 235
Kurds in Syria, 181-182, 183
Kushner, Jared, 166

La Follette, Robert, Senator, 228

ABOUT HAYMARKET BOOKS

Haymarket Books is a radical, independent, nonprofit book publisher based in Chicago. Our mission is to publish books that contribute to struggles for social and economic justice. We strive to make our books a vibrant and organic part of social movements and the education and development of a critical, engaged, and internationalist Left.

We take inspiration and courage from our namesakes, the Haymarket Martyrs, who gave their lives fighting for a better world. Their 1886 struggle for the eight-hour day—which gave us May Day, the international workers' holiday—reminds workers around the world that ordinary people can organize and struggle for their own liberation. These struggles—against oppression, exploitation, environmental devastation, and war—continue today across the globe.

Since our founding in 2001, Haymarket has published more than nine hundred titles. Radically independent, we seek to drive a wedge into the risk-averse world of corporate book publishing. Our authors include Angela Y. Davis, Arundhati Roy, Keeanga-Yamahtta Taylor, Eve Ewing, Aja Monet, Mariame Kaba, Naomi Klein, Rebecca Solnit, Olúfẹ́mi O. Táíwò, Mohammed El-Kurd, José Olivarez, Noam Chomsky, Winona LaDuke, Robyn Maynard, Leanne Betasamosake Simpson, Howard Zinn, Mike Davis, Marc Lamont Hill, Dave Zirin, Astra Taylor, and Amy Goodman, among many other leading writers of our time. We are also the trade publishers of the acclaimed Historical Materialism Book Series.

Haymarket also manages a vibrant community organizing and event space in Chicago, Haymarket House, the popular Haymarket Books Live event series and podcast, and the annual Socialism Conference.

ABOUT TOMDISPATCH.COM

After nearly a decade working together at TomDispatch.com, publishing some of the most thoughtful, powerful, and prescient writers of the post-9/11 era, legendary book editor Tom Engelhardt and award-winning journalist Nick Turse founded Dispatch Books in 2012.

Joining with Haymarket Books, the independent imprint has forged a storied history in a short amount of time, producing important, award-winning works of fiction and nonfiction. From Pulitzer Prize winner John W. Dower's searing indictment of US military power since World War II, *The Violent American Century*, and Ann Jones's up-close-and-personal look at the toll of recent wars on America's veterans, *They Were Soldiers*, to John Feffer's breakout dystopian thriller trilogy and Nick Turse's American Book Award–winning exposé of US military operations in Africa, *Tomorrow's Battlefield*, Dispatch Books has quickly distinguished itself as a home for influential authors and one of the premier imprints in progressive publishing.

ABOUT THE AUTHOR

Andrew Bacevich is professor of history and international relations emeritus at Boston University. A graduate of the US Military Academy, he served for twenty-three years as a commissioned officer in the United States Army. He received his PhD in American diplomatic history from Princeton. He previously taught at West Point and at Johns Hopkins. Bacevich currently serves as president of the Quincy Institute for Responsible Statecraft, a Washington-based think tank that he cofounded.

He is the author most recently of *After the Apocalypse: America's Role in a World Transformed* (2021). Earlier books include *The Age of Illusions: How America Squandered Its Cold War Victory* (2020); *Twilight of the American Century* (2018); *America's War for the Greater Middle East: A Military History* (2016); *Breach of Trust: How Americans Failed Their Soldiers and Their Country* (2013); *Washington Rules: America's Path to Permanent War* (2010); *The Limits of Power: The End of American Exceptionalism* (2008); and *The New American Militarism: How Americans Are Seduced by War* (2005). His essays and reviews have appeared in *Atlantic Monthly*, *Harper's*, *Foreign Affairs*, *New Left Review*, *The Nation*, the *New Republic*, TomDispatch, and the *London Review of Books*, among other publications.